SAMUEL RICHARDSON

Modern Critical Views

These and other titles in preparation

Modern Critical Views

SAMUEL RICHARDSON

Edited and with an introduction by
Harold Bloom
Sterling Professor of the Humanities
Yale University

CHELSEA HOUSE PUBLISHERS ◊ 1987
New York ◊ New Haven ◊ Philadelphia

Library of Congress Cataloging-in-Publication Data
Samuel Richardson.
  (Modern critical views)
  Bibliography: p.
  Includes index.
  Contents: Introduction / Harold Bloom — Richardson as
novelist / Ian Watt — The divided heart Lovelace / Martin
Price — [etc.]
  1. Richardson, Samuel, 1689–1761—Criticism and inter-
pretation. [1. Richardson, Samuel, 1689–1761—Criticism and
interpretation. 2. English literature—History and criticism] I.
Bloom, Harold. II. Series.
PR3667.S25   1987   823'.6   87-8069
  ISBN 1–55546–286–3 (alk. paper)

Contents

Editor's Note

This book gathers together a representative selection of the best modern criticism devoted to the novels of Samuel Richardson. The critical essays are reprinted here in the chronological sequence of their original publication. I am grateful to Marena Fisher for her assistance in editing this volume.

My introduction considers Clarissa Harlowe and Lovelace as agonists of the will, Protestant saint against Herculean libertine, who destroy both themselves and one another. Ian Watt begins the chronological sequence with a discussion of Richardson's epistolary technique and characterization in *Clarissa*. Martin Price gives his account of the ambivalent contest between Clarissa and Lovelace, which he sees as taking place between Pascalian orders of being, with Clarissa, representing the order of charity, triumphing over Lovelace's naturalism.

Lovelace is the subject of Anthony Winner's character analysis, which finds in him a fragmented and alienated energy, an ancestor of Balzac's Vautrin. *Clarissa*'s penultimate movement, its final duel of wills between the agonists before the heroine's slow dying commences, is studied by Mark Kinkead-Weekes, who locates Richardson's ruling principle in the individual's right to be precisely what she wills to be. A second essay by Kinkead-Weekes focuses on the central crisis in *Sir Charles Grandison*.

Pamela, Richardson's notorious romance of virtue rewarded, is read by Roy Roussel as the triumph of the familiar letter as a literary form. The "Pamela controversy," between the anti-Pamelists led by Fielding and Richardson's Pamelists, is outlined by Jina Politi. In a brief examination of marriage in *Sir Charles Grandison*, Jean H. Hagstrum notes that in this novel, for the first time, "true love is an extension of the familial."

Rita Goldberg returns us to *Clarissa* with a sustained meditation upon sex and enlightenment in the contest of Clarissa and Lovelace. In this book's final essay, the great fire-scene in *Clarissa* is read by Rosemary Bechler as the momentary triumph but ultimate defeat of "Lovelace the actor-dramatist," whose sublime effect is a trick and a lie and so a self-destructive misuse of his own elemental fire.

Introduction

I

I first read *Clarissa* as a Cornell undergraduate in the late 1940s, under the skilled direction of my teacher, William M. Sale, Jr., a fierce partisan of Richardson and a remarkable critic of fiction. Since I cannot read a novel other than the way that Sale taught me, it is not surprising that forty years later I hold on fast to his canonical judgment that *Clarissa* is the finest novel in the English language. Rereading it through the years, I find it the only novel that can rival even Proust, despite Proust's evident advantages. The long and astonishing sequence that ends the novel, Clarissa's protracted death and its aftermath, is clearly at one of the limits of the novel as an art. I find myself fighting not to weep just before the moment of Clarissa's death, but as a critic I submit that these would be *cognitive* tears, and would say little about me but much about Richardson's extraordinary powers of representation. It remains a mystery that Richardson, with no strong novelistic precursors, should have been able to make Clarissa Harlowe the most persuasive instance of a kind of secular saint, a strong heroine, in the entire subsequent history of the Western novel.

Ian Watt, still our best historian of the rise of the novel, emphasizes that one of Richardson's major advances upon Defoe was in solving the problem of plot by centering it upon a single action: courtship between the sexes. That action necessarily entails Richardson's other grand innovation: the novelistic representation of the protagonists' inwardness, a mode of mimesis in which Richardson had only the one inevitable precursor, Shakespeare. If Jan Hendrik van den Berg is right, then historical psychology is essentially the study of the growing inner self, from Luther's "inner man" (1520) through Shakespeare's almost fully secularized tragic heroes on to Rousseau's and Wordsworth's solitary egos confronting, with ecstasy, the estrangement of things in a "sense of nature." *Clarissa* (1747–48) preceded all of Rousseau's

1

publications, so that while Rousseau could have had something to tell Richardson about the sentiments and sensibility of inwardness, he did not teach the first great English novelist about the fictional representation of the inner life.

Whether anyone since has surpassed Richardson in this mimetic mode seems to me at least doubtful. George Eliot's Dorothea Brooke, Henry James's Isabel Archer, D. H. Lawrence's Ursula Brangwen, and even Virginia Woolf's Clarissa Dalloway, do not take us farther into the portrayal of a single consciousness than the original Clarissa brings us, and perhaps they all of them retreat to some degree from her full inwardness. Price remarks that "Richardson has transformed highly particularized characters so that their dense and familiar social setting fades away in the course of the slow disclosure of consequences." That transformation, in Clarissa and to some extent in Lovelace, replaces the social and historical context with a not less than tragic inwardness. If Clarissa is a saint and a martyr, then what she bears heroic witness to is not so much supernatural faith in Christ as it is natural faith in the heroic integrity of her own perpetually growing inner self.

II

Richardson's power as a novelist centers in the wildly antithetical and fiercely ambivalent relationship between Clarissa and Lovelace, who destroy both themselves and one another in what may be the most equivocal instance of a mutual passion in all of Western literature. I do not venture that assertion lightly, but no single love affair in Shakespeare, Tolstoy, or Proust seems comparable in its strength and complexity to the terrible agon that consumes Clarissa and Lovelace. We can no more speculate upon what a marriage between Richardson's protagonists might have been than we can visualize a world harmoniously ruled by a perpetually united Antony and Cleopatra. Lovelace and Clarissa are mighty opposites yet uncannily complementary, and it is Richardson's consummate art to have so created them that they must undo one another.

I begin with Lovelace, if only because his power of being, immense as it is, finally is eclipsed by the transcendental transformation of the gorgeously dying Clarissa. But that indeed is a finality; until Clarissa begins to die, the sheer force of her resistance to Lovelace compels him to become even more himself. Conversely, Lovelace's aggression greatly strengthens Clarissa, though the cost of her confirmation is her life. In the novel's most terrible irony, the slow dying of Clarissa directly causes a steady waning in Lovelace, a dwindling down from a heroic Satanist to a self-ruined libertine, drowning in remorse and confusion.

A. D. McKillop usefully traced Lovelace's literary ancestry to the libertine man-of-fashion in Restoration comedy and to the Herculean hero of Dryden's dramas, such as *Aureng-Zebe* and *The Conquest of Granada*. This lineage accounts both for some of Lovelace's obvious faults and for his few but authentic virtues: healthy disdain for societal appearances and for false morality, a curiously wistful longing for true virtue, and a brutal honesty. But a fusion of a Restoration witty rake and Herculean rhetorician is no more a match for Clarissa Harlowe than a Jacobean hero-villain would have been, and part of the novel's fascination is in watching Lovelace slowly realize that Clarissa is necessarily an apocalyptic defeat for him. The turning point is not the rape, but a moment late in Letter 266, when Lovelace suddenly apprehends the dialectical entrapment that he and Clarissa constitute for one another:

> A horrid dear creature!—By my soul, she made me shudder! She had need, indeed, to talk of *her* unhappiness, in falling into the hands of the only *man* in the world who could have used her as I have used her! She is the only *woman* in the world who could have shocked and disturbed me as she has done—So we are upon a foot in that respect. And I think I have the *worst* of it by much. Since very little has been my joy; very much my trouble: and *her* punishment, as she calls it, is *over*: but when *mine* will, or what it *may be*, who can tell?
>
> Here, only recapitulating (think, then, how I must be affected at the time), I was forced to leave off, and sing a song to myself. I aimed at a lively air; but I croaked rather than sung: and fell into the old dismal thirtieth of January strain. I hemmed up for a sprightlier note; but it would not do: and at last I ended, like a malefactor, in a dead psalm melody.
>
> High-ho!—I gape like an unfledged kite in its nest, wanting to swallow a chicken, bobbed at its mouth by its marauding dam!—
>
> What a devil ails me!—I can neither think nor write!—
>
> Lie down, pen, for a moment!—

The devil that ails him is the beginning of his own end, his falling outwards and downwards from his last shreds of a libertine ideology into the dreadful inner space of his defeat by Clarissa, his enforced realization that self-willing and self-assertion are permanently over for him. Clarissa, a great Puritan withholder of esteem, will not accept him at his own evaluation, and he begins to know that pragmatically they have destroyed one another. His actual death is a release from the death-in-life he has suffered since Clarissa's death:

He was delirious, at times, in the two last hours; and then several times cried out, Take her away! Take her away! but named nobody. And sometimes praised some lady (that Clarissa, I suppose, whom he had called upon when he received his death's wound) calling her, Sweet Excellence! Divine Creature! Fair Sufferer!—And once he said, Look down, blessed Spirit, look down!—And there stopped—his lips however moving.

At nine in the morning, he was seized with convulsions, and fainted away; and it was a quarter of an hour before he came out of them.

His few last words I must not omit, as they show an ultimate composure; which may administer some consolation to his honourable friends.

Blessed—said he, addressing himself no doubt to Heaven; for his dying eyes were lifted up—a strong convulsion prevented him for a few moments saying more—But recovering, he again with great fervour (lifting up his eyes, and his spread hands) pronounced the word *Blessed*—Then, in a seeming ejaculation, he spoke inwardly so as not to be understood: at last, he distinctly pronounced these three words,

LET THIS EXPIATE!

And then, his head sinking on his pillow, he expired; at about half an hour after ten.

Lovelace dies in his own acquired religion, which is the worship of the blessed Clarissa, whom he personally has converted into something considerably more than a saint or even an angel. Being himself pure will and having been conquered by an even purer one, he worships his conqueror as God. Dying as a Clarissian rather than a Christian, as it were, Lovelace sustains his final pride, a peculiar sense of glory that has gone beyond remorse and has little left in it of mere love. This is hardly expiation in any moral or spiritual sense whatsoever, as Richardson on some level must have known, but is certainly an aesthetic expiation, worthy of Baudelaire or of Proust.

III

Clarissa, as is radiantly appropriate, ends many trajectories beyond her lover's destination. I dissent from the entire critical tradition, from Watt and Price to my younger contemporaries, that has overemphasized Clarissa's supposed self-deceptions. Dr. Samuel Johnson first noted that Clarissa could not confront the truth of having fallen in love with Lovelace, but that hardly seems to me a duplicity in her, however unknowing. We cannot choose whom we are free to love, but Clarissa wars more strongly against every mode of overdetermination than any comparable character in secular fiction. What matters to her, and this is her greatness, is that her will cannot be violated, even by her own affections. *She refuses to see herself as anyone's victim—* whether Lovelace's, her family's, or her own turning against the self.

Lovelace becomes a wounded narcissist, and so is aggressive down to the end. But Clarissa could honestly say, if she wanted to, that it is not her narcissism but her eros that has been crucified. If Lovelace indeed represented her desire for what she did not have, and was not in herself, then her desire died, not so paradoxically, with the violation of her body. Lovelace becomes still more naturalistic after the rape, but she is transformed into a dualist and begins the process of dying to the body of this life. The issue has nothing to do with society and little to do with conventional reality. It is an aesthetic issue, the ancient agon of the Sublime mode, which always seeks to answer the triple question: more? equal to? less than? She was never less than Lovelace, hoped vainly he could be reformed into her equal, and knows now that she is far more than he is, and more indeed than anyone else in her world. At that height of the Sublime, she can only commence dying.

If her will is to remain inviolate, then its independence and integrity must be manifested by a death that is anything but a revenge, whether it be against Lovelace, her family, herself, or even against time. Rather, *her* death is the true expiation, which can bring forgiveness upon everyone else involved, though I surmise that she is more interested in forgiving herself even as she forgives the bewildered Lovelace. A Puritan saint, as Shaw's St. Joan shows, is rather more interested in her own integrity than in anyone else's suffering. The cost for Clarissa or for Shaw's St. Joan is an absolute, inner isolation, but is that not the essence of Protestantism?

There is nothing like Clarissa's virtually endless death-scene in all of literature, and while no one would wish it longer I do not wish it any shorter. Extraordinary as the actual moment of death is, in Letter 481, the most characteristic revelation of Clarissa's apotheosis is in Letter 475:

> Her breath being very short, she desired another pillow; and hav-
> ing two before, this made her in a manner sit up in her bed; and
> she spoke then with more distinctness; and seeing us greatly con-
> cerned, forgot her own sufferings to comfort us; and a charming
> lecture she gave us, though a brief one, upon the happiness of
> a timely preparation and upon the hazards of a late repentance,
> when the mind, as she observed, was so much weakened, as well

as the body, as to render a poor soul unable to contend with its own infirmities.

I beseech ye, my good friends, proceeded she, mourn not for one who mourns not, nor has cause to mourn, for herself. On the contrary, rejoice with me that all my worldly troubles are so near their end. Believe me, sirs, that I would not, if I might, choose to live, although the pleasantest part of my life were to come over again: and yet eighteen years of it, out of nineteen, have been *very* pleasant. To be so much exposed to temptation, and to be so liable to fail in the trial, who would not rejoice that all her dangers are over!—All I wished was pardon and blessing from my dear parents. Easy as my departure seems to promise to be, it would have been still easier had I had that pleasure. BUT GOD ALMIGHTY WOULD NOT LET ME DEPEND FOR COMFORT UPON ANY BUT HIMSELF.

This is certainly the purest Protestantism, and we might still be tempted to call this pride, particularly since Clarissa reminds us that she is all of nineteen years old. But we do Clarissa violence to name her total knowledge as a form of pride. The Protestant will by now has been blamed for practically everything that has gone wrong in our spiritual, intellectual, economic, and political life, as well as our sexual life, and the United States is the evening land of Protestantism and so the final stage for the travails of its will. Clarissa, as she dies, shows us the other side, the glory of the Protestant will. If God would not let Clarissa depend for comfort upon any but himself, then he gave her the ultimate accolade of the Protestant will: to accept esteem only where it chose to bestow esteem, and only on its own terms.

IAN WATT

Richardson as Novelist: *Clarissa*

Early in 1741 Richardson explained to Aaron Hill that he had written *Pamela* in the hope that it "might possibly introduce a new species of writing." This claim antedates that of Fielding, made the following year in the preface to *Joseph Andrews*, and indicates that, unlike Defoe, Richardson was a conscious literary innovator.

There was certainly no accidental quality about *Clarissa*, whose plot was already in his mind in 1741, and whose actual composition occupied him fairly continuously from 1744 to 1749 when the last volumes were published: nor can there be any doubt that in *Clarissa*, even more completely than in *Pamela*, Richardson resolved the main formal problems which still confronted the novel by creating a literary structure in which narrative mode, plot, characters and moral theme were organised into a unified whole. For, although *Clarissa* contains something like a million words and is almost certainly the longest novel in the language, Richardson was justified in asserting that "long as the work is, there is not one digression, not one episode, not one reflection, but what arises naturally from the subject, and makes for it, and [carries] it on."

I

Richardson's use of the letter form in *Clarissa* was much better adapted to the presentation of personal relationships than was the case in his first

From *The Rise of the Novel*. © 1957 by Ian Watt. University of California Press, 1957.

novel. In *Pamela* there was only one main correspondence—that of the heroine and her parents; as a result there was no direct presentation of Mr. B.'s point of view, and our picture of Pamela herself was completely one-sided. This posed a very similar critical problem to that in *Moll Flanders:* it was difficult to know how far the heroine's own interpretation of her character and actions was to be accepted. The parallel, indeed, can be continued, for the fact that Richardson had essentially only one narrative source, Pamela herself, meant not only that he occasionally had to intervene himself as editor and explain such matters as how Pamela got from Bedfordshire to Lincolnshire, but, more important, that the epistolary convention itself gradually broke down, the letters turned into "Pamela's Journal," and the later parts of the novel therefore produced a kind of narrative effect not unlike that of the autobiographical memoir in Defoe.

In *Clarissa*, however, the epistolary method carries the whole burden of the story which is, therefore, as Richardson says in his Postscript, a "dramatic narrative" rather than a "history." Its main and obvious difference from drama, indeed, is a significant one: the characters express themselves not by speaking but by writing letters, a distinction which is entirely in keeping with the inward and subjective nature of the dramatic conflict involved. This conflict is also such as to justify the way Richardson organised his narrative "in a double yet separate correspondence, between two young ladies of virtue . . . and two gentlemen of free lives"—the basic formal division is both an expression of the dichotomisation of the sexual roles which is at the heart of Richardson's subject, and an essential condition of the candid self-revelation by the characters which would have been inhibited by a mixed correspondence.

The use of two parallel series of letters, then, has great advantages, but it also presents considerable difficulties; not only because many of the actions have to be recounted separately and therefore repetitively, but because there is a danger of dispersing the reader's attention between two different sets of letters and replies. Richardson, however, handles the narrative sequence in such a way as to minimise these disadvantages. At times the attitudes of the protagonists to the same events are so different that we have no sense of repetition, while at others he intervenes editorially to explain that some letters have been suppressed or shortened—the distinction, incidentally, between such intervention, which is limited to clarifying the handling of the original documents, and that which occurs in *Pamela*, where the author becomes the narrator, is an important one.

Richardson's main method of resolving the narrative problem, however, is to give us large groups of letters from one side or the other and to organise these major compositional units in such a way that there is a significant relationship between the action and the mode of its telling. At the outset, for example, the letters between Clarissa and Anna Howe occupy most of the first two volumes. It is only when their characters and background have been fully established, and Clarissa has taken the fateful step and placed herself in Lovelace's power, that the main male correspondence begins and at once reveals the full danger of Clarissa's situation. The climax of the story brings another very effective piece of counterpoint: the rape is announced briefly by Lovelace, but the reader has to undergo several hundred pages of anguished expectation before hearing a word of Clarissa's account of the affair, and the events that preceded it. By then her death is already in sight and it precipitates another significant reordering of the epistolary pattern: the rigid canalisation of correspondences is broken down by a flood of letters surrounding Clarissa with admiring and anxious attention, while Lovelace becomes a more and more isolated figure, to have his eventual death reported by a French travelling valet.

Richardson prevents the fundamental simplicity of his handling of the main epistolary structure from becoming obvious or boring by a great variety of auxiliary devices. There is, first of all, the contrast between the totally different worlds of the male and female correspondences; and within them there are further contrasts of character and temperament: Clarissa's anxious restraint is juxtaposed to Anna's pert volubility, and Lovelace's Byronic alternations of mood are set off against the increasingly sober tenor of Belford's letters. From time to time further contrasts of tone are provided by the introduction of new correspondents, such as Clarissa's heavy Uncle Anthony, Lovelace's illiterate servant Joseph Leman, the ridiculous pedant Brand or by the inclusion of incidents of a contrasted kind, varying from the full-dress description of the moral and physical squalor of Mrs. Sinclair's death to the social comedy of some of the disguise scenes in which Lovelace participates.

For—contrary to general opinions—Richardson had considerable humorous gifts. Much has been made of his unintentional humour, and *Clarissa* is certainly not free from it—witness the letter where Clarissa informs her Cantabrigian brother that she is "truly sorry to have cause to say that I have heard it often remarked, that your uncontrolled passions are not a credit to your liberal education." But there is also a great deal of effective conscious humour in the novel; Fielding found "much of the true comic force" in the widow Bevis, and some very lively and sardonic irony is obtained, especially in the central portions of the book, from the interplay of characters and of their very different standards and assumptions. One brief example must suffice. After the dinner in Mrs. Sinclair's parlour before Clarissa realises the true nature of the establishment, Lovelace dryly reports Clarissa's approving comment on the dissolute Sally Martin's quite imaginary prospective alliance with a woollen draper: "What Miss Martin particularly said of marriage, and of her humble servant, was very solid." The comment enforces the pathos of Clarissa's charitable ignorance, and yet leads us on to savour the total irony of the scene, an irony which depends upon the fact that it is Lovelace who is writing mockingly to Belford about Clarissa's penchant for the "very solid."

Richardson also shows great skill in varying the tempo of the narrative: after a very prolonged preparation, for example, the rape is reported so swiftly that it comes as a surprise whose full impact reverberates through the atmosphere of slowly developing leaden horror that ensues. Such calculated alternations combine with the tenor of the action itself to produce a curious and wholly characteristic literary effect. Richardson's very slowness communicates a sense of continual tension held lightly in check: the poised, almost processional, tempo of the narrative with its sudden lapses into brutality or hysteria is itself the perfect formal enactment of the universe which *Clarissa* portrays, a universe where the calm surface of repressive convention and ingrown hypocrisy is momentarily—but only momentarily—threatened by the irruption of the secret violences which it provokes but conceals.

Richardson was as careful and skilful in his characterisation as in his epistolary technique. He claimed in the postscript that "the characters are various and natural; well distinguished and uniformly supported and maintained"; and his assertion is very largely justified. All characters of any importance are given a complete description, which includes an account, not only of their physical and psychological nature, but of their past life and of the ramifications of their family and personal relationships; while in the "Conclusion Supposed to be Written by Mr. Belford" Richardson anticipates a later convention of the novel by acknowledging his responsibility for all his *dramatis personae* and rounding off his narrative with a brief account of their later careers.

Many modern readers, it is true, have found Clarissa too good and Lovelace too bad to be very convincing, but this was not the view of Richardson's contemporaries, who infuriated him, as he recounts in the postscript, by their tendency, on the one hand, to condemn the heroine as "too cold in her love, too haughty, and even sometimes provoking," and on the other to succumb to the hero's rakish charms. "Oh that I could not say, that I have met with more admirers of Lovelace than of Clarissa," Richardson lamented to Miss Grainger; and this despite the fact that he had already added footnotes to his original text so as to emphasise Lovelace's cruelty and duplicity.

This very different attitude to Richardson's protagonists lasted until well into the nineteenth century: Balzac, for example, thought it appropriate in 1837 to illustrate the point that there are always two sides to a question by asking, with what was certainly meant to be a rhetorical flourish—"Who can decide between a Clarissa and a Lovelace?"

On the other hand, there is no doubt that it was a major part of Richardson's intention to establish Clarissa as a model of feminine virtue—he stated very explicitly in the preface that she was "proposed as an exemplar to her sex"—and that this interposes considerable barriers between us and the heroine. When we are told that Clarissa knew some Latin, was distinguished for the correctness of her orthography, was even "a perfect mistress of the four rules of arithmetic," we find it a strain to muster the proper awe. Clarissa's systematic apportionment of time seems ridiculous, with its fantastic bookkeeping carried on by such entries as "debtor to the article of benevolent visits, so many hours" if perchance she has skimped on philanthropy by running over the three hours allotted daily to epistolary amusements; we are gratified rather than otherwise when Clarissa bewails the fact that her fall has deprived her of the pleasure of visiting the "cots of my poorer neighbours, to leave lessons for the boys and cautions for the elder girls"; and we pine for more substantial concessions to human frailty than are indicated by Anna Howe's admission that her friend did not excel "in the executive part" of painting.

None of these things would have seemed so ridiculous to Richardson's contemporaries. Theirs was an age of very deep class distinctions; an age when the position of women was still such as to make any effective intellectual achievement on their part a legitimate cause of admiration; an age when the ceremonies of benevolence were commonly performed with a blandly patronising pomp. Even Clarissa's care in the management of her time, though extreme by any standard, would probably have found wide approval as a laudable schematisation of an established Puritan tendency.

The ideals of Richardson's time and class, then, combined with the somewhat limited literary perspective prevalent in his day according to which the didactic function of art was best served by making characters paradigms of vice or virtue, go far towards explaining much that we find incredible or uncongenial in Clarissa's personality. But in any case such a defence is only necessary for a small part of the book—the beginning and especially the end when she is overwhelmed in the obituary pieties of her friends; during most of the narrative our attention is deflected from her perfections towards the tragic consequences of her error of judgement in leaving the parental roof in the company of Lovelace. Nor is this all: with a psychological penetration

which shows how, if the need arises, Richardson the novelist can silence
Richardson the writer of conduct books, it is made clear that this error of
judgement was itself the result of Clarissa's very excellencies: "So desirous,"
she taunts herself, "to be considered an *example*! A vanity which my partial
admirers put into my head! And so secure in my own virtue." Indeed, with
a supreme objectivity, Richardson connects his heroine's downfall with her
attempt to realise the aims of the campaign of sexual reformation described
above. Clarissa eventually comes to realise that she fell into Lovelace's power
because of her spiritual pride, which led her to believe "that I might be an
humble means in the hands of Providence to reclaim a man who had, as I
thought, good sense enough at bottom to be reclaimed."

In the case of Clarissa, then, Richardson's strong tendency towards making his characters exemplifications of some rather obvious moral lesson is
to a large extent redeemed by his equally strong if not stronger tendency
towards a very powerful imaginative projection into a much more complicated
psychological and literary world. There is a similar qualification of his didactic
tendency in his portrayal of Lovelace—Richardson refused, for example, to
satisfy the narrow moralists who wanted him to add atheism to Lovelace's
other sins, on the grounds that this would have made it impossible for Clarissa
even to consider him as suitor. But the main objections to Lovelace's character
are of a somewhat different order: we object not so much to his exemplary
viciousness as to its artificial, self-conscious and single-minded quality.
Richardson undoubtedly had Lothario in Rowe's *Fair Penitent* (1703) in mind,
as well as several real persons of his acquaintance; he had "always" been
"as attentive . . . to the profligate boastings, of the one sex as . . . to the
disguises of the other": and as a result produced a character who is not so
much a real individual as a conflation of a variety of rakish traits that Richardson derived partly from personal observation and partly from his considerable
reading in the drama.

Yet, although the artificial and composite elements in Lovelace's
character cannot be denied, there is, as we shall see, much else that is convincingly human about him; and, as with Clarissa, an appreciation of the
contemporary social context does much to relieve Richardson of the grosser
charges against the credibility of his creation. For the eighteenth-century rake
was very different from its twentieth-century counterpart. Lovelace belonged
to an age before the public schools had enforced a code of manly reticence
upon even the most hypertonic of aristocratic cads; nor did cricket and golf
provide alternative channels for the superfluous energies of the leisured male.
Lady Mary Wortley Montagu tells us that in 1724 one of Richardson's possible models for Lovelace, Philip, Duke of Wharton, was the moving spirit

in a "committee of gallantry," the Schemers, who met "regularly three times a week to consult on gallant schemes for the advantage and advancement of that branch of happiness"; and there is much other evidence to suggest that a single-minded devotion to the chase was the exception rather than the rule among the gentry of the time, and that many of the younger set differed from Squire Western only in preferring a sport that had no closed season and where the quarry was human and feminine.

The moral theme of *Clarissa* is open to objections somewhat similar to those against its characterisation, but there can at least be no doubt that Richardson's purpose, as stated in the title, is carried out considerably more carefully than is the case in *Moll Flanders*. The title reads: *Clarissa: or The History of a Young Lady: Comprehending the Most Important Concerns of Private Life, and Particularly Showing the Distresses that May Attend the Misconduct Both of Parents and Children, in Relation to Marriage.* What follows bears this description out: both parties are wrong—the parents in trying to force Solmes on their daughter, and their daughter in entertaining the private addresses of another suitor, and leaving home with him; and both parties are punished—Clarissa dies, and is shortly followed to the grave by her remorseful parents, while the fates bring to her sister and brother respectively the appropriate scourges of a faithless husband and a wife who brings, not the anticipated fortune but only "a lawsuit for life."

In the postscript, however, Richardson also laid claim to a much larger moral purpose. Considering that "when the Pulpit fails other expedients are necessary," he resolved to "throw in his mite" to reform the infidel age and to "*steal in* . . . the great doctrines of Christianity under the guise of a fashionable amusement." Whether this lofty ambition is achieved is open to serious question.

The crux of the matter is Clarissa's death. In the postscript Richardson adversely criticises previous tragedy on the grounds that "the tragic poets have . . . seldom made their heroes . . . in their deaths look forward to a future hope." He, on the contrary, prides himself that he is "well justified by the *Christian system*, in deferring to extricate suffering virtue to the time when it will meet with the *completion* of its reward" and goes on to discuss the theory of poetic justice, with copious quotations, notably from Addison's essay on the subject in the *Spectator*. This has led B. W. Downs to argue that Richardson was merely continuing the "virtue rewarded" theme of *Pamela* with the single difference that he post-dated "the reward," and paid it "in different currency from that in common use at B—— Hall": that Richardson, in fact, merely "substituted a transcendental for a sublunary audit."

Although a transcendental audit is aesthetically more satisfying in the circumstances than the very sublunary one which is found, not only in *Pamela*, but in many eighteenth-century works which attempt to combine the tragic mode with a happy ending, it must be admitted that Richardson has at best a shallow notion of religion: as a writer in the *Eclectic Review* (1805) said of him, with damning brevity: "his views of Christianity are general and obscure." On the other hand, if all examples of Christian art—or theology for that matter—in which some form of transcendental reward played an important part were to be rejected, there would be very little left, especially from the eighteenth century; we cannot fairly condemn Richardson too strongly either for sharing the complacent piety of his age or for failing to overcome the very general tendency of the Christian view of the afterlife to modify the usual effect of the death of the tragic hero.

In any case, the overpowering sense of waste and defeat actually conveyed by Clarissa's death, combined with the fortitude she displays in facing it, actually succeed in establishing a true tragic balance between the horror and the grandeur of Clarissa's death, a balance which reveals an imaginative quality of a much higher order than the jejune eschatology of Richardson's critical defence in the postscript would suggest. Here again, however, the modern reader encounters what seems to be an insuperable obstacle—the tremendous scale on which every detail of Clarissa's death is described, up to her embalming and the execution of her will. The reality of this obstacle must be in part admitted: to devote nearly one-third of the novel to the heroine's death is surely excessive. On the other hand, Richardson's emphasis can be to some extent explained on both historical and literary grounds.

Puritanism had been opposed to all the joyous festivals of the church, but it had approved of protracted rituals and even of emotional abandon where death and burial were concerned. Consequently the scope and importance of funeral arrangements had increased until, by Richardson's day, they had attained an unprecedented elaboration. Once again, therefore, it would seem that what appears to be a false note to us in *Clarissa* is also evidence of how Richardson, for good and ill, acted as a sounding board for the dominant notes of his age, and in this case, incidentally, for a note which has echoed from the Pyramids to the cemeteries of twentieth-century Los Angeles.

The later part of *Clarissa*, in fact, belongs to a long tradition of funeral literature. J. W. Draper has shown how one specifically Puritan contribution to poetry was the Funeral Elegy; and deathbed reflections were often published separately as pamphlets for evangelical purposes. Eventually both these sub-literary genres developed into a larger literary trend which exploited all the thoughts and emotions concerned with death and burial; and it was the decade in which *Clarissa* was published that saw the triumph of this movement in such works as Blair's *The Grave* (1743), Edward Young's *Night Thoughts on Life, Death, and Immortality* (1742–45) and Hervey's very popular *Meditations among the Tombs* (1746–47), the last two of which Richardson printed.

Theological works dealing with death were also among the best-sellers of the time—among them Drelincourt's *On Death*, to which Defoe's *The Apparition of Mrs. Veal* was commonly appended. It was undoubtedly part of Richardson's intentions to supply another work of this kind, a conduct book for death and burial. He wrote to Lady Bradshaigh hoping that she would place *Clarissa* on her shelf with Jeremy Taylor's *Rule and Exercises of Holy Living and Holy Dying;* and would have been happy to know that Thomas Turner, grocer of East Hoathly, and a devotee of Drelincourt, Sherlock and other specialists in the literature of death, accorded him this status: "My wife read to me that moving scene of the funeral of Miss Clarissa Harlowe," he wrote in 1754, and concluded, "Oh, may the Supreme Being give me grace to lead my life in such a manner as my exit may be in some measure like that divine creature's."

The reason for this emphasis on death seems to have been the belief that the growing secularisation of thought could best be combated by showing how only faith in the future state could provide a secure shelter from the terrors of mortality; for the orthodox at least, death, not ridicule, was the test of truth. This was one of the main themes of Young's *Night Thoughts;* and Richardson himself was responsible for the insertion into Young's *Conjectures on Original Composition* of the story of how Addison had called a young unbeliever to his bedside so that he could "see in what peace a Christian can die." To us Clarissa's preoccupation with her own coffin can only seem morbid affectation; but it must have seemed a convincing confirmation of her saintly fortitude to an age which made Newgate criminals about to be executed kneel round a coffin on their last Sunday alive while the "condemned sermon" was preached.

To his contemporaries, then, Richardson's funerary emphasis would have seemed justified for its own sake; and we, perhaps, can only try to regard it in the same light as we do a good deal of baroque memorial sculpture—forget the crushing banality of the symbolism and notice only the elaborate assurance of its presentation. At the same time we must recognise that there are strong literary reasons why Richardson should have placed such an emphasis on the death of his heroine. A very considerable length of time is required before we can forget the sordid scenes through which Clarissa has passed and remember only the final radiance, the "sweet smile" that remains on her face when Colonel Morden opens the coffin. A very complete description is necessary before we can fully appreciate, in Belford's words, "the infinite difference, on the same awful and affecting occasion, between a good and a bad conscience." Clarissa meets her end with tragic serenity, asking Belford to tell Lovelace "How happily I die:—and that such as my own, I wish to be his last hour." But Lovelace falls suddenly and unprepared, whereas by his unhurried emphasis Richrdson has contrived to give Clarissa's death all the appearance of an act of the will—it is no hasty surrender to man's mortality but a beautifully staged collaboration with the powers above that have already marked her for their own.

II

In *Clarissa*, then, Richardson solved many of the formal problems of the novel, and brought the new form into relation with the highest moral and literary standards of his day. The epistolary method, it is true, lacks the pace and crispness of Defoe's narrative manner, but *Clarissa* is what *Moll Flanders* is not, a work of serious and coherent literary art, and one which, by the almost unanimous consent of his contemporaries at home and abroad, was the greatest example of the genre ever written: Dr. Johnson called Richardson "the greatest genius that had shed its lustre on this path of literature," and considered *Clarissa* "the first book in the world for the knowledge it displays of the human heart," while Rousseau wrote in the *Lettre à d'Alembert* (1758) that "no one, in any language, has ever written a novel that equals or even approaches *Clarissa*."

That this is not the modern view does not prove that it is wrong; but it is undeniable that the moral and social preoccupations of the age obtrude themselves much more insistently in *Clarissa* than in the novels of Defoe or of Richardson's great contemporaries, and thus tend to render it much less immediately palatable to the modern reader (Defoe's moralising, we have seen, is usually viewed ironically today; while Fielding, Smollett and Sterne, being primarily comic or satirical writers, do not demand our acceptance of their positive standards in the same way). This, combined with the enormous length of *Clarissa*, and Richardson's occasional tendency to a harrowing moral and stylistic vulgarity in which Dreiser is perhaps his only peer among the great novelists, has denied the first masterpiece of the novel form the tribute which it so freely earned in its own day, and to which it is still largely entitled.

It is entitled to it primarily because Richardson's very responsiveness to the dictates of his time and his class, which did much to render *Clarissa* unpalatable today, also helped to make it a more modern novel in a sense than any other written in the eighteenth century. Richardson's deep imaginative commitment to all the problems of the new sexual ideology and his personal devotion to the exploration of the private and subjective aspects of human experience produced a novel where the relationship between the protagonists embodies a universe of moral and social conflicts of a scale and a complexity beyond anything in previous fiction; after *Clarissa* one has to wait until Jane Austen or Stendhal for a comparable example of a work which develops so freely and so profoundly under the impetus of its own fictional imperatives.

Richardson was, as has often been noted, obsessed by class distinctions. Not consciously perhaps; he seems rather to have combined an acute sense of class differences with something of the moral democracy of the earlier Puritans which eventually led to the Victorian view as expressed by G. M. Young that "the great dividing line . . . is . . . the respectable and the others." Some such duality is perhaps responsible for the very unsatisfactory treatment of the class issue in *Pamela*: virtuous indignation at upper-class licentiousness jars very unpleasantly with the heroine's abject regard for Mr. B.'s social status. In *Clarissa*, however, and perhaps because there is nothing like the same social distance between hero and heroine, Richardson achieves a much more powerful rendering not only of the social conflict itself, but of its moral implications.

Both Clarissa and Lovelace come from the wealthy landed gentry and have aristocratic connections. Those of the Harlowes, however, are only on the mother's side, and they are in no sense the equivalent of Lovelace's uncle, Lord M., or his titled half-sisters. The Harlowe "darling view," as Clarissa bitterly explains, is that of "*raising a family* . . . a view too frequently . . . entertained by families which having great substance, cannot be satisfied without rank and title." The chief repository of this ambition is James, the only son: if the family fortune, combined with those of his two childless uncles, can be concentrated on him, his enormous wealth and its accompanying political interest "might entitle him to hope for a peerage." Lovelace's courtship of Clarissa, however, threatens the realisation of this aim. Lovelace has even higher expectations, and James is afraid that his uncles may encourage the match by diverting some of their fortunes from him to Clarissa. For this reason, combined with a personal animosity towards Lovelace and perhaps an envious fear lest his sister outstrip him in the race for a coronet, James uses every possible means to make his family force Clarissa to marry Solmes. Solmes is very rich but he is meanly born, and in return for such a grand alliance will not expect any more dowry from Clarissa than her grandfather's estate, which is already hers and whose loss therefore cannot in any case be avoided.

At the outset, therefore, Clarissa is placed in a complicated conflict of class and family loyalties. Solmes is most unpleasantly typical of the rising middle class: mercenary with the squalid concentration of *"an upstart man . . .* not born to the immense riches he is possessed of," as Clarissa scornfully reports. He is totally devoid of social grace or intellectual cultivation, repulsive physically and a poor speller to boot. Lovelace, on the other hand, seems to possess the very qualities which Clarissa misses in her own environment: a generous landlord, a "person of reading, judgement and taste," and what is more, his suit is primarily motivated not by economic interest but by genuine personal admiration of Clarissa's beauty and accomplishments. As a potential lover he is immensely superior to the males of the Harlowe milieu—not only to Solmes but to her previous suitors and to Anna Howe's rather tame admirer Hickman; and there is therefore every reason why Lovelace should at first represent for Clarissa a very desirable escape from the constrictions of the Harlowe way of life, and the immediate threat of being forced to marry Solmes.

Events soon demonstrate, however, that Lovelace actually menaces her freedom and self-respect even more dangerously, and this for reasons also closely connected with his social affiliations. Primarily, of course, it is his aristocratic licentiousness, and his cynical distaste for matrimony, which are at issue, but they are accompanied by a quite conscious enmity to the moral and social attitudes of the middle class in general. Clarissa's sexual virtue is his great "stimulative" as he says, and it must be regarded as an expression of the moral superiority of her class: "were it not for the *poor* and the *middling*," he comments, "the world would probably, long ago have been destroyed by fire from Heaven." He has already deceived and ruined a Miss Betterton, of a rich trading family that "aimed at a new line of gentry"; and one of the factors which poisons his love of Clarissa is his resolve to win a much greater victory for his caste against the Harlowe family that has insulted him, and that he despises as a house "sprung up from a dunghill, within every elderly person's remembrance."

Clarissa, therefore, is without allies, and this is fitting since she is the heroic representative of all that is free and positive in the new individualism, and especially of the spiritual independence which was associated with Puritanism: as such she has to combat all the forces that were opposed to the realisation of the new concept—the aristocracy, the patriarchal family system, and even the economic individualism whose development was so closely connected with that of Puritanism.

The authoritarian nature of the family is what precipitates Clarissa's tragedy. Her father goes beyond what was generally agreed to be his legitimate paternal rights: he demands not only that she give up Lovelace but that she marry Solmes. This she must refuse, and in an interesting letter to her Uncle John enumerates the absolute dependence of her sex upon their marriage choice, and concludes that "a young creature ought not to be obliged to make all these sacrifices but for such a man as she can love."

The patriarchal authoritarianism of the Harlowe family is exacerbated by the unrestrained dominance of the dictates of economic individualism; and Clarissa is caught between the two. Much of the initial animosity that her brother and sister feel towards her is based on the fact that their grandfather has singled her out to inherit his estate. In doing so, of course, he has disregarded primogeniture, and the fact that his grandson James is the only relative who could possibly continue the family name; instead he has chosen Clarissa, a younger granddaughter, and this purely on grounds of personal preference, that is on grounds of an individual, not a family relationship. At the same time Clarissa's plight is increased by James's hatred of the traditional system of dowries: "daughters," he likes to say, "are chickens brought up for the tables of other men," and he cannot bear to think that to achieve this, "the family stock must be impaired into the bargain."

The combination of family authority with the attitudes of economic individualism not only denies Clarissa any freedom of choice, but even leads her family to treat her with calculated cruelty, on the grounds that, as her Uncle Anthony puts it, she prefers "a noted whoremonger . . . before a man that is merely a money-lover." Richardson here suggests how rigid middle-class morality, combined with a primary regard for material considerations, express themselves in a concealed and self-righteous sadism; and this was recognised by one member of his circle, Jane Collier. In her *Essay on the Art of Ingeniously Tormenting* (1753)—an early study of the minor persecutions of genteel family life—she comments on "How much must an old Harlowe enjoy himself in loading a Clarissa with money, clothes, jewels, and etc., whilst he knows, that all she wants from him, is kind looks, and kind words."

A perfectly realised scene depicting this kind of persecution occurs when her sister Arabella tortures Clarissa by pretending not to understand why she is unwilling to talk about the trousseau which has been ordered for her wedding with Solmes. Clarissa, who has been confined to her room for disobedience, thus reports the visit of Arabella and her aunt:

> My sister left my aunt musing at the window, with her back towards us; and took that opportunity to insult me still more barbarously: for, stepping to my closet, she took up the patterns which my mother had sent me up, and bringing them to me, she

spread them upon the chair by me; and, offering one, and then another, upon her sleeve and shoulder, thus she ran on, with great seeming tranquillity, but whisperingly, that my aunt might not hear her. *This*, Clary, is a pretty pattern enough: but *this* is quite *charming*! I would advise you to make your appearance in it. And *this*, were I you, should be my wedding night-gown, and *this* my second dressed suit! Won't you give orders love, to have your grandmother's jewels new set? Or will you think to show away in the new ones Mr. Solmes intends to present to you? He talks of laying out two or three thousand pounds in presents, child! Dear Heart, how gorgeously you will be arrayed! What! Silent my dear!

Clarissa escapes from such oppressions and the struggle is transferred to the purely individual plane. Even here, however, she is under great disadvantages. The mere fact that she has left home to protect her own freedom and not out of love for him gives deep offence to Lovelace's pride; while the main issue that separates them, that of marriage, presents peculiar difficulties. As far as Lovelace is concerned, to consent to marriage is to yield Clarissa too easy a triumph: it means that "a man is rather to be *her* prize, then she *his*." Lovelace therefore tries by every stratagem to make her love "come forward and show itself," to have the attraction of his maleness fully acknowledged; and it is only when this fails, and he fears that "she presumes to think that she can be happy *without* me" that he uses force, hoping that then at least family pressure and public opinion will force her to remain with him.

The way that Lovelace exploits every disadvantage of her situation means that Clarissa continues to be confronted with the issue which parental tyranny first raised—the power of all the forces which deny her sex their just equality with men. She is indeed, as Richardson implies during Belford's discussion of *The Fair Penitent*, engaged in the same cause as Rowe's heroine Calista, and asks with her:

> Wherefore are we
> Born with high souls, but to assert ourselves,
> Shake off this vile obedience they exact,
> And claim an equal empire o'er the world?

Unlike Calista, however, and because she is pure and guiltless, Clarissa is eventually able to conquer her Lothario with spiritual weapons. At first Lovelace proclaimed himself "a very Jew" in believing "that women have no souls," but he is finally convinced of the reality of considerations which had not previously entered his mind: Clarissa's behaviour as she undergoes her terrible trials persuades him that "justly did she tell me . . . that her soul was my soul's superior." Such is the wholly unexpected result of his experiment to vanquish her with the methods he has previously employed so successfully against other members of Clarissa's sex: for the first time he has been brought up against the fact that the individual is ultimately a spiritual entity and that Clarissa is a finer one than he.

In a sense, therefore, Clarissa's triumph is one in which her sex is irrelevant and looks forward to the new and inward ethical sanction which an individualistic society requires, and of which Kant was to be the philosophical spokesman. His categorical imperative was based on the premise that "persons, because their very nature points them out as ends in themselves . . . must not be used merely as means." Lovelace uses Clarissa, as he uses everybody else, as a means to gratify his pride in his caste, his sex and his intellect; Clarissa at first fails in the eyes of the world because she does not use others as means, but eventually she proves that no individual and no institution can destroy the inner inviolability of the human personality. This realisation completely cows him: as he confesses, "I never knew what fear of man was—nor fear of woman neither, till I became acquainted with Miss Clarissa Harlowe; nay, what is *most* surprising, till I came to have her in my power."

If Richardson had stopped here, *Clarissa* would have been a work analogous to such later portrayals in the Puritan tradition of the tragedy of feminine individualism as George Eliot's *Middlemarch* and Henry James's *Portrait of a Lady*. The three novels reveal the all but unendurable disparity between expectation and reality that faces sensitive women in modern society, and the difficulties that lie before anyone who is unwilling either to be used, or to use others, as a means. Richardson's fascinated absorption in the sexual issue, however, produced a treatment of the theme which is starker, less reticent, and, perhaps, even more revealing.

Clarissa is, among other things, the supreme embodiment of the new feminine stereotype, a very paragon of delicacy. This is a crucial factor in her relations with Lovelace, who carefully contrives not to propose marriage in such a way as would enable Clarissa to agree without compromising her delicacy, which she refuses to do: "Would he have me catch at his first, his *very* first word?" she asks on one occasion, and on another, when Lovelace cruelly asks if she has any objections to delaying a few days until Lord M. can attend the wedding, she is forced by her sense of "due decorum" to answer, "No, no, You cannot think that I should imagine there can be reasons for such a hurry." As a result, even Anna Howe thinks that Clarissa is "over-nice, over-delicate," and she strongly urges that Clarissa "condescend to clear up his doubts." Richardson, however, points out in a footnote that "it was not possible for a person of her true delicacy of mind to act otherwise than she did, to a man so cruelly and insolently artful": and in fact Lovelace understood this very well, as he explained to Belford: "Never, I believe, was there so true, so delicate a modesty in the human mind as in that of this lady . . . this has been my security all along."

The reinforced taboo on women avowing their feelings in courtship is, therefore, primarily responsible for the way that the deadlock between Clarissa and Lovelace drags out so long, becoming uglier and more desperate in the process. Richardson, indeed, with remarkable objectivity, even makes Lovelace challenge the whole basis of the code. He wonders whether women should really be proud of having "wilful and *studied* delays, *imputed to them*" over marriage: "are they not," he suggests, "indelicate in their affected delicacy; for do they not thereby tacitly confess that they expect to be the greatest gainers in wedlock; and that there is *self-denial* in the pride they take in delaying."

Lovelace is himself a representative of the masculine stereotype against which the feminine code is a defence. He believes, for example, that the hypocritical bashfulness of the "*passive* sex" justifies his own in using forceful methods. "It is cruel to ask a modest woman for her consent," he writes, and finds a kind of support in the views of Anna Howe who believes that "our sex are best dealt with by boisterous and unruly spirits." Clarissa sees that a larger issue is at stake, and pleads that a "modest woman" should "distinguish and wish to consort with a modest man" such as the unexciting Hickman: but Lovelace knows better; women do not really desire such a lover—"a *male virgin*—I warrant!" For, as he rather wittily puts it, a virtuous woman can "expect . . . the confidence *she* wants" if she marries a rake, whereas she cannot but consider the virtuous male "and herself as two parallel lines; which, though they run side by side, can never meet."

Lovelace himself, like the rakes and heroes of Restoration drama, gives his allegiance to a debased form of romantic love, thus underlining his historical role as the representative of the Cavalier attitude to sex, in conflict with the Puritan one represented by Clarissa. Sexual passion is placed upon a different and higher plane than the institutional arrangement of marriage, and so, although the divine Clarissa Harlowe can almost make him think of "foregoing the *life of honour* for the *life of shackles*," his darling hope is "to prevail upon her to live with [him] what [he] call[s] the life of honour," in which he will promise "never to marry any other woman," but in which their felicity will be uncontaminated by the rites of matrimony.

That, at least, is his scheme: to win her on his own terms; with always the possibility that he can marry her afterwards, once his personality and his code have had their triumph. "Will not the generality of the world acquit me, if I *do* marry?" he asks. "And what is that injury which a *church rite* will not at any time repair? Is not the *catastrophe of every story that ends in wedlock accounted happy?*"

As the world goes, Lovelace is perhaps as close to the average view as Clarissa, and his attitude finds some support in the story of *Pamela.* But Richardson was now in a much more serious mood, and, as he announced in the preface, was now determined to challenge "that dangerous but too-commonly-received notion, *that a reformed rake makes the best husband.*" So he introduced the rape when Clarissa is unconscious from opiates, which is perhaps the least convincing incident in the book, but which serves a number of important moral and literary purposes.

First, and most obviously for Richardson's didactic purpose, it puts Lovelace wholly beyond the pale of any conception of honour, and proclaims to all the barbarity which lies below the genteel veneer of rakery; this Lovelace himself comes to realise, and curses himself for having taken the advice of Mrs. Sinclair and her crew. Not, of course, out of moral compunction, but because it is an admission of complete defeat: in his own eyes, since, as he says, "there is no triumph in *force.* No conquest over the will": and in the eyes of the world, since as John Dennis cynically remarked, "A rape in tragedy is a panegyrick upon the sex . . . for . . . the woman . . . is supposed to re-main innocent, and to be pleased without her consent; while the man, who is accounted a damned villain, proclaims the power of female charms, which have the force to drive him to so horrid a violence."

Once Lovelace has found that, contrary to his expectation, it is not a case of "*once overcome . . . for ever overcome,*" Clarissa is able to demonstrate the falsity of his view of the feminine code, and defy him in the famous words, "That man who has been the villain to me that you have been shall never make me his wife." Clarissa's sense of her own honour is much more important than her reputation in the eyes of the world; the code, in fact, is not a hypocritical sham; Lovelace's assumption that "the for-better and for-worse legerdemain" would "hocus pocus . . . all the wrongs I have done Miss Harlowe into acts of kindness and benevolence to Mrs. Lovelace" is completely disproved, and he succumbs to such "irresistible proofs of the love of virtue for its own sake."

If this were all, the conflict in *Clarissa* would still, perhaps, be too sim-ple for a work of such length. Actually, however, the situation is much more complex and problematic.

Freud showed how the artificiality of the modern sexual code "must incline [the members of society] to concealment of the truth, to euphemism, to self-deception, and to the deception of others." In *Pamela* this self-deception produces irony: the reader contrasts the heroine's pretended motives with her transparent but largely unconscious purpose. In *Clarissa*, however, a similar unawareness of sexual feeling on the heroine's part, which by others may be interpreted as gross lack of self-knowledge, if not actual dishonesty, becomes an important part of the dramatic development, deepening and amplifying the overt meaning of the story.

Johnson observes of Clarissa that "there is always something which she prefers to truth." But Anna Howe justly points out that as far as women's communication with men is concerned, this duplicity is imposed by the sexual code: for, as she says, if a woman writes "her heart to a man practised in deceit, or even to a man of some character, what advantage does it give him over her!" The real tragedy, however, is that the code also makes Clarissa withhold her sexual feelings from Anna Howe, and even from her own consciousness, and it is this which creates the main psychological tension in the early volumes, for which Johnson particularly admired Richardson. The correspondence of Clarissa, and, to a lesser extent, of Lovelace, is an absorbing study because we can never assume that any statement should be taken as the complete and literal truth. Perhaps one of the reasons for Johnson's admiration was that, although as we have seen he believed that a man's "soul lies naked" in his letters, he also knew that "There is . . . no transaction which offers stronger temptations to fallacy and sophistication then epistolary intercourse."

The counterpoint of these unconscious duplicities in the early volumes is built upon the fact that Anna believes that Clarissa is in love with Lovelace, and does not believe Clarissa's protestations that her elopement was entirely accidental and involuntary on her part. After the marriage has been long delayed, Anna Howe even thinks it necessary to write to Clarissa: "What then have you to do but to fly this house, this infernal house! Oh that your heart would let you fly the *man*!" Lovelace, it is true, seizes the letter, and Clarissa escapes on her own initiative. Nevertheless, until half the book is done, there is a genuine ambiguity about the situation in everyone's mind; we are fully entitled to suspect Clarissa herself of not knowing her own feelings: and Lovelace is not altogether wrong in suspecting her of the "female affectation of denying [her] love."

As the story develops, Clarissa herself gradually makes this discovery. Very early she has cause to wonder "what turn my mind had taken to dictate so oddly to my pen" in the course of a letter about Lovelace; and her debates with Anna Howe about her real attitude to him eventually force her to question whether her original hope that she could reform Lovelace was not actually a mask for less creditable motives. "What strange imperfect beings!" she reflects. "But *self* here, which is at the bottom of all we do, and of all we wish, is the grand misleader." "Once you wrote," she confesses to Anna Howe, "that men of his cast are the men that our sex do not *naturally* dislike: while I held that such were not (however *that* might be) the men we *ought* to like." She cannot deny that she "could have liked Mr. Lovelace above all men," and that there may be some justice in the tenor of Anna's raillery that she did not "attend to the throbs" of her heart; her principle that we should "like and dislike as reason bids us" was not so easy to practise as she imagined; and she convicts herself "of a punishable fault" in having loved him, punishable because "what must be that love that has not some degree of purity for its object?" But, as she realises, "love and hatred" are not "voluntary passions," and so, although without any full clarification of her feelings, she admits "detection" by Anna of her passion for Lovelace: "*Detection*, must I call it?" she wonders, and adds defeatedly: "What can I call it?"

Throughout the novel Clarissa is learning more about herself, but at the same time she is also learning more about the much blacker deceptions of Lovelace. The minor reticences and confusions revealed in the feminine correspondence are insignificant compared to the much grosser discrepancies between Lovelace's pretended attitudes to Clarissa and the falsehoods and trickeries which his letters reveal. The masculine code allows him to practise, and even openly avow, his complete lack of truth and honour in his pursuit of the opposite sex. As Belford points out, "*our honour*, and *honour* in the *general acceptation* of the word are two things," and Lovelace's honour is such that he has "never lied to man, and hardly ever said truth to woman." As a result of these revelations we realise that the code which might seem to make Clarissa too prudent is not prudent enough when measured against the outrageous means which men allow themselves to gain their ends. But if Clarissa's code fosters the self-ignorance which helps to place her in Lovelace's power, it at least does not involve conscious deception; and so Lovelace is forced to see that since Clarissa cannot "stoop to deceit and falsehood, no, not to save herself," Belford was right when he asserted that "the trial is not a fair trial."

The sophistries both conscious and unconscious produced by the sexual code, then, helped Richardson to produce a pattern of psychological surprise and discovery very similar in nature to that in *Pamela*, although the counterpoint between feminine self-deception and masculine trickery is of a much more extended and powerful kind. But Richardson's explorations of the unconscious forms taken by the sexual impulse also took him much further; and he added to the already complex series of dualities embodied in the relationship of Lovelace and Clarissa quite another range of meanings which may be regarded as the ultimate and no doubt pathological expression of the dichotomisation of the sexual roles in the realm of the unconscious.

The imagery in which the relation between the sexes is rendered indicates the basic tendency of Richardson's thought. Lovelace fancies himself as an eagle, flying only at the highest game; Belford calls him "cruel as a panther"; while Anna sees him as a hyena. The metaphor of the hunt, indeed, informs the whole of Lovelace's conception of sex: he writes to Belford, for example: "we begin when boys, with birds, and when grown up, go on with women; and both, perhaps, in turn, experience our sportive cruelty." Then he gloats as he pictures "the charming gradations" by which the bird yields to its captor as he hopes Clarissa will yield to him, and concludes, "By my soul, Jack, there is more of the savage in human nature than we are commonly aware of." But Jack is already aware of it, in Lovelace's case at least, and replies: "Thou ever delightedst to sport with and torment the animal, whether bird or beast, that thou lovedst and hadst a power over."

Sadism is, no doubt, the ultimate form which the eighteenth-century view of the masculine role involved: and it makes the female role one in which the woman is, and can only be, the prey: to use another of Lovelace's metaphors, man is a spider, and woman is the predestined fly.

This conceptualisation of the sexual life has had an illustrious literary history since Richardson. Mario Praz has seen *Clarissa* as the beginning of what he calls "the theme of the persecuted maiden," a theme which was taken up by de Sade, and played an important part in Romantic literature. Later, in a somewhat milder form, this picture of the sexual relationship established itself in England. The Victorian imagination was haunted by the perpetual imminence of attacks on pure womanhood by cruel and licentious males, while, in a Rochester or a Heathcliff, the feminine and Puritan imaginations of Charlotte and Emily Brontë produced a stereotype of the male as a combination of terrifying animality and diabolic intellect which is equally pathological.

The complement of the sadistic and sexual male is the masochistic and asexual female; and in *Clarissa* this conception is present both in the imagery connected with the heroine and in the underlying implication of the central action. As regards imagery, Clarissa, significantly, is symbolised not by the rose but the lily: Lovelace sees her on one occasion as "a half-broken-stalked lily, top-heavy with the overcharging dews of morning," and Clarissa later arranges that her funeral urn be decorated with "the head of a white lily snapped short off, and just falling from the stalk." In the realm of action, the rape itself, when Clarissa is unconscious from opiates, may be regarded as the ultimate development of the idea of the feminine sexual role as one of passive suffering: it suggests that the animality of the male can only achieve its purpose when the woman's spirit is absent.

Even so, Clarissa dies; sexual intercourse, apparently, means death for the woman. What Richardson intended here is not wholly clear, but it may be noted that he had already shown a remarkable awareness of the symbolism of the unconscious in *Pamela*. When the heroine is still terrified of Mr. B. she imagines him pursuing her in the shape of a bull with bloodshot eyes; later, when a happy resolution is in sight she dreams, appropriately enough, of Jacob's ladder. It is significant, therefore, that just before her elopement, Clarissa should have a dream in which Lovelace stabs her to the heart; then, she reports, he "tumbled me into a deep grave ready dug, among two or three half-dissolved carcasses; throwing in the dirt and earth upon me with his hands, and trampling it down with his feet." The dream is primarily a macabre expression of her actual fear of Lovelace; but it is also coloured by the idea that sexual intercourse is a kind of annihilation.

This connection haunts the later part of the story. Though afraid of Lovelace, she goes off with him; and later, when his intentions are becoming more evident, she several times offers him knives or scissors to kill her with. One of these occasions is thus reported by Lovelace: "baring, with a still more frantic violence, part of her enchanting neck, Here, here, said the soul-harrowing beauty, let thy pointed mercy enter." Unconsciously, no doubt, Clarissa courts sexual violation as well as death; and when the violation comes its equation with death is apparent to both parties. Lovelace announces, "The affair is over. Clarissa lives"—as though the contrary might have been expected; while later Clarissa directs that if Lovelace insists "upon viewing *her dead* whom he ONCE before saw in a manner dead, let his gay curiosity be gratified."

In a sense the coming death to which Clarissa here refers is a working out of her own initial masochistic fantasy: having equated sex and death, and having been violated by Lovelace, her self-respect requires that the expected consequence ensue: her decline is as the physician says, clearly not a bodily matter but "a love case." Not much is said about the covert and implacable cause why her fate cannot be otherwise, but there is never any doubt about the fact itself: anything else would prove her deepest self to have been wrong.

This, of course, is not the only cause of her death, which has a very complex motiviation. It is, for example, quite consistent with Richardson's beliefs that Clarissa should prefer death to the burden of her sexual desecration, even though it is, as Lovelace says, "a mere *notional violation*." But there is also more than a hint that what Clarissa cannot face is not so much what Lovelace has done or what the world may think about it, but the idea that she herself is not wholly blameless.

This idea is most clearly expressed in one of the fragments which she writes in her delirium after the rape:

> A lady took a great fancy to a young lion, or a bear, I forget which—but of a bear, or a tiger, I believe it was. It was made her a present of when a whelp. She fed it with her own hand: she nursed up the wicked cub with great tenderness; and would play with it without fear or apprehension of danger . . . But mind what followed: at last, somehow, neglecting to satisfy its hungry maw, or having otherwise disobliged it on some occasion, it resumed its nature; and on a sudden fell upon her, and tore her in pieces, And who was most to blame, I pray? The brute, or the lady? The lady, surely! For what *she* did was *out* of nature, *out* of character, at least: what it did was *in* its own nature.

Lovelace, being a man, had done only what was to be expected: but Clarissa had acted out of nature in toying with him. Looking back, she perhaps remembers that Anna Howe, mocking her own claim that "she would not be in love with him for the world," had ironically congratulated her on "being the first of our sex that ever I heard of who has been able to turn that lion, Love, at her own pleasure, into a lap-dog." And this bitter reminder that she was wrong may have caused her to look within and glimpse the truth that even she was not above what Lovelace calls the "disgraceful" weaknesses "of sex and nature." With such a belief poisoning her mind, the need to be delivered from the body becomes imperative; she must act out in a very literal fashion the words of St. Paul in *Romans*: "I delight in the law of God after the inward man. But I see another law in my members, warring against the law of my mind . . . O wretched man that I am! Who shall deliver me from the body of this death?"

In a historical perspective, it seems clear, Clarissa's tragedy reflects the combined effects of Puritanism's spiritual inwardness and its fear of the flesh, effects which tend to prevent the development of the sexual impulse beyond the autistic and masochistic stages. Freud and Horace are agreed that *Naturam expellas furca, tamen usque recurret*—a sentiment, incidentally, which was familiar to Richardson since Lovelace quotes it—and it is not surprising, therefore, that Clarissa's *Liebestod* should suggest that the erotic impulse has been channelled in varied and divergent directions. The perverse sensuous pleasure which she takes in every detail of the preparations for her coming death is primarily due to the feeling that she is at least about to meet the heavenly bridegroom: "I am upon a *better preparation* than for an earthly husband," she proclaims. "Never bride was so ready as I am. My wedding garments are bought . . . the easiest, the *happiest* suit, that ever bridal maiden wore." But her pleasure in her own approaching demise also has a strong narcissistic quality. Belford reports that "the principal device" she chose for her coffin "is a crowned serpent, with its tail in its mouth, forming a ring, the emblem of eternity": emblem of eternity, doubtless, but also emblem of an endlessly self-consuming sexual desire.

Opinions may well vary over the details of the meaning of the psychopathological aspects of *Clarissa*, but there can at least be no doubt that this was one of the directions which Richardson's imagination took, and that he there demonstrated a remarkable insight into the by now notorious sophistries of the unconscious and subconscious mind. Further evidence of this is to be found in the scenes after the rape, and in Clarissa's incoherent letter to Lovelace: Fielding praised it as "beyond anything I have ever read." Another great contemporary admirer, Diderot, specifically pointed to the exploration of the deeper recesses of the mind as Richardson's *forte*—a testimony which carries considerable authority in the light of his own treatment of the theme in *Le Neveu de Rameau*. It was Richardson, Diderot said, "qui porte le flambeau au fond de la caverne; c'est lui qui apprend à discerner les motifs subtils et déshonnêtes qui se cachent et se dérobent sous d'autres motifs qui sont honnêtes et qui se hâtent de se montrer les premiers. Il souffle sur le phantôme sublime qui se présente à l'entrée de la caverne; et le More hideux qu'il masquait s'aperçoit." Such certainly is the nature of the voyage of discovery which we take in *Clarissa*; and the hideous Moor is surely the frightening reality of the unconscious life which lies hidden in the most virtuous heart.

Such an interpretation would imply that Richardson's imagination was not always in touch with his didactic purpose; but this, of course, is in itself not unlikely. The decorous exterior, the ponderous voice of the lay bishop, expresses an important part of Richardson's mind, but not all of it; and, his subjects being what they were, it is likely that only a very safe ethical surface, combined with the anonymity of print, and a certain tendency to self-righteous sophistry, were able to pacify his inner censor and thus leave his imagination free to express its profound interest in other areas of experience.

Some such process seems to have occurred in Richardson's portrayal of Lovelace as well as of Clarissa. There was probably a much deeper identification with his rake than he knew, an identification which left traces in such a remark as this of Lovelace: "Were every rake, nay, were every man, to sit down, as I do, and write all that enters into his head or into his heart, and to accuse himself with equal freedom and truth, what an army of miscreants should I have to keep me in countenance!" Elsewhere, the prodigious fertility of Lovelace's sexual imagination surely suggests a willing cooperation on the part of his creator's far beyond the call of literary duty: Lovelace's plan, for instance, of wreaking his revenge on Anna Howe, not only by ravishing her, but in having her mother abducted for the same fell purpose is a monstrously gratuitous fancy which is quite unnecessary so far as the realisation of Richardson's didactic intentions are concerned.

The ultimate effect of Richardson's unconscious identification, however, would seem to be wholly justified from an aesthetic point of view. The danger in the original scheme of the novel was that Lovelace would be so brutal and callow that the relationship with Clarissa would be incapable of supporting a developing and reciprocal psychological pattern. Richardson, however, diminished the disparity between his protagonists by supplying their personalities with psychological undertones which do something to qualify the apparently diametrical opposition between them. He mitigated Clarissa's perfections by suggesting that her deeper self has its morbid aspects—a suggestion which actually increases the pathos of her story but which brings her closer in a sense to the world of Lovelace; and at the same time he led us to feel that, just as his heroine's virtue is not without its complications, so his villain's vices have their pitiable aspect.

Lovelace's name—in sound as in etymology—means "loveless"; and his code—that of the rake—has, like Clarissa's, blinded him to his own deepest feelings. From the beginning one side of his character is continually struggling to express its love for Clarissa openly and honourably, and it often almost succeeds. Clarissa, indeed, is aware of this undercurrent in his nature: "What *sensibilities*," she tells him, "must thou have suppressed! What a dreadful, what a judicial hardness of heart must thine be; who canst be capable of such emotions as sometimes thou hast shown; and of such sentiments as sometimes have flown from thy lips; yet canst have so far overcome them all, as to be able to act as thou hast acted, and that from settled purpose and premeditation."

This division in Lovelace between conscious villainy and stifled goodness provides yet another satisfying formal symmetry to the conduct of the narrative. For, just as Clarissa began by loving Lovelace unconsciously and then was forced to see that, in truth, he did not deserve it, so Lovelace begins with a feeling in which hate and love are mixed, but comes eventually to love her completely, although only after he himself has made it impossible for her to reciprocate. Clarissa could perhaps have married Lovelace, very much on her own terms, had she known her own feelings earlier, and not been at first so wholly unaware, and later so frightened, of her sexual component; so Lovelace need not have lost Clarissa, if he had known and been willing to recognise the gentler elements in his personality.

The ultimate reason why this was impossible is, indeed, the exact complement of that which causes Clarissa's virtual suicide: both their fates show the havoc brought about by two codes which doom their holders to a psychological attitude which makes human love impossible, since they set an impenetrable barrier between the flesh and the spirit. Clarissa dies rather than recognise the flesh; Lovelace makes it impossible for her to love him because he, too, makes an equally absolute, though opposite, division: if he wishes "to prove her to be either angel or woman," Clarissa has no alternative but to make the choice she does, reject her physical womanhood, and prove, in Lovelace's words, that "her frost is frost indeed." At the same time for him also the only possibility of salvation lies in the rejection of his own illusion of himself which, like Clarissa's, is ultimately a projection of false sexual ideology. "If I give up my contrivances," he writes in a moment of heart-searching, "I shall be but a common man." But, of course, he is, like Clarissa, so deeply attached to his own preconceptions of himself that he cannot change; the deadlock is complete, and, as he confesses, "what to do with her, or without her, I know not."

For Lovelace also, therefore, death is the only way out. His end, it is true, is not a suicide, but it is like Clarissa's in the sense that he has in part provoked it, and that he has been forewarned in a dream, a dream where, thinking at last to embrace her, he sees the firmament open to receive her and then, left alone, the floor sinks under him and he falls into a bottomless Inferno. His unconscious premonition is confirmed by the event, but not before he has made expiation, admitting to his slayer Colonel Morden that he has provoked his destiny, and imploring Clarissa's Blessed Spirit to look down with pity and forgiveness.

So ends a relationship that, in this at least like those of the great lovers of myth and legend, endures beyond death. Clarissa and Lovelace are as completely, and as fatally, dependent on each other as Tristan and Isolde or Romeo and Juliet; but, in keeping with the novel's subjective mode of vision, the ultimate barriers that prevent the union of Richardson's star-crossed lovers are subjective and in part unconscious; the stars operate on the individual through varied psychological forces, forces which are eventually, no doubt, public and social, since the differences between the protagonists represent larger conflicts of attitude and ethnic in their society, but which are nevertheless so completely internalised that the conflict expresses itself as a struggle between personalities and even between different parts of the same personality.

This is Richardson's triumph. Even the most apparently implausible, didactic or period aspects of the plot and the characters, even the rape and Clarissa's unconscionable time a-dying, are brought into a larger dramatic pattern of infinite formal and psychological complexity. It is this capacity for a continuous enrichment and complication of a simple situation which makes Richardson the great novelist he is; and it shows, too, that the novel had at last attained literary maturity, with formal resources capable not only of supporting the tremendous imaginative expansion which Richardson gave his theme, but also of leading him away from the flat didacticism of his critical preconceptions into so profound a penetration of his characters that their experience partakes of the terrifying ambiguity of human life itself.

MARTIN PRICE

The Divided Heart:
Clarissa and Lovelace

In Samuel Richardson's *Clarissa* (1748) the theme of the divided heart—or in Clarissa's own phrase, the "unexamined heart"—is given formal rigor and tragic consequences. Clarissa's elevation of spirit arouses fear and jealousy in her family; and, as the Harlowes impose their will more and more cruelly, Clarissa finds herself drawn to Lovelace. Her desires to reclaim his faulty nature and to escape her family combine to make her Lovelace's victim. Once he has raped her, she puts beneath consideration all earthly solutions to her plight. She chooses to die, to become the bride of Christ; and her coffin becomes her marriage bed.

Lovelace is trapped by Clarissa in turn. He is a libertine who cannot endure the hindering of his will; he needs to control and subdue others, and he finds tremendous, almost sexual, pleasure in deceit and disguise. Yet there is an element of self-hatred in Lovelace, too, that attracts him to virtue. He must disprove its existence or be conquered by it, and he hardly knows which he wishes the more. The appeal of Clarissa is precisely her power to resist, and thus to conquer him; but he must test her to the utmost. If he can have her on his own terms, he will have preserved his old identity and shown up the claims of a higher order. If he is conquered by her, he will find a new identity; and it is clear that he half hopes this may happen. But the rape destroys both possibilities; in taking Clarissa by force, he has not conquered her will, and his effort to resolve the problem by offering her marriage only wins her scorn.

After the rape, Clarissa moves toward sainthood, and Lovelace discovers

From *To the Palace of Wisdom: Studies in Order and Energy from Dryden to Blake*. © 1964 by Martin Price. Southern Illinois University Press, 1964.

the emptiness of his satanism. She is now hopelessly "above" him. The orders of being have been completely sundered, and there is no possible reconciliation. The power of the book comes of the terrible force that each of these two characters exerts on the other. Each makes the other a supreme instance of a moral type. They are led to absolute self-assertion, and they "stand in contrast," as Alan D. McKillop puts it, "to many of the surrounding characters who are bogged down in convention and give automatic responses, facile and superficial answers to the questions that beset the principals" (*The Early Masters of English Fiction*).

Lovelace is one of the great characters of English fiction, and we can begin to understand him by looking back to the Restoration heroes. "Lovelace inherits the cynicism and the fluency of the fashionable libertine of Restoration comedy," McKillop observes. "But he is also the superman of the heroic play; he has the lawless egotism common both to the heroes and the villains of the genre." Dryden is Lovelace's favorite poet, and he quotes from *The Conquest of Granada*, *Aureng-Zebe*, *Tyrannic Love*, and *Don Sebastian*. Like the Restoration heroes, Lovelace has a skeptical distrust of the false order that the world conspires to maintain. Like Almanzor or Dorax, he despises cant and hypocrisy. Of the Harlowes he writes: "*soul!* did I say—there is not a soul among them but my charmer's." His difficulties with them arise from his refusal to be "a sly sinner, an hypocrite." He scorns those "*tame spirits* which value themselves upon reputation, and are held within the skirts of the law by political considerations only." When he defends his conduct against his converted and repentant friend, Belford, he can point to the way of the world:

> Out upon me for an impolitic wretch! I have not the art of the least artful of any of your Christian princes, who every day are guilty of ten times worse breaches of faith: and yet, issuing out a manifesto, they wipe their mouths, and go on from infraction to infraction; commit devastation upon devastation; and destroy—for their glory! And are rewarded with the names of *conquerors*, and are dubbed *Le Grand*; praised, and even deified, by orators and poets, for their butcheries and depredations.

One need not take Lovelace's protestations at face value, but one must recognize an aspect of generosity in his defiant boldness. He is a liberal landlord who refuses to rack his tenants. He spends money lavishly, but never to the point of losing his independence of his family. He and Belford, even as libertines, recognize "the noble simplicity, and natural ease and dignity," of the Scriptures, and Lovelace finds scriptural quotations in the works of modern authors who seek to appropriate them "like a rich vein of golden ore which runs through baser metals." There are moral grounds, in short, for Lovelace's disdain of conventional respectability. Is he worse in his treatment of Clarissa than was "the *pious* Aeneas" in his behavior to Dido? Or the good Protestant Elizabeth in her behavior to Mary of Scotland? "Come, come, Belford," he concludes, "I am *comparatively* a very innocent man."

Much of this is pretext and self-justification, but by no means all. Like many libertines Lovelace has an impossible standard of goodness. When he cites Mandeville, he refers to him as his "worthy friend"; and, like Mandeville, he makes the idea of virtue so remote and unattainable that men must despair of achieving it. But Lovelace is not so untroubled as Mandeville. While he glories in his contrivances and in his deception of Clarissa, he is still scarcely able to control his impulse to surrender to her. He snatches her hand and violently exclaims, "take me, take me to yourself; mould me as you please; I am wax in your hands; give me your own impression, and seal me for ever yours. We were born for each other!—you to make me happy, and save a soul—I am all error, all crime." He boasts to Belford that this is all play-acting, that he played the role so intensely because he could scarcely control his passion at the time. But a few days later he finds himself proposing marriage "by an involuntary impulse, in defiance of premeditation, and of all his proud schemes." Later, he looks at Clarissa's tearful uplifted face and asks himself, "And can I be a villain to such an angel!—I hope not."

As libertine, Lovelace is consistently naturalistic. He invokes a barnyard analogy to describe the lover: "he struts over her with an erected crest, and with an exulting chuck-a chuck-aw-aw-w, circling round her with dropped wings, sweeping the dust in humble courtship." And while he dwells on his treatment of Clarissa as the taming of a caged bird, he invokes a larger view of natural cruelty, with Hobbesian overtones: "How usual a thing is it for women as well as men, without the least remorse, to ensnare, to cage, and torment, and even with burning knitting-needles to put out the eyes of the poor feathered songster" which "has more life than themselves (for a bird is all soul)." The cynicism with which Lovelace regards his fellow men ("Have I not often said *that human nature is a rogue*," betrays the bitterness of disappointment, even of moral outrage.

In his treatment of Clarissa, it is impossible to separate the sexual excitement Lovelace finds in her resistance from the moral excitement he finds in her virtue. He must prove to himself that she is only a woman, and women have never finally been able to resist him. But he senses the disaster that impends: "Why was such a woman as this thrown in my way, whose very fall will be her glory, and perhaps not only my shame, but my destruction?" And

the torture increases. "By my soul, I cannot forgive her for her virtues! There
is no bearing the consciousness of the infinite inferiority she charged me with.
But why will she break from me, when good resolutions are taking place?
The red-hot iron she refuses to strike—Oh, why will she suffer the yielding
wax to harden?" When the pressure of her virtue becomes more than he can
endure, Lovelace resorts once more to the reductive explanation: " 'Tis pride,
a greater pride than my own, that governs her."

When, after the rape, Clarissa refuses marriage, Lovelace at last confronts what he has both yearned and feared to see: "Such irresistible proofs
of the love of virtue *for its own sake*," he tells her, "did I never hear of,
nor meet with, in all my reading." It is to this theme he constantly returns:

> Oh, my damned incredulity! That, believing her to *be* a woman,
> I must hope to *find* her a woman! Oh, my incredulity that there
> could be such a virtue (virtue for *virtue's* sake) in the sex, found-
> ed I my hope of succeeding with her.

Clarissa comes, at last, to accomplish her purpose of awakening him out
of his "sensual dream." He still fluctuates between the resurgent libertine,
hectically defiant and skeptical, and the repentant worshiper, possessively
trying to make Clarissa his own even after her death—"Clarissa Lovelace
let me call her." But he dies completely possessed by Clarissa, as much her
captive as she had been his: "Look down, Blessed Spirit, look down!"

Lovelace's pride and need to control others are only one aspect of his
nature. The other is the vacuity his self-assertion and swagger have been used
to conceal. The weakness of Lovelace's pride (Clarissa has remarked on this)
is made clear in the final scenes. "Oh the triumphant subduer," he exclaims.
"Ever above me! And now to leave me so infinitely below her!" He can examine his heart at last: "to bring her down from among the stars . . . that
my wife, so greatly above me, might not despise me; this was one of my reptile motives, owing to my *more* reptile envy, and to my consciousness of
inferiority to her!"

The character of Clarissa has been more fully explored by critics, and
there has been growing agreement about the nature of Clarissa's "unconscious
duplicities." We can never assume, Ian Watt points out, that any statement
she makes "should be taken as the complete and literal truth." Until "the
book is half done . . . we are fully entitled to suspect Clarissa herself of not
knowing her own feelings." Or as Dr. Johnson put it, "There is always
something which she prefers to truth." If Richardson seems at times to deny
this weakness in his heroine, we can invoke Leslie Fiedler's formula: Richardson knows what she really feels "though he does not quite know he knows

it." The result of this "happy state of quasi-insight" is that Richardson "never falsifies the hidden motivations of his protagonists." Certainly one feels that Richardson is more accurate than his rather prim consciousness might have been expected to permit.

Clarissa is clearly attracted by Lovelace, and for good reason. His generosity and recklessness are in marked contrast to the tight, ritualized, status-seeking regimen of the Harlowes. Even his intrigues, which show him in a shabbier aspect, make him the counterpart of a Restoration comic hero in a world of shoddy hypocrites more culpable than himself. In such a world, Clarissa tries to maintain independence and freedom of choice. But she herself is a person of strong will, who terrifies her mother and is capable of a measure of malice to her genuinely malicious sister. One discovers only gradually the full degree of Clarissa's complicity in encouraging Lovelace's clandestine letters. Her motives are not necessarily what they seem to herself. Her friend Anna Howe can recognize Clarissa's incipient love for Lovelace before Clarissa is ready to face it. "Yet, my dear," Anna writes, "don't you find at your heart somewhat unusual make it go throb, throb, throb, as you read just here! If you do, don't be ashamed to own it. It is your *generosity*, my love, that's all."

Clarissa's "native generosity and greatness of mind" (as Anna Howe puts it), only stimulate the repressiveness of the Harlowes. The ugly and rich Solmes whom the Harlowes would force Clarissa to marry is their own counterpart:

> Mr. Solmes appears to me (to all the world indeed) to have a very narrow mind and no great capacity: he is coarse and indelicate; as rough in his manners as in his person: he is not only narrow, but covetous; being possessed of great wealth, he enjoys it not; nor has the spirit to communicate to a distress of any kind. . . . Such a man as this, *love!* Yes, perhaps he may, my grandfather's estate.

Clarissa becomes the vicim of the materialism as well as the willfulness of the Harlowes; she is left no room for self-assertion except in flight. Lovelace vows that his only object is "to restore [her] to her own free will."

The suffering of Clarissa becomes the cause of her greatness. She comes to recognize and acknowledge the feelings that have controlled her. Just as Lovelace is reveling in his successful deception of Clarissa, she is writing to Anna Howe of her trust in him and confessing her affection: "I think I could prefer him to all the men I ever knew, were he but to be always what he has been this day. You see how ready I am to own all you have charged me with, when I find myself out." But in the fragments she writes in distraction after the rape, she strikes a deeper vein. To her sister, she writes:

> I thought, poor proud wretch that I was, that what you said was owing to your envy.
> I thought I could acquit my intention of any such vanity.
> I was too secure in the knowledge I thought I had of my own heart.
> My supposed advantages became a snare to me.
> And what now is the end of all?

We are perhaps too eager today to see Clarissa accepting dark motives that have been hidden within her before. She does, certainly, acknowledge her pride and stubbornness of will as well as the appeal of Lovelace's frankness and generosity. But what she most dramatically accepts is responsibility for what has happened. She refuses Lovelace's offer of marriage, and she preserves her freedom now in the only way she can, by her readiness to die: "She who fears not death is not to be intimidated into a meanness unworthy of her heart and principles!" "The man whom once I could have loved, I have been enabled to despise," she writes. "My will is unviolated." She has won through to integrity: "No credulity, no weakness, no want of vigilance, have I to reproach myself with. I have, with grace, triumphed over the deepest machinations." As Lovelace puts it, "has not her triumph over me, from first to last, been infinitely greater than her sufferings from me?" Her triumph is completed, however, not with despising Lovelace but with forgiving him. It is a generous forgiveness in which she acknowledges once more that she "could have loved him."

There is a danger, in reading Richardson, of allowing facile sophistication to displace more essential awareness. Richardson, like Defoe, seems a writer whose sensibility outruns his conscious art, and it is tempting to impose our own clearer designs upon what he has produced. Several critics have turned his novel into a great Puritan myth of love, as if we were to encounter, in Clarissa and Lovelace, after a long journey through time, the great ancestors. To do this is to import into the novel an historical awareness that may be enormously compelling, as it is in Leslie Fiedler's discussion, but that tends to obscure the response the novel demands in its own terms. We may prefer our historical myth to the novel Richardson wrote, but we should know we are making a choice. And I am not sure that it is the right choice.

The ambiguous motivations of Richardson's characters are the stuff of which tragedy is made, and we must respect this tragic possibility. Is it more apt to say that Clarissa "courts sexual violation as well as death" than to say that an Oedipal Hamlet courts failure as well as death? Perhaps. Richardson is no Shakespeare. Yet the evidence for Clarissa's unconscious desires looks more impressive when it is collected in lists of stock symbols than it does when it is examined in context. Again and again we have the savage irony of Clarissa's defense of her freedom exciting Lovelace's possessive desire. It is Lovelace who brings a febrile sexuality to the scenes he describes:

> she wildly slapped my hands; but with such a sweet passionate
> air, her bosom heaving and throbbing as she looked up to me,
> that although I was most sincerely enraged, I could with transport
> have pressed her to mine.

This moment follows upon the notorious passage where Clarissa asks for death: "Then, baring, with a still more frantic violence, part of her enchanting neck, Here, here, said the soul-harrowing beauty, let thy pointed mercy enter."

Clarissa, six days after the rape, has just tried to escape from the brothel where Lovelace is holding her prisoner. He has seized her at the door and brought her back, "choked with grief and disappointment." Richardson has the dramatic shrewdness to make her desperation take the form of sexual provocation for Lovelace, and the force of the scene seems to me divided if one makes Clarissa a counterpart of Pope's Eloisa, a woman tempted by the very passions she is trying to fight. We must accept, with whatever difficulty, the fact that Clarissa, who at the outset was a robust and marriageable young woman of strong feelings, has begun the process of moving toward sainthood. She has accepted more than her share of guilt for making the abduction and the rape possible, and, having asserted an heroic degree of responsibility, she has begun the defense of her integrity that is the only expiation allowed her. McKillop has pointed out the importance in the last half of the novel of "isolation as an essential part of the tragedy of personality" (*Early Masters*).

Clarissa displays a certain artistry in improving the pathos of her final situation; but the pathos comes from the inability of either Lovelace or, more important for her, the Harlowes, to recognize her nature. She has been driven by the world about her into the purest realization of the order of charity. Except for Belford, there is no one to see what she has become. Lovelace is all too aware at intervals of her terrifying superiority, but he must bury this haunting awareness by explaining it away in natural terms. He even hopes that she has become pregnant so that nature will overcome her austere principles, "all her cant of *charity* and *charity*." The Harlowes are locked up in the self-righteousness that is a nasty travesty of what Clarissa has genuinely attained. The loneliness of Clarissa's condition cannot be overstressed. If she prepares herself as the bride of Christ we need not shake our heads with post-Freudian condescension; she is herself making clear the disjunction between kinds of love, between the order of charity and Lovelace's order of the flesh or the Harlowes' love of power.

Richardson holds surprisingly well to the balance between Clarissa's triumph and her tragic catastrophe. One must think back to those protracted but intense scenes of family council, or to the confidences with Anna Howe, to recall how vividly Richardson has made Clarissa an actual personality. It is because she is so sharply presented in characteristic speech and gesture, strong in will and limited in self-awareness (far more limited than Anna Howe, and a forerunner of such later heroines as George Eliot's Dorothea Brooke and Henry James's Isabel Archer) that her emergence through suffering to sainthood seems a waste of powers as well as the discovery of new ones. Lovelace begins by regarding her quizzically, as a "charming frost-piece" and an exciting challenge. He ends in a state of absolute awe, with the dying word "Blessed." Clarissa has ascended above the possibilities of earthly life, and Richardson uses figures like Anna Howe and Hickman to make clear the severity, even cruelty, of this ascent as well as its glory. (One may recall T. S. Eliot's less successful treatment of a comparable instance, the bizarre martyrdom of Celia Coplestone in *The Cocktail Party*.)

Richardson has transformed highly particularized characters so that their dense and familiar social setting fades away in the course of the slow disclosure of consequences. The Harlowes and Lovelace represent a conflict of social classes, and Clarissa—like Polly Peachum—the rebellion of feeling against righteous bourgeois acquisitiveness. Unlike Polly, Clarissa is of divided mind; she still honors the filial relationship, even when her father has morally failed its demands. It is hard to make *Clarissa* into the great bible of the bourgeoisie; the sinister nature of middle-class success has never been more harshly presented than in the Harlowes.

Nor can we properly draw out of Clarissa's defense of her integrity as a person a myth of bourgeois sexual morality. Dorothy Van Ghent has proposed that "Clarissa's whiteness, her debility, and her death are correlatives of the sterilization of instinct and the impotence that are suggested as the desirable qualities of family and social life" (*The English Novel*). Leslie Fiedler has written brilliantly about those "secret scriptures" that the popular novel becomes, "holy books" in which "the Pure Young Girl replaces Christ as the savior, marriage becomes the equivalent of bliss eternal, and the seducer is the only Devil." One can surely recognize the stereotypes that both critics trace back to their origins in Richardson, but the fact that they may have their origins there does not mean that they are what Richardson has created. Clarissa's withdrawal into sainthood is not offered as the pattern of the good woman in the world. There is little reason to assume "sterilization of instinct" in the marriages of Anna Howe and Hickman or of Charlotte Montague and Belford. Richardson's moralizing is oppressive, and he tends to displace charity into chastity; but the novel *Clarissa* succeeds in making charity its genuine concern and all else its "inescapable conditions."

ANTHONY WINNER

Richardson's Lovelace:
Character and Prediction

Both the suggestiveness and the problematic realism of Lovelace's character [in *Clarissa*] are supported largely by his lack of fixity and role in his socio-historical situation. Cut off both from the spiritual meanings which for Richardson provide the unique mode of fulfillment open to human energies and aspirations and from the roles and meanings espoused by society, Lovelace is trapped in the cul-de-sac of self. His predicament is that of one forced not only to write "to the moment," but to live to it alone—to reinvent himself in response to each vibration of sensation or each fragment of vision. He anticipates the fragmented, alienated energy often typical of counter-enlightenment, post-Providential protagonists. Unlike his heirs, of course, his dilemmas are controlled by the terms of the anagogic drama in which Richardson casts him and which (as in his failure to understand Clarissa's reference to her father's house) he cannot comprehend. Nonetheless, he is as much a figure of pathos as a butt of moralistic condemnation. He transcends the context of those stupidly blind to the evidence of things not seen, those faithless fools too curious for their own good, to mix with the sad company of those later *hommes fatals* whose intimations of vision or design are frustrated by the seeming nature of things. The vehement inconsistencies of his warring passions point toward what will later become the situation of the sheer bafflement of desire infuriated by the absence of any commensurate object.

Nowhere is this clearer than in his attitude toward women, their role,

---

From *Texas Studies in Literature and Language* 14, no. 1 (Spring 1972). © 1972 by the University of Texas Press.

and their honor. For Richardson, in an equation almost immediately debased into prurient melodrama by popular fiction, woman's honor in its fullest meaning is the physical vesture of a God-given soul. The earthly extension of honor is the complex phenomenon we know as character. Knowledge of this equation is the central issue in Lovelace's failed education: what he ought for his salvation to have learned. His experience leads him to the verge of understanding, as when he admits before the court of his family "that till I knew *her*, I questioned a soul in a sex, created, as I was willing to suppose, only for temporary purposes." He cannot, however, escape the usual terms of his mechanistic materialism. He has insisted that since Clarissa's "will is unviolated," it is nonsense "to suppose that such a mere *notional* violation as she has suffered, should be able to cut asunder the strings of life." Scoffing at the "romantic value" Clarissa places upon her "*honour*," he remarks: "people's extravagant notions of things alter not *facts*." Yet not only Clarissa's apparent exemption from the general rule but also the demands of his own program compel him to allow: "That if a person sets a high value upon anything, be it ever such a trifle in itself, or in the eyes of others, the robbing of that person of it is *not* a trifle to *him*. Take the matter in this light, I own I have done wrong, great wrong, to this admirable creature."

In the comment on Clarissa's violation, the physical emerges as notional and the will becomes factual. In the remarks on value, the subjectively notional is permitted the status of fact. Apart from Lovelace's characteristic inability to sustain coherent thought, these inconsistencies indicate both a pervading need for some system of value and the almost self-imposed frustration of that need by the absolutistic materialism adopted as a defense and vengeance against social and mediated modes of evaluation. One of the crosses romantic criminality must bear is its reliance on conventional society for a norm against which to define its action: if Lovelace dismisses the spiritual meaning of women's honor, he must still accept some form of received social valuation. For it is this valuation that lends his warfare a socioeconomic dimension and reality. The basis for Richardson's reestimation of women is Christian realism, not socioeconomics. But Lovelace's inability to comprehend the former establishes the latter at the center of the action. Clarissa is a potential angel because her relation to society appears to him as disjunctive as his own: women have been reduced to chattel just as heroes have been demeaned as criminal dross. Theoretically, Lovelace offers freedom from bondage and a joint rebellion against the enslaving world. Yet the meaning he assigns Clarissa merely inverts that assigned by the world: grimly and parodistically imitating the materialism of society at large, he can phrase her value only in terms of a private variation on this ubiquitous materialism.

Though he yearns for the inifinite value he half-glimpses in her, he spurns the divine pathway to his goal and is forced into behavior that can only be a function of the finite and an inversion of the social.

The process of alienation and isolation to which he subjects Clarissa reflects directly on the society whose depersonalizing idea of women lends itself, by omission or commission, to the implementation of private tyranny. At home, where her trial began, Clarissa had no rights or value except as property. Lovelace extends this strange destiny until there is no refuge in the world: "In the first place, the man, who has had the assurance to think me, and to endeavor to make me, his *property*, will hunt me from place to place and search after me as a 'stray; and he knows he may do so with impunity, for whom have I to protect me from him?" Lovelace reports her as asking "whether I am to be controlled in the future disposal of myself? Whether, in a country of liberty, as *this*, where the *sovereign* of it must be guilty of *your* wickedness; and where *you* neither durst have attempted it, had I one friend or relation to look upon me; I am to be kept here a prisoner, to sustain fresh injuries?" The hierarchical order that once protected women having broken down, there is no earthly escape. Society, abetting the criminal, becomes criminal—and the model Richardson here provides for a dramatization of social injustice at the service of an evil figure of force becomes the well-spring for numbers of subsequent libertarian treatments of righteous brigands in revolt and for the vision of society as a Gothic institution explicit in works such as Godwin's *Things as they are; or, The Adventures of Caleb Williams*. Moreover, since family and society have degraded Clarissa into property, Lovelace's idealization of her as property appears initially a relative improvement.

The treatment accorded Clarissa, as Leslie Fiedler has shown, can readily be viewed as a representation of the denial by the aristocracy of the rights and identity of her class. The conflict between her and Lovelace, with its warring systems of value, verges on political drama. Such a reading, however, risks distortion of the primary manners conflict between woman and hero. Richardson's sense of Lovelace's dilemma harks back to the confinement of heroic and absolutistic occupation within domestic tragedy: to a plot wherein Lovelace plays Iago to his own Othello; wherein he renders love as a physical possession and casts away a pearl worth more than his rakish tribe. Losing Clarissa, he loses the only true complement to himself and, anagogically, his chance for salvation.

> All that the charmer of my heart shall say, that will I put down:
> every motion, every air of her beloved person, every look, will

I try to describe; and when she is silent I will endeavor to tell thee her thoughts, either what they are, or what I would have them be—so that, having *her*, I shall never want a subject. Having lost her, my whole soul is a blank: the whole creation round me, the elements above, beneath, and everything I *behold* (for nothing can I *enjoy*), are a blank without her!

Oh, return, return, thou only charmer of my soul! Return to thy adoring Lovelace! What is the light, what the air, what the town, what the country, what's anything, without thee? Light, air, joy, harmony, in my notion, are but parts of thee; and could they all be expressed in one word, that word would be CLARISSA.

O my beloved CLARISSA, return thou then; once more return to bless thy LOVELACE, who now, by the loss of thee, knows the value of the jewel he has slighted.

Possessive imperialism is scarcely abated in this grand equation of the woman once judged soulless with the soul of all creation Lovelace would rule. But the possession of Clarissa has supplanted the overreaching of warlike stratagems as his subject; his own notion has accorded infinite value to the trifle, the recalcitrant fact, she once was. She has become the tangible ideal, and as such is an apotheosized property—there is no question of class or of problematic womanhood. In the ranting pathos of his loss Lovelace emerges as the ancestor of those protagonists of romanticism who would transmute the material into the ideal—of those who turn to criminal rebellion because God is not to be possessed in His creations. Beyond Lovelace stand figures such as E. T. A. Hoffmann's Don Juan, who

hoped to still, in love, the longing that burned in his heart. . . . Through the cunning of man's hereditary enemy, the thought was planted in Don Juan's soul that through love, through the pleasures of the flesh, there could be achieved on earth that which exists in our hearts as a heavenly promise only, and which amounts to just that longing for infinity that weds us to Heaven. Fleeing restlessly from one more beautiful woman to another . . . believing himself always deceived in his choice, hoping always to realize the ideal of ultimate satisfaction, the Don was doomed to find all earthly life dull and shallow in the end . . . he revolted against the delusion which at first had spelled the highest of life's ambitions for him, only to betray him so bitterly at last. The enjoyment of woman no longer offered him any satisfaction of his sensuality, but had become an opportunity atrociously to outrage Nature and the Creator.

The transformation of the Don Juan into a Tristan *manqué* is the work of later generations. Lovelace may more appropriately be viewed as a perversion of the eighteenth-century premise of feeling: the substitution of emotional for rational values. *Clarissa* is at one and the same time the fictional source of a sentimental revolution and a largely pejorative examination of the implications of such a revolution. Richardson's celebrated empathy with feminine premises and psychology is carried over into Lovelace, who joins the traditional emotionalism of women to masculine force. At the service of passion rather than reason, this force can be countered only by grace. As Clarissa writes *in articulo mortis* to the Reverend Doctor Lewen: "I have, through grace, triumphed over the deepest machinations. . . . The man whom once I could have loved, I have been enabled to despise: and shall not *charity* complete my triumph? And shall I not *enjoy* it? And where would be my triumph if he *deserved* my forgiveness? Poor man! He has had a loss in losing me! I have the pride to think so, because I think I know my own heart." Having nearly completed her earthly purgation, Clarissa judges with the justified pride of Christian triumph; her charity is a refraction of God's mercy to mankind. Charity is the divine idea nurtured by and adumbrated in terrestrial sentiment. And sentiment should be the complement of manliness such as Lovelace's; virile force must be tempered by sentiment, which one critic [Harrison R. Steeves] defines as a *"consciousness* of feeling," "a stimulated consciousness of emotion." But Lovelace travesties the sentimental faith, derived out of Shaftesbury, that our feelings are functions of the Providential nature of things, that the issue of emotion will be benevolent. Within this faith, the motions of the feeling heart are continuous with spiritual reason. Clarissa cannot love in contradiction to her God-given "lights" because for her love and reason are in unison. Unfortunately, however, she is exemplary, not natural. And in the natural world the validation of emotion and feeling consequent upon the code of sentiment can unleash chaos and nightmare. Lovelace's rampant feelings are wholly discontinuous with reason; the forceful male equivalent of what his century calls the female Quixote, he becomes monstrous.

The centrality of women and of psychological representation in *Clarissa* should not obscure Richardson's allegiance to pure spiritual reason as opposed to mundane emotion, his ultimate concern with soul rather than character. The treatment of Anna Howe is intended to stress the flaws of merely natural psychology. Though in no sense evil, she is a creature of feelings—which often express themselves (as do Lovelace's) in a gay and lively "wit"—and thereby a figure of potential disorder, a benign rebel against her duties as a daughter and a fiancée. She predicts the major tradition of democratic feminism in the novel, is a collateral ancestor of Dorothea Brooke and Isabel Archer. But Richardson is a Christian, not a democratic, feminist. Extravagance such as Miss Howe's can threaten the hierarchy of order and duty upon which terrestrial life, however uncomfortably, must rely, and Clarissa's repetitious chiding appears a reliable index of Richardson's disapproval.

Anna Howe's way is that of the world, while Clarissa's distresses and final triumph point toward heaven. Her progress constitutes a type of theodicy. The evil of earth is countervailed by and must be understood from the vantage of her divine father's house. But spiritual explanation leaves the grossness and ambiguity of mundane fact well behind. And it is this fact, with Lovelace as its example and explicator, that subsequent novelists tend to borrow and rework. Secure in his divine certitudes, Richardson plumbs deep indeed into earthly inversions, their psychologies and roles. Individual, problematic psychology, the delicate particularities of feeling, are the achievement of the novel but also the nemesis of its characters. Individual psychology is a blind to truth, a stumbling block to grace. Paradoxically for a work that opens the novelistic doors to the registration of feeling, the inner world appears a Pandora's box. The issue of emotion sundered from grace is sensationalism; the seamy side of mere sensibility abuts on Gothicism.

Feeling unchecked mounts into a predominant passion, the monomania that intrigues so many eighteenth-century writers. The misdirection of the soul's energies into such passion ultimately deprives both the monomaniac and his object, if human, of soul. Lovelace's career describes this plot, illuminates the inevitable course, the suicidal or murderous fate, of unleashed emotion. He predicts not just the villains of worldliness and the criminal mechanists who debase the Enlightenment's "Système de la Nature," but also Goethe's Young Werther and his numerous progeny. Unlike Lovelace, the foiled epic hero, Werther, of course, is an essentially passive, lyric figure. Yet when, under the impetus of Ossian, Werther's yearning emotions rise to the threshold of action, they recall Lovelace's warlike stratagems of feeling. In his delirious suicide letter, Werther proclaims: "You are mine, Lotte, forever. . . . Husband—that's a word for this world, and for this world it's a sin that I love you and would wrench you out of [your husband's] arms into mine. A sin? Very well then, and I punish myself for it. I have tasted this sin in all its divine rapture, I have sucked its balm and strength into my heart. From now on you are mine—mine, Lotte!" It is only the hysteria of defeated yearning, of emotion shorn of tenable outlet, that leads to Werther's suicide but also a maddened self-punishment for the sin of absolute possessiveness. Extreme feeling characteristically overturns any barriers blocking its object; that, in Goethe's portrait, such feeling should turn against itself in punishment is an assumption of moral sentimentalism. Emotion transmogrified by frustration and released at the pitch of Werther's last scene with Lotte may as plausibly turn against her, against all society, against God. The raving suicide letter dilutes but does not alter the basic implication of Lovelace's crude delirium upon hearing of Clarissa's death: "my ever-dear and beloved lady should be opened and embalmed. . . . her *heart*, to which I have such unquestionable pretensions . . . I *will* have. I will keep it in spirits. It shall never be out of my sight. . . . Whose was she living?—Whose is she dead, but mine? . . . Whose then can she be but mine?" Lovelace's passionate imperialism is, to be sure, far from Werther's desire to participate wholly and organically in nature. Yet both heroic activism displaced into feeling and a career premised upon the infinite fulfillment of lyric emotion verge on criminal depredation. In Goethe, the crime is forefended by suicide; in Richardson, the reverberations of the criminal nightmare are stilled by Clarissa's heavenly triumph. Both works, however, suggest a black fission whereby sentiment is split: its spiritual element winging back to the empyrean; its human emotionalism, divested of right reason, bestially stalking earth.

Unlike Werther, Lovelace is for his creator an extreme and appalling extension of the character of an entire society, ultimately of the postlapsarian world. He is the estrangement of the energies of this world from grace, truth, and order. Clarissa, "looking steadfastly at the awful receptacle," her coffin, can believe "that there is such a vast superiority of weight and importance in the thought of death, and its hoped-for happy consequences, that it in a manner annihilates all other considerations and concerns." She has gone beyond mundane multidimensionality, transcended the disintegrative psychology created in man's Fall. Lovelace, wholly bound by this psychology, is both more "natural" and, novelistically, more suggestive. Like Milton's Satan, he incarnates his own hell. "As health turned its blithe side, and opened my prospects of recovery, all my old inclinations and appetites returned; and this letter, perhaps, will be a thorough conviction to thee that I *am* as wild a fellow as ever, or in the way to be so." Not only is Lovelace at times majestically infernal, he is usually complexly so: for the hell he embodies is the terrible totality of the falsities, ambiguities, and disjunctions of the novelistic world Richardson dramatizes. He is a towering Babel of human potentialities, of builders' blocks that can never be fit architecture, certainly never mount to heaven. He possesses the "vitality of a myth and the validity of a proverb tested on the pulses." But the myth resides in the delimiting resonance of Comte's contention that "society has become the only Divinity," and the proverb leads to the dark sayings of such criminally wise figures as Balzac's Vautrin. For later writers who have lost the faith and option of Richardson's theocentric moralism, Lovelace can stand as typical rather than unique. His inverted and contorted vision becomes the norm of post-Providential, fallen omniscience.

MARK KINKEAD-WEEKES

The Inquisition
(The Final Instalment)

Once more, Richardson's first audience had to wait, this time for seven months, before the final instalment [of *Clarissa*] appeared. The news leaked out, however, that there was to be a tragic ending, and there was a spate of appeals of mercy. They came from young ladies and gents and clergymen, writing under flowery or classical pseudonyms. Lady Bradshaigh threatened: "If you disappoint me, attend to my curse:—May the hatred of all the young, beautiful and virtuous, for ever be your portion! may you meet with applause only from envious old maids, surly bachelors, and tyrannical parents! may you be doomed to the company of such! and, after death, may their ugly souls haunt you! Now make Lovelace and Clarissa unhappy if you dare." A more practical threat lay in the promise of many correspondents not to buy the last volumes unless Richardson changed his mind, and as a businessman he must have known very clearly how much better a happy ending would have sold. Moreover the appeals also came from authors like Fielding, Thomson, Lyttleton and Cibber. Many of the objectors invoked the theory of "poetic justice," and theoretical considerations would have their due weight with a novelist pledged to moral instruction. But to his lasting credit Richardson remained unmoved, though passages in the novel itself are directed at the objections, and his efforts to write a postscript and get his friends to help him answer them, show how seriously he took it all.

Yet anybody who had really responded to the novel should have known that tragedy was inevitable, for all the surface suspense. In the fourth volume the shadows had begun to close; in the fifth the actors become fixed in the

From *Samuel Richardson: Dramatic Novelist.* © 1973 by Mark Kinkead-Weekes. Cornell University Press, 1973.

parts of a play which both have written but neither understands. There soon begins to be something of the inevitability of nightmare, where human actions hold the attention, yet at the back of one's mind seem curiously stylised, because the outcome already exists in one's apprehension and cannot really be affected by anything that happens.

Briefly, in Hampstead, the action takes place on a social stage again, after the prolonged single combat of Clarissa's captivity. She seems to have escaped from Lovelace's power, yet it is not so. For we are made aware once more of the capitulation Richardson saw everywhere in his society to rank, influence, and wealth. The moment Lovelace arrives in Hampstead all citadels fall before him. The people he has to deal with are not Harlowes obsessed by greed or pride; the innkeeper and his wife, Mrs Moore, Miss Rawlins, even the jolly widow Bevis, are all kind, respectable, middle-class folk. But Will has only to mention that his master is "one of the finest gentlemen in the world" for the innkeeper and his wife to pity Lovelace before they see him, and to be "ready to worship" when they find his "person and dress having answered Will's description." He goes off in his chariot the short distance along the Heath to Mrs Moore's because "What widow, what servant, asks questions of a man with an equipage?" In the first stormy scene with Clarissa he has only to insist on his letters from *Lord* M and *Lady* Betty and *Lady* Sarah to have the women half on his side, and when he finally puts the "ostentatiously coroneted" letter from Lord M into Miss Rawlins's hands it "clench'd the nail. Not but that, Miss Rawlins said, she saw I had been a wild gentleman."

Lovelace now begins to reap the benefit of his previous plots to make her seem to have consented to pass as his wife. He manages to shout her down several times in the first stormy scene when she is insisting that he has no right to persecute her; but he is also able to say himself, uncontradictably, that Tomlinson has reported their marriage. Behind this is a clear power situation. He can produce nine witnesses to swear that she has passed as Mrs Lovelace, and if he has legal rights as her husband, the people at Hampstead have to be very careful how they go about offending a man of his status and influence. Clarissa's character also plays into his hands again, particularly her delicacy and to some extent at the back of it her pride. She is obviously ashamed to tell a story which in outline, without the complications, which do—heaven knows—take a long time to make clear, shows her to have run away from her family with Lovelace, to have lived with him for some time, and to have left him because of an attempt her modesty makes it impossible for her to describe. Richardson steers dangerously close to disaster when Clarissa, in her first private conversation with the women, does not categorically deny Lovelace's well-tried stories about the unconsummated marriage—though she expresses her scorn. Yet when she does, immediately afterwards, publicly challenge him to declare that they are indeed married, the strength of his position is clear. All he has to do is to be sweetly reasonable: "But, my dear, will you be pleased to consider what answer half a dozen people whence you came, could give to your question? And do not now, in *the disorder of your mind*, and in the height of passion, bring into question before these gentlewomen a point you have acknowledged before those who know us better." She may cry out "I own no Marriage with thee!—Bear witness Ladies, I do not," but she cannot deny what her heart has already reproached her for. The fact that she cannot, with the "explanation" of the unconsummated marriage and the confirmation of Tomlinson's carefully doctored letter, is enough to ensure that she gets no help from women already overawed by Lovelace's rank, and ensnared by his charm and plausibility.

Richardson again risks improbability, but is perhaps just saved by the consistency with what we know of his heroine. There is a familiar double criticism. Lovelace remarks on "that Security which Innocence gives, that nevertheless had better have in it a greater mixture of the Serpent with the Dove . . . A dear silly Soul . . . to depend upon the goodness of her own heart, when the heart cannot be seen into but by its actions; and she, to appearance, a Runaway, an Eloper, from a tender, a most indulgent Husband!—To neglect to cultivate the opinion of individuals, when the whole world is governed by appearance!" The criticism of a world so governed is clear enough, but the criticism of Clarissa is plain as well. It is not enough for her to wrap herself in her own innocence; in the world as it is, Clarissa is betrayed not only by her physical cowardice but by the theoretic and idealistic nature of her views. She is betrayed also by her good qualities: her modesty, her unwillingness to speak at all if she cannot speak the whole truth, and by her self-reproach for having already lent herself to deception. Once again the art exposes the uncomfortable fact, for its author, that Clarissa's moral nature unfits her to cope with situations that less admirable characters would have made short work of.

On the other hand, though we can appreciate the masterly psychology of Lovelace, and the clever way he plays on the romantic susceptibilities as well as the self-interest of the women, we should notice how his strategy has become purely a matter of keeping Clarissa in his power. He is being forced out of "appearance" himself. He can prevent her escape by hedging her about with servants, keeping the women perplexed by his tissue of lies and half-truths, tampering with Anna's correspondence, and finally forging letters from her and his relatives, but the tactics that serve him best for retaining power are those which serve him worst if he should hope again to convince her of his love and penitence. When he starts out of his old man's disguise at Mrs Moore's, like Milton's Satan touched by Ithuriel's spear, the scene is not only Lovelace-theatrical but symbolic. His "own form" is not yet clear to Clarissa, but it begins to be clearer from that moment. The "fire-scene" has been a turning point for her willingness to trust him, and the more he surrounds her with deception and force, the less likely it is that she will ever trust him again.

Even Tomlinson cannot help now. He and his master may bring all the familiar big guns to bear: the "fact" that reconciliaton can only be undertaken by her uncle if they marry, the threat from James Harlowe and the threat to him if she renounces Lovelace, the hopes of Lovelace's family, the whole allure of their relationship and the resulting ease of social reacceptance. Clarissa shows how much these can still move her, but she can no longer be persuaded. She is ready now to confess that she could not have agreed to marry him if she had not loved him, and that she would have shown her feelings more clearly if she had not been driven back into her shell when she needed encouragement. Her obvious difficulty in sustaining her decision to give him up shows the continuing power of those feelings, and the pain of renouncing her happier prospects. But she cannot trust him now; indeed, begins to be ominously suspicious of Tomlinson. The fire-plot has shown her that Lovelace does not respect her personality, "he could not love the creature whom he could insult as he has insulted me." He cannot make her happy, nor she him, and to marry him might cause her to fall into error. It is not the physical attempt itself that matters but its implications, especially the fact that the complicity of the women at Sinclair's suggests deliberate design. The fact that she still cares for him in spite of it makes things worse, not better. "If I had never valued him, he never would have had it in his power to insult me; nor could I, if I had never regarded him, have taken to heart as I do, the insult (execrable as it was) so undeservedly, so ingratefully given" (omitting Richardson's italics). The counters of value may change with the centuries, but the relationship between them does not, and we should have no difficulty in understanding the accuracy of Clarissa's diagnosis of the meaning of the fire-plot, even on the facts she knows. She is brought to agree to see Lady Betty when she arrives, but that is all.

The pain this costs her shows, however, that even now there might have been some hope for Lovelace if he had been able to be open, and to put his trust in her own decision and her generosity. When, with another of his momentary bursts of sincerity, he wholeheartedly begs forgiveness (with real tears!), and whispers to Tomlinson "By my Soul, man, I am in earnest," he actually produces a moment of indecision in Clarissa. But Lovelace is now the trapped one. He is still under pressure from his old obsessions, but what has finally trapped him is the net of his own contrivances. He has put it "out of my *own power* to be honest. I hate compulsion in all forms; and cannot bear, even to be *compelled* to be the wretch my choice has made me!—So now, Belford, as thou hast said, I am a machine at last, and no free agent." If, as the now squeamish Tomlinson urges, he gets "Lady Betty" to persuade Clarissa to marry him, and gets Tomlinson accepted as her uncle's deputy, he can be "honest" to the extent of marriage. Yet the revelation of the extent of his designs must finally come; and how will she take that, when she has reacted so strongly to the little she knows already? The risk of losing her love seems almost as great with honesty as with dishonesty, though Tomlinson for one can now see that only violence will serve if Lovelace does mean to go on with his plans. Lovelace at last begins to realise that if she really finds him a villain she may refuse and abhor him. He is plagued by conscience and begins to see that even "victory" will undo him. He reflects how happy he could be "had it been given to me to *be* only what I wished to *appear* to be." He begins to sense that his love may not be of the "*Right sort*," though he has little enough idea of what the right sort might be. But it is too late to turn back.

At this point the "garden scene," the last oasis of calm, allows us to see just what Lovelace has lost. Clarissa speaks to him quietly and much more openly than ever before. She sums up the evidence she has of his premeditated plots, and insists that she cannot marry where there is such disunion of minds. Yet her feeling for him is quite apparent now in her face and eyes, she lets him hold her hand, she openly shows her distress at the loss of relationship with his family and she confesses, with hesitation and embarrassment but unmistakably, that she still cares for him and finds it painful to renounce him now. But she will not err "wilfully and against the light of my own judgement." If she can acquit herself of this she will be "more happy than if I had all that the world accounts desireable." As Lovelace listens, it seems to him that "Her whole person was informed by her sentiments. She seemed to be taller than before. How the God within her exalted her, not only above me, but above herself!" Yet she will not be called "Divine creature." "All human excellence, said she, is comparative only. My Mind, I believe, is indeed superior to yours, debased as yours is by evil habits: But I had not known it to be so, if you had not *taken pains* to convince me."

This, in its way, is an extraordinary achievement; the modern reader is aghast that Richardson should think of taking such a risk. Yet he succeeds triumphantly here as he had so consistently failed in *Pamela*. The thing is said quietly, as the fact it indeed is. It is said in rebuttal of praise. And it is said curiously without personality, and wholly without animus or conceit. Lovelace has many times accused her of "conscious superiority," meaning a synonym for arrogance, an indication of the proud and scornful Beauty. It is Richardson's achievement now to transform the phrase. This is superiority in an absolute sense; and it is conscious without hypocrisy, circumlocution, or disguise. Yet it is at this moment wholly insulated from self-applause and indeed from self. She is superior not because of her basic nature nor even because of his—Richardson has none of Fielding's oddly Calvinist assertion of good and bad *nature*—but because of the effect on him of what he has chosen to do. She is superior, as Lovelace himself can see, because she allows the God *in* her to exalt her, and we shall find this formulation significant.

That Lovelace should see all this; and yet feel that he has created a situation where he is likely to lose her love whatever he does, and even if he should succeed in marrying her, is the foundation of his tragedy. Yet he prevents us from feeling it as we might because he manages to prevent himself, eventually, from feeling it at all. His characteristic response is to clamp the rake's mask back more and more firmly on to the human face, in order to hide the truth from himself. There is now however a certain awareness and admission of what he is doing. He tells Belford how Tomlinson's opposition (like Belford's earlier) served to confirm the very purposes it set out to change. "Had he left me to myself, to the tenderness of my own nature . . . had he sat down, and made odious faces, and said nothing; it is very possible that I should have taken the chair over against him . . . and have cried and blubbered with him for half an hour together. But the varlet to *argue* with me!—To pretend to *convince* a man, who knows in his heart that he is doing a wrong thing!—He must needs think that this would put me upon trying what I could say for myself; and when the excited compunction can be carried from the *heart* to the *lips*, it must evaporate in words." Verbalisation is a kind of anaesthetic. So he converts his battle with his conscience into a humorous stagey knockabout; and his thoughts about love into a "debate" in which debating points score. He relapses into his gayest and most cynical vein on hearing Belford's news of the death of his uncle, but we can see that the cynicism is being used to escape facing the situation it so splendidly verbalises as "the necessity I am under of committing either speedy Matrimony, or a Rape"! When he succeeds in capturing the vitally important letter from Anna that Clarissa has been waiting for, we can watch him using it to whip himself up to vengeance as he had used its predecessors. Finally he succeeds in recapturing his old persona, in convincing himself in the old rake's way that she is ruled not by virtue but pride. "She cannot bear to be thought a *woman* . . . And if, in the last attempt, I find her *not* one, what will she be worse for the trial?—No one is to blame for suffering an evil he cannot shun or avoid." He gives way again to the gratification of his "predominant passion" because it is in his power; and argues with his old wholehearted levity that he is conferring a benefit on her by procuring her the penitential life she seems to want—at the expense of which he waxes very witty. If we should wonder at this success in clamping the mask back so fully—"Why, Jack, I cannot but say, that the Westminster Air is a little grosser than that at Hamstead." He is back in the brothel, and in the attitudes the prostitutes so sedulously foster. He gives way again to his full aversion to marriage in sporting with the wording of the marriage licence which has now arrived, and in outlining his grand proposal to reform the marriage laws to permit an annual change of partners. Finally he gives rein to his immense delight in acting and intrigue as he coaches his two high-grade tarts for their impersonation of Lady Betty and Charlotte, in order to decoy Clarissa back to town.

What we watch is the deliberate self-blinding of an intelligence; the fixing into the rake's persona of a man whose experience and understanding had been enlarged well beyond it, but who refuses to face the facts of his situation or the truth of his emotions. Once this has happened, Clarissa never stands a chance. She has no reason to distrust his "relatives," or imagine that he could descend to using their reputations to despicable ends. It is easy enough to get her into the coach for the expedition to "Lady Betty's" lodgings. It is harder of course to get her back into "Sinclair's" on their "accidental" passing there; but when we get the whole story nearly a volume later, it is clear that the drugging begins in the coach, with the hartshorn and water she is given for her faintness and her near hysteria.

Lovelace's letters describing the scenes that follow are only seen in their full repulsiveness afterwards, when we know the whole story, but even without this they are repulsive enough. He never seems shoddier than when he rehearses, to extinguish the last possibility of pity, the old gramophone record of his reasons for vengeance; or resolves not to be made a fool of before the prostitutes; or pleads, after his stagily protective show of indignation when Sinclair has been allowed to terrorise his victim, that "her coming in was without my orders." But what is finally ugliest above Lovelace now is his tone. For what his "to the moment" letters (composed retrospectively, though just before the rape takes place) reveal above all, is his savouring enjoyment. He is taken up with his own suspense as the sadist is. He enjoys replaying the part of not knowing what is happening—"What shall we do now! We are immersed in the depth of grief and apprehension!"—significantly identifying himself with his victim to share for the moment the flavour of her terror. He obviously loves the scurry, the hectic emotions, the part-playing; he revels in his starring role in his own dramaturgy. Richardson may perhaps be releasing through Lovelace something in himself, something that probably exists at the back of the mind of any dramatic artist; and something which in this hectic form looks forward in particular to the sentimental excesses of the latter part of the century: what Richardson himself called "sporting with distress." But the important difference is that Richardson is showing how far Lovelace has succeeded in blinding himself so completely to the meaning, and even curiously to the reality of what he is doing. He is "quite astonished" at "so sincere, so unquestionable a repugnance," but it makes no difference because the reality of Clarissa's feeling never locks home in his mind. The strength of his self-obsession is shown by the flimsiness of his excuses: "Yet how should I know that it would be so till I tried?—And how, having proceeded thus far, could I stop, were I *not* to have had the women to goad me on, and to make light of circumstances, which they pretended to be better judges of than I?" He can achieve moments of absolutely blank calm because of his ability to unrealise: "Dreading what might happen as to her intellects, and being very apprehensive that she might possibly go thro' a great deal before morning . . . I humoured her." Language could hardly be more anaesthetised.

There is sadism behind his delight in playing with his victim. But at the very heart of Lovelace, as deep as one can go, what Richardson succeeds in showing is the inability, finally, to believe in the reality of other people, their personalities, and their emotions. Behind the Restoration playacting, behind the rake's ideology, behind the power-urge and the sadism, is an obsessive egotism so complete that nothing else exists for it.

After the rape, with Clarissa deranged and insensible, he half glimpses that it is what *she* feels about her virginity that matters, but with horrible obsession he still cannot see what he has done, and can still occupy himself with thoughts of his darling notion of cohabitation. At the moment which moved Fielding so much, when Clarissa half comes to, and holds up the licence "in a speechless agony" Lovelace's language again expels reality. "She seemed about to call down vengeance upon me; when, happily, the Leaden God, in pity to her trembling Lovelace, waved over her half-drowned eyes his somniferous wand, and laid asleep the fair Exclaimer, before she could go half thro' with her intended imprecation." He can speak of the "*little* Art" that has been used, and of its "*generous* design (if thou'lt allow me the word on such an occasion) in order to lessen the too quick sense she was likely to have of what she was to suffer." It was a "little *innocent* trick," and "Who the devil could have expected such strange effects from a cause so common, and so slight." It is not finally the rape itself, nor even the utter obsessiveness, that makes one feel as though one is moving through some nightmarish quagmire. It is the fact that Lovelace can succeed to the extent he does in dehumanising his own reactions.

We must however be clear about the significance of the rape, and why it happens as it does. How can Lovelace go through with a sexual act from which he can gain no possible sexual satisfaction, since he is not a sex maniac, and admits himself with characteristic brutality that "there is no difference to be found between the skull of King Philip, and that of another man"? It cannot be a trial of her virtue either, in the sense of finding out whether she can be seduced, for the same reason: her will is paralysed. We discover later that she is already "stupid to their hands" from the first dose of the drug in the coach, before she is given what turns out to be the overdose in her tea. The drug makes her alternately drunken and numb, but not unconscious. She remembers vaguely seeing the women moving about while she is being raped, but goes into fits and a coma thereafter.

Yet the rape is, precisely, a trial of virtue itself, in that it is an attempt to disprove the existence of a moral *nature*. It is a last desperate effort to prove the rake's creed true, and preserve Lovelace from having to give up his whole idea of himself. The blind obsession, the mind forever tramping the treadmill of its own assumptions and seeking feverishly to force down any glimpses of a different truth, are an index of how crucially Lovelace's ideology is tied up with his deepest psychological needs. What is at stake is the mainspring of his life, what makes life worth living for him. He *must* go on, to stake everything on a last desperate throw to prove he is right about her, and himself. He cannot make her consent, but if his basic assumptions are right that doesn't matter. For he knows that she loves him, and if he can only reveal to her what she "really" is, even without her consent, everything else will follow as of course. If the basic nature of woman is sexual, and her morality is only a veneer of custom and education reinforced by pride, then the physical violation which puts her at a stroke beyond the pale of custom, and is a complete humiliation, will allow her "true" nature to emerge. The experience of sexual penetration itself should result in an irreversible change; hence "once subdued, always subdued." (There is a modern analogy here with Terence Rattigan's *Ross*, where the experience of rape reveals T. E. Lawrence's homosexuality to him, wholly outside any question of consent.)

The most agonising question Richardson can ask about his heroine is whether her virtue is real or not, and the rape is the beginning of his inquisition. Each of Lovelace's basic assumptions will be tested against her reactions to her violation. Again, and very curiously, the rape in *Clarissa* is like the half-attempted rape in *Pamela* in being "sexual" only in a rather peculiar sense. It takes place in public, in the presence of Mrs Sinclair and probably Sally and Polly. This is partly because of Lovelace's need for an audience to play up to, to the bitter end. It is also partly because Richardson's whole concept of morality and immorality is public. But the central reason is that the rape is a public trial in the strict sense; the first stage in proving a hypothesis about the true nature of Woman. If we want an analogy we should think of a scientific experiment carried out in front of an expert audience. It is the most extraordinary climax of any novel in English. Yet is is not so for any desire to shock, let alone titillate, by the *outré*. It is because, for Richardson, the rape of his heroine enables him to expose her innermost nature. It is the beginning of his answer to the most basic of all questions: the Psalmist's, What *is* Man?—or Woman?

II

He begins to open up Clarissa's mind by using derangement as Shakespeare had done, to reveal the unconscious. Indeed, since the ravings of later tragedy are little more than emotional indulgence, this is the first honest attempt to deal with the unconscious since Lear and Ophelia. Richardson clearly understood how much lay hidden in the mind that the daylight consciousness either repressed or failed to understand . . . but which dreams, or derangement, could reveal.

Clarissa's nightmare in the first instalment, if we look back at it now, reveals its full significance. She dreams that "my Brother, my Uncle Anthony, and Mr Solmes, had formed a plot to destroy Mr Lovelace; who discovering it, and believing I had a hand in it, turned all his rage against me. I thought he made them all fly into foreign parts upon it; and afterwards seizing upon me, carried me into a church-yard; and there, notwithstanding all my prayers and tears, and protestations of innocence, stabbed me to the heart, and then tumbled me into a deep grave ready dug, among two or three half-dissolved carcases; throwing in the dirt and earth upon me with his hands, and trampling it down with his feet."

This is obviously a product of its circumstances. She has just heard from her aunt and Betty about the plans for the fatal Wednesday; has overheard her brother and sister exulting in the success of their plans; and, spurred on by her apprehensions and by a wholly new rancour, has written her letter agreeing to use Lovelace's help to escape. But immediately afterwards she is seized by deep misgivings, she cannot get to sleep, and when she does her nightmare expresses her fears, in a significant form. In her unconscious mind she clearly perceives that she is only a pawn in the struggle of Lovelace and her family to destroy one another, in which the destructive urges of pride and revenge dominate, and do indeed drive her family to "foreign parts." Her dream separates out this truth from the complications of her duty, her love for her family, and her dawning love for Lovelace which inhibit her daylight understanding, so that in the dream she can see the subterranean motives clearly. They are by no means the whole truth, but they are true. Unfortunately, the daylight Clarissa thinks very slightly of dreams, for if she had managed to lock home in her mind what part of it knew, her subsequent behaviour might have been rather different, and wiser.

Further beneath the surface however, the nightmare clearly has sexual significance too. An anticipatory irony manifests itself when the rape is over. The rape is what stabs her to the heart; the grave is the pit he digs for her and the bed in which she experiences the "death" of drugs and sex, and the annihilation of her previous life and reputation. (This will of course ultimately become a literal death too.) The two or three carcasses are the women she is levelled with, whose flesh is already corrupt, and the dirt and the trampling hardly require a gloss. At the moment of the dream however, all we need say is that Clarissa already unconsciously perceives the character of the "love" that will eventually lead to the rape and prove the dream prophetic. In realising his darker motivation, she sees that his "love" is something desecrating, hence the churchyard, and destructive of her personality and her purity. One must sound a note of caution here: this is a perception about Lovelace, not necessarily about sex itself, though clearly her fear of sex would enter into it. When we remember what Lovelace hopes to prove by the rape, however, it enables us to predict the way she will regard it, and the impossibility that it could have the effects he hopes for.

Her derangement allows us to test the prediction. The most obviously striking thing about her first few "papers" is however something unexpected. Clarissa in our experience has developed a real intellectual stature; we think of her as an analytic *mind*, collected, firm, penetrating. We forget her age. And there is about her emotional life an aura of reserve. We have seen a good deal into it in crisis, but have also seen how blind she can be to the state of her own heart, and how her feminine code has encouraged her to conceal many of her feelings and emotional problems not only from others, but from herself. It is against the background of this experience over four volumes of the novel that her first few papers gain their touching quality. It is as though we had never really seen her before; for the derangement shows itself less in her lack of connection, though that is there, than in the childlike tone. The first few papers are written by her emotions. The educated, highly developed mind, the self-sufficiency, the analytic intelligence, suddenly drop away. What we see is a lost and bewildered teenage girl, confused and grief-stricken, all assurance and sophistication gone, seeking desperately for reassurance and love in the only direction she can, and failing to find any. Anna, we remember, has not written (as far as Clarissa knows) since before the escape to Hampstead. Her father has cursed her to perdition, both here and hereafter. Her lifelines of affection are cut, or lead nowhere. She tries to believe that they still exist to be laid hold of again. But she cannot—and here we see the first effect of the rape—not only because she cannot communicate, but because the "self" of her past relationships is gone. She cannot focus on what has happened; she "cannot tell" the "dreadful, dreadful things" that have been done to her, partly because she cannot bear to think of them, and partly because she doesn't yet fully understand. "But I am no longer what I was in any one thing—In any one thing did I say? Yes but I am; for I am still, and I ever will be, *Your true*—." But she cannot sign the name that should have followed, and the paper is torn in two and thrown away. For a moment she can assert continuity with the past, since her love for Anna is unaltered; but it breaks down, for the self that feels now is not the same as Anna's friend. Similarly, in the second paper, her love for her father remains real and because of it she asserts that the bond between father and child cannot be broken. "Yes, I *will* call you Papa, and help yourself as you can—for you are my own dear Papa, whether you will or not—And tho' I am an unworthy child—yet I *am* your child—." But again she cannot go on, and the paper is scored across and discarded. For, once more, "I don't know what my name is!—I never dare to wish to come into your family again!" The rape has damaged her sense of her own identity, her sense of herself as a continuous personality, and with that, the relationships nearest her heart. Lovelace seems to be right. Her first reaction is indeed to feel that an irreversible change has taken place. We are however being made to realise imaginatively what sort of experience this is in its agony and confusion, and to measure the disorientation that can convert the Clarissa we knew into this stricken child—it already seems unlikely that it could issue in the slick conversion of Lovelace's brutal theory.

The third paper is written very simply, but after its first sentence it is wholly coherent and ordered, and in it she does begin to understand. Having reached for help outside herself, and failed, she is forced to seek a foothold in her own being, and she finds one. Her moral nature (be it "original" or a "second nature") is still real to her, its values apply, and it gives her a language she can use to understand what has happened: the language of moral fable. Lovelace is hopelessly wrong after all. Her moral nature is no sham veneer; it is authenticated by her suffering because it is the only bedrock reality that remains. The first thing she understands by its aid is inimical to his hopes of a change in her nature, for it is an assertion that her nature is utterly different from his. In her fable the young girl is savaged by the tiger she has fed and loved since infancy; but "who was most to blame, I pray? The Brute, or the Lady? The Lady, surely!—For what *she* did was *out* of nature, out of character, at least: What *it* did was *in* its own nature." This is admittedly a crude and immature view of another human being (and it is not Richardson's, as we have seen), but it is natural enough at this point. Yet it is not the view of Lovelace that matters so much as the insight into herself. Far from revealing a "real" sexuality that her morality has glossed over, the effect of the rape is to enable her to see that it could never have happened if she had not betrayed her real nature, or at least the "character" that re-formed whatever nature she had to start with. What happens is the opposite of what Lovelace expected. It is not her morality which is false, but her love which was wrong. She sees, behind that love, something in herself which courted disaster, which was blindly prepared to ignore the "hungry maw" and the brute nature she had to deal with, which even boasted her own power to subdue. *That* was finally to blame. Lovelace was right to believe that the rape would show her what she is "really like." But we can already guess what the something laid bare inside herself is; or at any rate we can see that it isn't the sexuality Lovelace expects.

The fourth paper identifies it beyond question: it is spiritual pride. The paper is couched in the language of Puritan introspection this time; the "thees" and "thous" indicating a necessary objectivity. "How art thou now humbled in the dust, thou proud Clarissa Harlowe! Thou that never steppedst out of thy Father's house but to be admired! Who wert wont to turn thine eye, sparkling with healthful life, and self-assurance, to different objects at once, as thou passedst, as if (for so thy penetrating Sister used to say) to plume thyself upon the expected applauses of all that beheld thee! Thou that usedst to go to rest satisfied with the adulations paid thee in the past day, and couldst put off every-thing but thy Vanity!—." By the light of this self-arraignment, in the fifth paper, she is even able to reach out to Bella in the understanding that however much her sister's penetration was owing to her jealousy, what she saw was true. "I was too secure in the knowledge I thought I had of my own heart. My supposed advantages became a snare to me. And what now is the end of all?" This is of course to some extent unfair and exaggerated, as the experience of remorseful introspection usually is. Yet the rape has enabled her to see deeper into her heart than ever before, and to detect for herself something that Richardson has already clarified in the experience of his fiction.

The sixth paper is interesting because it confirms the analysis in the way it most needs confirmation: by showing at the moment of her greatest insight that she remains ensnared by what she has seen. She thinks that the rape has put marriage forever beyond her reach. But in bringing this home to herself pathetically—indeed with sentimental indulgence—she reveals that her thoughts of marriage, religious and responsible though we know them to have been, are also intertwined with pride and vanity. "No court now to be paid to my smiles! No encouraging compliments to inspire thee with hope of laying a mind not unworthy of thee under obligation! No elevation now for conscious merit, and applauded purity, to look down from on a prostrate adorer, and an admiring world, and up to pleased and rejoicing parents and relations!" One can imagine the tear-ducts of many of Richardson's first feminine readers beginning to work overtime at this point, but the tears would surely have been thrown away. We have only to remember the "garden scene" to make a placing comparison. What is giving its last spasm here is the product of those aspects of the feminine code which fostered the very pride and vanity she has taken herself to task about. The paper is a farewell to something whose falsehood she has just revealed, yet whose power over her she cannot help reinforcing by the syrupy sweetness of her last indulgence of it.

Again Lovelace has been right about her pride; but the next three papers turn to him, and the first, paper seven, is the knell of his hopes from the rape. For however one might interpret it in detail, it expresses the most powerful revulsion against what he has done to her. The mode this time is poetic image, partly because Clarissa cannot confront her sexual experience directly, and partly because of the intensity of her feelings. The indirection does however cause a certain difficulty, especially since this must be the crux for interpreting her attitude to sex. The simplest way to read the paper is as an expression of revulsion at sex itself, by way of Lovelace. In this reading the ambiguity of the "Thou" which is the first word—is the caterpillar an image of sexual appetite? or is it Lovelace? as indeed it turns out to be—is unimportant. I used to read in this way, making rather unfavourable comparisons with the treatment of worm, storm, and rose in Blake's great poem of Experience, which may well derive from it. But I now think such a reading would be both superficial and significantly mistaken. For what it leaves out of account is just the most striking feature: that from the first image onwards, the emphasis is not on violation or desecration of purity, but on the destruction of potential fertility, growth, warmth, and colour. "Thou pernicious Caterpiller, that preyest upon the fair leaf of Virgin Fame, and poisonest those leaves that thou canst not devour"—the second clause surely says something different from and deeper than the first? What Lovelace has done is not simply to desecrate her virginity, but to poison or kill a vitality his "love" is incapable of making its own. A caterpillar's petty gnawings spoil a leaf that a man could enjoy in its entirety. This is not sex seen as desecration like the first apostrophe, but *rape as seen as a desecration of true sex*, and the difference is crucial. Moreover the point, once taken, is confirmed and strengthened by all the images that follow. The "fell Blight," the "Eastern Blast," the "overspreading Mildew," not only destroy "the early promises of the shining year" (which are already a potentiality of growth and fertility, not a state), but they also mock the toil and blast the joyful hopes of the "Husbandman"—and it is not fanciful to see a grim pun. The crops don't exist for their own sake and beauty; they do exist to be harvested, and so enrich the life of man. But they demand laborious pains and toil to cultivate them to fullness of growth, and to harvest them at the proper time and in the proper way; they are not to be snatched or spoilt, blighted, or made to decay before they have reached their full ripeness. Similarly the crime of the "fretting Moth" is to corrupt the "fairest garment" which is meant to be worn, not just to be beautiful in itself. And the crime of the "eating Canker worm" in the opening bud of the rose of love, is that it prevents the rose from reaching its full rich red (which is not the colour of virginity), but turns it to "livid yellowness," the colour of disease and pallid unfulfilment. I labour the point, but it is there, it is far too easily missed, and without it the full irony of Lovelace's "proof" is lost. He is, as we have been noticing all along, so curiously near the truth in his predictions; but the narrow margin of error makes a world of difference. Clarissa does feel that an irreversible change has taken place which has revealed her true nature to herself. She has been proud, and the experience is indeed one of utter humiliation. But each of these means something quite different from his expectations. It is her moral nature which is the reality to her, and her love for him the aberration. Her pride lay in believing in her own power, believing that her love could overcome his destructive brutality; her new humility will renounce all such hopes in victory over herself, not abasement before her "conqueror." She does indeed admit her sexual nature, if only under the cloak of image; yet, if I am right, her idea of sex is deeper and more human than his, in its insistence that sex should be growth, fertility, harvest, warmth, richness—and by these values his idea of sex as ego-endorsement can only be seen as poisonous, corrupt, and diseased.

Now in her eighth paper she can speak to Lovelace simply and directly about the way she had looked at him at first, and had allowed her love to grow through her readiness to find in him the qualities she wanted to find.

"But, Oh! you have barbarously and basely conspired against that Honour, which you ought to have protected: And now you have made me—What is it of vile, that you have *not* made me?—Yet, God knows my heart, I had no culpable inclinations!—I honoured Virtue!—I hated Vice!—But I knew not, that you were Vice itself!" The strength of the grasp she has regained of her moral nature can be gauged now. She has come out of derangement, from the emotions of the lost, hurt child, through the languages of moral fable, Puritan introspection, and the intensity of image, to a point where she can write with clear and ordered simplicity. She doesn't name what he has done to her but she does try to face it. Having condemned herself for pride and blindness she now finds nothing culpable in her love itself, apart from these. Her view of her own vileness, and of him as "Vice itself," are less than satisfactory, but even here she qualifies still further in the ninth paper. The essential difference between them is the difference between their hearts. "Had the happiness of any the poorest Outcast in the world, whom I had never seen, never known, never before heard of, lain as much in *my* power, as my happiness did in *yours*, my benevolent heart would have made me fly to the succour of such a poor distressed." It is quite clear that Lovelace has entirely misread her, and that the effect on her of what he has done can only be to make her condemn and despise him beyond recall.

The last of her papers is scrawled over with quotations from the poets; from Otway, Cowley, Garth, Dryden, Lee and Shakespeare. Having searched herself for the meaning of what has happened, she finally uses the poetry of others as an emotional catalyst and relief. So Hamlet's horror at his mother's lust is an index to her feelings; Cowley's *Despair* helps her to express her own at being forced back from insensibility into the cage of a conscious body; and several others bring out the longing for death which (as we have seen before) is her immediate emotional reaction to the hateful prospect of her life. What such use of quotations makes one suspect, however, is confirmed by what three of them say: she is still afraid of her feelings. The first shows her longing to escape from consciousness and memory; the other citation from *Hamlet*, the Ghost's "I could a Tale unfold / Would harrow up thy soul!—" is chiefly remarkable for the dash; and the adaptation to Anna of lines from *Venice Preserved* speaks of the divided soul warring within her. She has always been emotionally reserved; has always had difficulty in seeing into her own heart. Her moral insight may have become clearer and clearer, but her emotions are still turgid, confused, and terrifying. Yet the quotations help her to begin to get them outside herself and look at them; and at the end of the paper she finds some words from the *Absalom and Achitophel* of Lovelace's favourite bard, which help her to sound a note of acceptance that will become the novel's dominant chord:

For Life can never be sincerely blest.
Heav'n punishes the *Bad*, and proves the *Best*.

What we have been watching is a personality disintegrated and remade; a successful search for reorientation after what Richardson clearly thought was the most damaging and challenging blow a woman could suffer. Only now does he show us the real derangement which these ten papers have brought her out of: her letter to Lovelace which, apart from its ordered postscript, probably antedates them all and represents the last stage of her delirium. It is really disordered. She cannot keep her mind at all on what she writes, for "My head is gone. I have wept away all my brain." She thinks Lovelace may have poisoned Anna, may be in Faustian league with the devil. She is incoherently terrified of Mrs Sinclair, and desperately pleads to be sent away from her hateful house to some private lunatic asylum where she can be hid forever from the world. Mixed up with this is the dawning insight into her own responsibility, and pride, which her suffering reveals to her. But at the heart of the letter is a moment of sheer self-revelation, of what it *feels* like to know that she has been raped; and there is no moment like it in the eighteenth-century novel. "O Lovelace! if you could be sorry for yourself, I would be sorry too—But when all my doors are fast, and nothing but the key-hole open, and the key of late put into that, to be where you are, in a manner without opening any of them—O wretched, wretched Clarissa Harlowe! For I never will be Lovelace—let my Uncle take it as he pleases."

As soon as one realises what this is about, the maidenly groping for language becomes deeply moving. The whole of her upbringing, her feminine code, and the ethics of her age, have inhibited all thought or mention of sex; have encouraged her native reserve; have taught her to think of her body as a fortress locked against attack; have made her regard any sexual approach before marriage as an encroaching liberty, to be resented as an insult. The experience of rape is the agony of knowing that the opening in her body, in spite of the fact that her senses and her intellect have been wholly unmoved, has enabled Lovelace to "be where you *are*"—not "were"—to be always part of her inner consciousness, having touched her most private being. There is a deep psychological truth here; and not for a hundred and fifty years could the English novel begin to approach again a "new way of writing" which could probe its characters as deeply as this. Clarissa could only make such a self-revelation in derangement, but to bring it off at all is an astonishing feat in the mid-eighteenth century.

Richardson has moved behind sex, behind "character," behind morality. His imagination told him here that what was really the issue in the situa-

tion he had created was the sacredness of a human being's innermost self—
whether we use the new word "psyche" or the old word "soul." What is really unforgivable about Lovelace is not the raped virginity, the ruined reputation, the moral turpitude. It is that he cannot conceive or respect the essentially private inner core of personality that each individual has a right to
dispose of as only he or she may wish. He has not treated her as a human
being but as a mere object, a function of his ego, and this she will never accept. We can now see that this also lay behind the Harlowes and Solmes;
that it is what the whole novel has been about. Yet to answer his ultimate
question, what is "Clarissa" *essentially*? and to prove the existence of that
inner core, Richardson has had to challenge himself to disintegrate his heroine,
to break her down to the last possible distillation before her personality disappears into the mechanism of madness. No novelist better earns his right to
his ultimate beliefs by his courage in putting them imaginatively to the test—
not even Henry James, whom he resembles in so many respects, though James
is a much more accomplished artist. It does not matter whether one agrees
that a moral nature may be innate; or whether one simply sees Clarissa remak-
ing her personality into the shape she wishes it to have. It doesn't even matter, in the last analysis, whether one admires or detests that shape. At the
heart of Richardson's novel is the assertion of her right to be what she wishes
to be, and one is bound to respect the integrity that drives him so far, in
order to earn the right to make it.

MARK KINKEAD-WEEKES

Crisis, Resolution,
and the Family of the Heart

W̲e are ready to judge the challenge Richardson posed himself, to reconcile "ought" and "is" in the far more testing circumstances posed to Sir Charles by the Porretta family in Bologna.

This is the central crisis of [*Sir Charles Grandison*] as a whole, because "ought" and "is" have been brought together in a highly challenging situation. The more one has been prepared to make allowances for Richardson's chosen method, and to try to read the "Sir Charles" story in terms of its own criteria, the more important it will be now that Richardson should justify that method by a convincing testing of "ought" by "is." In the interval between the library scene and the arrival of Sir Charles in Bologna, he has produced a way of reconciling the two kinds of insight and imagination. Harriet's moral drama established a clear grasp of what she ought to feel as well as do, without in any way excluding a realistic exploration of the cost in conscious struggle, of trying to raise herself to her chosen role. Now, in Italy, Richardson poses his hero with an even more awkward problem; the most delicate he could devise—so difficult, indeed, that the normally assured moral paragon has to confess to the Countess that he hardly knows what he ought to do. Instead of a clash between right and wrong, or even between the "great" and the merely "good," he is caught at a crossroads with no clearly marked route. In the situation itself there is room for considerable disagreement among equally moral judges; and Richardson invites the response of serious casuistry more strongly still by deliberate delaying tactics. While the crisis is taking place we are given a number of clues to the hero's thinking, but

From *Samuel Richardson: Dramatic Novelist.* © 1973 by Mark Kinkead-Weekes. Cornell University Press, 1973.

no full-scale discussion of the problem as a whole. Only after it is all over and he has returned to England will Sir Charles be allowed to argue a full case for his conduct, to Jeronymo and to Harriet. There is little doubt that this is because Richardson was determined to test his readers as well as his hero. So the problem of "ought" itself is more awkward than ever before. On the other hand, in the library, and as he faces his grilling by the Countess, Sir Charles's very uncertainties have begun to bring him alive in terms of the art of "is." Expectations of a wholly new kind in his story have arisen: and because there is no straightforward "ought," only a collision of opposed impulses and loyalties to two excellent women, the crisis seems bound to be one of consciousness at least as much as conscience. Whatever role Sir Charles chooses should hardly be less painful and costly than Harriet's, and will have to be convincingly earned in terms of inner conflict, and psychological as well as ethical "delicacy." "A man divided in himself, not knowing what I *can* do, hardly sometimes what I *ought* to do" . . . the confession to the Countess of D holds inner conflict and problems of principle in a newly exacting tension; and the treatment and solution of the crisis will have to satisfy us in the same double way.

Richardson's preparation for the crisis, the treatment of achieved role in Harriet, suggests a suitable critical method: to establish first the nature of the role Sir Charles chooses to play, then the nature of his feelings, and finally a judgement how far there has been a reconciliation of the demands of "ought" and "is."

The crisis falls into four distinct phases, marked by separate batches of letters to Dr Bartlett. In the first, the real concern is with Clementina's prospects of recovery under the influence of Grandison's return. The question of marriage is left deliberately open. In the second phase, the family is won over to the belief that she must be indulged in all her wishes, and the decision is left entirely to her. In the full expectation that she will choose to marry her chevalier, the terms are finally agreed, on the basis he had originally proposed. The last letter of this batch is sent away the day before he goes to hear her answer. In the third phase, Clementina astounds everyone by refusing him on religious grounds. At first both sides agree not to try to influence her; but after the Bishop and her Confessor have broken the conditions by responding to her appeal to them as Catholics, Sir Charles makes a final effort to persuade her that her ʿaith would not be at risk if she married him. In the final phase, he has accepted her decision, and waits only to make sure that she will hold to her resolution. He urges her, as a brother, not to think of taking the veil.

What did Sir Charles mean by telling the Countess that his journey to

Italy was "indispensable"? "As generosity, as justice, or, rather, as Providence leads, I will follow." He obviously thinks it would be unjust and ungenerous to allow the Family's rejection of his terms to prevent him offering his help in the recovery of the stricken brother and sister, even though only some of the Porrettas have asked him to return. But when he told the Countess that both girls were free, while he was bound, he clearly meant that he felt bound not only to try to restore Clementina from her mental breakdown, but also to marry her if she and her family wish it. (There is in any case a direct connection, since the implicit assumption is that he can help precisely because she loves him so much.) He makes it clear to the Marchioness that this must be so in justice: "I never yet made an offer, that I receded from, the circumstances continuing the same." Harriet had made the same point long before. Since the very obligation of the terms he had offered, which Clementina had never refused, made it impossible to make any move toward Harriet, he feels that the only circumstances that have changed are his accession to the title and to his father's estates—and if the terms were just when they were offered, his new wealth and position cannot be allowed to make any difference. If justice requires him to be ready to stick to his offer, however, generosity demands that he should put self-interest out of the question. So he assures the Marchioness that the family are free from obligation; he overcomes the general's hostility by insisting that he will accept no decision in his favour that is not endorsed by all the Porrettas; and when the bright hopes of Clementina's recovery cause a change in her mother's behaviour, because she fears he may take advantage, he proves his disinterestedness by himself suggesting that he should try the effect of short absences. He goes to Florence for a fortnight, then to Naples for three weeks, to see whether her recovery is as dependent on him as it appears. If this "justice" and "generosity" put him in the hands of the Family, he also insists that he is in the hands of Providence above all. He must have no wish for himself; if Jeronymo can be restored physically and Clementina mentally, may "Providence dispose as it pleases of me!"

The interesting point about this chosen role is its *passivity*. Whatever we may have thought of Richardson's hero up till now, he has been a remarkably active moral agent. Yet the essence of his solution to the dilemma he is in seems to be that he has no right to make any decision.

But as the first phase becomes the second, with the family's conviction that Clementina must be allowed to choose for herself, the role acquires more initiative. The discussion of terms calls on him to suppose Clementina his, and to make a series of decisions on that assumption. Here there was much room for contemporary controversy especially over his compromise about possible children, that the sons should be brought up as Protestants, but the daughters as Catholics. What seems most important however is simply to establish the careful balance in this, and all Sir Charles's thinking. If it is just that Clementina should be secured in her faith, with her own confessor, and her own personal attendants to provide a Catholic circle around her; it is no less just that Sir Charles should protect his household against zealous attempts at conversion, and should refuse to compromise his rights as its head. He clearly attempts a meticulous evenhandedness. But generosity is also guaranteed, in his attitude to his wife, her servants, and his "in-laws," and in the whole range of the financial settlements, where he makes it clear that self-interest has no part. For the mid-eighteenth century, his proposals strike one as notably liberal.

As the third phase opens, moreover, there seems to be a temporary change from the passive to the active. Just before he leaves to see Clementina, Sir Charles adds an interesting gloss to his trust in Providence, but he tells Count Belvedere that his attitude must change now. "I have been willing to consider the natural impulses of a spirit so pure, though disturbed, as the finger of Providence. I have hitherto been absolutely passive: In honour I cannot now be so." Once the objections of the family have been removed, it no longer seems just or generous to be a passive "offering" to Clementina. But then she gives him her famous paper, beseeching him to be great enough to help her follow her conscience. He is dumbstruck at first: "Never was I so little present to myself." The Porrettas underline what Clementina had made clear, that it is wholly in his power to make her surname what he pleases. They consider themselves still bound to him, and offer congratulations on her confession of her love. But Sir Charles himself is sure that he ought to revert to his previous passivity, and that her plea of conscience must override all others. "God only knows, whether the ardent heart would be punished or rewarded, by the completion of its wishes: But this I know, that were Clementina to give me both her hand and her heart, and could not, by reason of religious doubts; be happy with me, I should myself be extremely miserable; especially if I had been earnest to prevail upon her to favour me against her judgment." He readily consents to his part of the bargain that no effort to persuade her be made from either side; but when her brother the bishop and her confessor break the conditions, he does feel that honour obliges him to make one matching effort. But it is strictly circumscribed both in motive and point. The only valid motive is his concern for her female delicacy. When Clementina has the original conditions put to him for the first time as from herself, he is anxious, in refusing them, not to seem to refuse *her*, and allows it to appear that the family have merely sounded him out. Now the same concern for her delicacy prompts him to argue that a woman has a right to expect the man who claims to love her, to make one effort to assure her that she could be happy with him. At worst this will test her resolution, and they will both be easier in their minds afterwards. But he must not argue the merits and demerits of the two Faiths, and he must respect her conscience throughout—all he can and should do is make a last effort to assure her that her conscience has nothing to fear from marrying him. He fails, because the very effect of his tenderness seems to justify her distrust of her own power to hold out for what, when she is not with him, she knows to be the "irresistible impulse" of her conscience. From this point Sir Charles accepts her decision absolutely. He must become her brother again, and it can only be in that capacity that he can urge her not to think of becoming a nun.

Richardson's first surprise for us at the crisis, then, is that the role of "ought" his very active hero chooses is a role of extraordinary passivity. It might therefore seem that the less Sir Charles can act, the more important it will become to show us the inner struggle of consciousness in the strong man who can hardly lift a finger in the circumstances he finds himself trapped in. But Richardson's second surprise is that, while he makes it perfectly clear that a severe struggle is taking place, we are only allowed to see the ripples on the surface of his prose to Dr Bartlett. The conflict in the depths is unexplored.

Sir Charles in his first two letters only mentions Harriet to congratulate himself on not having tried to involve "that loveliest of women" in his difficulties, and to say that he is "ready to think" that she will not be able to resist the persuasions of the Countess and her noble son. But between the two letters he has been taken ill, "by a hurry of spirits; by fatigue; by my apprehensions for Jeronymo; my concern for Clementina; and by my too great anxiety for the dear friends I had so lately left in England. You know, Dr Bartlett, that I have a heart too susceptible for my own peace, tho' I endeavour to *conceal* from *others* those painful sensibilities, which they cannot relieve." I think there is no doubt that we are meant to read between the lines here. The phrasing of both mentions of Miss Byron has the air of a man repeating a lesson to himself of which he has some need; and the "sensibilities" and the "too great anxiety" clearly spell "Harriet" at least as much as anything else. At the same time we are given his motive for not opening his heart in his letters. After his first visit to Clementina and his quarrel with the general, he is taken ill again, badly enough to need to be bled. To his worries about Harriet and the stricken brother and sister has to be added a growing resentment of the Porrettas' failure to match his own attempts at justice and generosity.

In the second phase, Richardson allows his hero a momentary slip, but so ambiguously that we cannot be sure what it means. Mrs Beaumont has been telling him that "there is a man whom she wishes to be Clementina's," and Sir Charles goes on, "There is a woman—But—do thou, Providence, direct us both! All that thou orderest must be best!" This looks like the first indication that Sir Charles's heart is really with Harriet all the time; but it is broken off before we can be certain. There is however a further hint in the next letter to keep suspicion alive; when the fancifulness of Clementina's dress, hinting the disorder of her mind, also brings the contrast with Harriet home to him. He is careful to equate the two girls, remembering the "unaffected elegance" of Clementina as she used to be, but the reservation has its significance all the same.

But if at first we are only given this kind of hint, after the second phase even less is available. As the apparent certainty mounts that he will marry Clementina, hints of what he actually does feel are replaced by statements of what he ought to feel. The conclusion of the last letter of this batch, which leaves everyone in England in such cruel suspense, shows very clearly the switch to the language of ought and ought not. "What, my dear Dr Bartlett, would I give, to be assured, that the most excellent of English-women, could think herself happy with the Earl of D.—— . . . Should Miss Byron be unhappy, and through my means, the remembrance of my own caution and self-restraint could not appease the grief of my heart. But . . . What are these suggestions of tenderness—Are they not suggestions of *vanity* and *presumption*? They *are*. They *must* be so. I will banish them from my thoughts, as such. Ever-amiable Miss Byron! friend of my Soul! forgive me for them!" We have the exact equivalent here of Harriet's "wish" in the library that Clementina might marry Sir Charles. But the idea that it would be presumption to worry about Harriet's happiness would seem to lock the door on any hope of our witnessing the inner struggle, which alone could validate the wish and remove all hint of hypocrisy.

And so indeed it proves. From now on there is no mention of Harriet in connection with himself. After Clementina's refusal Sir Charles is indisposed again, but there is no hope of knowing whether feelings about Harriet still play any part in his sufferings. Indeed, when his last attempt to persuade the Italian girl fails, the evidence seems to be that his emotions are concentrated on Clementina. He is "greatly dissatisfied with myself, yet hardly knowing why. I thought I wanted somebody to accuse, somebody to blame—Yet how could it be Clementina? . . . It is difficult, my dear Dr Bartlett, at the instant in which the heart finds itself disappointed of some darling hope, to avoid reflexions that, however, can only be justified by self-partiality." The "darling hope" seems to indicate that Harriet is no longer in contention in his heart, and that the "greatness" of Clementina's refusal has also been the moment when Sir Charles fell wholly in love with her. Yet the next sentence is suspicious, because it is framed so completely in the language of "ought." "What must I be, if, led as I have been, by all her friends to hope, I had not been *earnest* in my hope!" The assumption that he could not feel anything besides the "right" feeling is one that begs all the important questions. Now he has not only closed the doors of his heart to us, he has closed them to himself as well.

At the crisis then, Richardson not only makes his hero choose an almost completely passive role, but also allows him to prevent us from discovering what really goes on in his heart and mind. At best we are given only veiled hints and guesses by implication; but then even these are obliterated by his determination to admit only what he ought to feel, not what he actually does. Instead of the equivalent of Harriet's struggle to earn her moral role, and to learn to feel as she ought by overcoming other feelings, we are confronted with a closing-off of consciousness, leaving only "public" words and behaviour to judge.

We have yet, of course, to hear Sir Charles's final confession of what did go on in his heart and mind, in those accounts to Jeronymo and Harriet that Richardson held back until after his return to England. But since Richardson went to such lengths to test his readers, it might be valuable to take up the challenge on the basis of what we know now. My readers might like to examine their own responses at just this point, and formulate what they would like to have said at one of those gatherings in the grotto at North End . . .

The main objections of Sir Charles's handling of the crisis are likely to concentrate on three points. The first of these is put by Uncle Selby, and even more strongly by Olivia, writing before Sir Charles leaves Italy. "Unworthy Grandison! . . . You who could leave her" (i.e., Harriet), "and, under colour of honour, when there was no pre-engagement, and when the proud family had rejected you, prefer to such a fine young creature, a romantic Enthusiast." This is to question whether Sir Charles need have felt bound to Clementina at all. The second objection would allow some obligation, but sees a gross oversimplification in the notion that circumstances have not changed. For Harriet has fallen in love with him, and he cannot be wholly blind to the signs of this, even if he cannot know it as surely as we do. What about his obligation to her, then? Thirdly, it can hardly be questioned that his own feelings have been engaged, as they were not when he proposed terms to the Porrettas. Is not this a change of circumstance of the most crucial kind?

If we imagine the debate at North End, however, and a reply from the kind of reader the Master longed for, one can conceive answers on the basis of what we already know, without needing to appeal yet to whatever Sir Charles may have to say for himself.

The crucial point in answering the first objection is that Clementina herself has never been given the chance to say "yes" or "no" to Sir Charles's proposal. *That* is why he cannot consider himself released by the family's rejection of his terms, especially since her mental breakdown was obviously connected with her love for him. The answer to the second objection is that he could not possibly be held responsible for Harriet's feelings in the same way, since he has, wholly honourably, done everything in his power to avoid engaging her affections. Moreover, possibly the clearest single piece of evidence we have of his thinking at the crisis was concerned precisely with Harriet's happiness. But that reminds us, not only that he cannot know what we know about her heart, but also that he has to guard against the vanity and presumption of even suspecting she could have fallen so deeply in love, when he had made no move. To the third point, about his own feelings, the answer would be that if it were right to believe that only Clementina could release him from his proposal, and that he was responsible for her mental stability and happiness as he could not be for Harriet's, then it would be right to suppress whatever he felt for Harriet if Clementina accepted him.

It is at just this point, however, that the argument becomes more subtle and more interesting. For if the last point be granted, and Sir Charles's problem became that of reconciling a principled decision with his conflicting feelings towards the two girls, it would seem as important for his integrity that his feelings for Harriet should be proved delicate, true and tender, as that they should be convincingly overruled. Now how could this be proved unless they *engage* with his feelings for Clementina; unless the pain of their suppression guarantees their genuineness; and unless the question of whether they *can* be effectively overcome is openly raised and resolved? For this affects the delicacy and tenderness of his feelings for Clementina too. If we are expected to admire Clementina for facing up to the question of whether she could make Sir Charles happy in the light of her religious scruples, can we admire Sir Charles for never apparently facing up to the question of whether he could make Clementina happy in the light of his feelings for Harriet? Lastly, ought there not to be at least a question of whether the existence of those feelings should be confessed?—whatever the decision might be in the light of Clementina's precarious stability.

What is significant about this development of the argument is the way that questions of "ought" have become utterly inseparable from questions of "is": the need to know what Sir Charles actually does feel, at the time. If he is to convince us imaginatively of his ideal goodness, it cannot be sufficient to judge on the basis of his actions alone, or his feeling for Clementina alone. He is under no "obligation" to Harriet; but the integrity of his behaviour to *Clementina* is inextricably bound up with the conflict between his feelings for the two girls. Moreover the obvious danger of the passivity he chooses, even if it be judged right, is that he will seem to have become merely a creature of circumstance and not a moral agent at all, unless we can be convinced of the integrity of his heart. And what have we to go on, since Richardson has allowed him to close the door on that heart, and firmly avert his own eyes from introspection?

The signs begin to point to a crucial and damaging miscalculation at the heart of the novel; for the only possible rescue will lie in Sir Charles's own retrospective self-justification, and there may well be a doubt as to whether this could be a really effective substitute for convincing experience of his consciousness at the time.

The letter to Jeronymo is no help at all. It confirms that Clementina was his first love; that he imputed her sufferings to her love of him; and that consequently he felt his honour involved in keeping himself free until her destiny was decided. But when he met Harriet, this obligation caused him "uneasiness" for the first time, though he was not sure of succeeding with the English girl even had he been free. So much we already knew . . . the only interesting thing is the hint of evasiveness in the word "uneasiness." But as Sir Charles goes on to give us the first new insight, the evasiveness becomes even more marked. "Shall I, my dear Jeronymo, own the truth?—The two noblest-minded women in the world, when I went over to Italy . . . held almost an equal interest in my heart." Which was more equal than the other? The fact that he is writing to Clementina's brother makes the evasion suggest that it must have been Harriet. This would make it all the more important that Italian delicacies should be satisfied about the rightness of his then coming within an ace of marrying Clementina; but Sir Charles continues overly diplomatic. As Clementina's recovery confirmed her feeling for him and the importance of his attachment to her, he says that he "contented" himself with wishing the English lady a worthier husband than he could be in his embarrassed situation, and when the whole family wished their daughter to be his, "I had not a wish but for your Clementina." But this is to beg precisely the real question of the *nature* of the resolution of conflicting feelings, and the conviction it can carry. It is not enough to think one ought to feel something, and then assume that every other feeling is banished—if this could be done, it would say very little for the integrity of the heart that could manage it. On this interpretation of "almost equal," the best that could be said for the diplomacy of the letter is that it succeeds in blurring the issue for Clementina. When she reads and comments on it some time later, she reacts to Sir Charles's confession of his feeling for Harriet by a spasm of outraged delicacy, that he remained tied to her only through compassion. But when she comes to "almost equal," she construes it in her own favour, and the further question vanishes. But even so, in the rarefied atmosphere of delicacy in which we are moving, it should not vanish quite so easily—one would expect her to ask searching questions about the nature of "contented" and "not a wish" that she does not ask—or at the very least to wonder why Harriet was never mentioned to her at all. And, in any case, which *is* the right interpretation of Sir Charles's riddling phrase? The only thing we can be certain of, is that he has not owned the whole truth.

We are left then with his very last chance, his statement to Harriet— and it is left exceeding late. But it starts well: "altho' what I have to say, may, I presume, be collected from what you know of my story . . . something, however, may be necessary to be said . . . of the state of my own heart . . . And I will deliver myself with all the truth and plainness which I think are required." At least there should be no ambiguity now. He confesses his attraction to her from the first moment, but that it was his growing knowledge of her mind and behaviour that led him into a "gentler, yet a more irresistible passion," especially since there seemed "no *probable* hope" of Clementina. But because of his obligation to the Italian girl, he took himself to task, and saw as little of Harriet as he possibly could. He detected the wishes of his sisters and Lord L, and sometimes thought that he could hope for Harriet's love by their interest, but he would not permit himself to hope, and resolutely made himself ascribe all signs of Harriet's favour to her natural goodness of heart, and to her powerful sense of gratitude. But, finding that his feeling for her continued to increase, he had no way left but "to strengthen my heart, in Clementina's cause, by Miss Byron's assistance." *That* is why he told her the story in the library, knowing that this would deprive him of any hope of encouragement to break his obligation, and that it would engage Harriet's generosity on Clementina's behalf.

So far, this is distinctly good. We could not have inferred the motive with absolute assurance, but it is wholly convincing, because with it all the signs of Sir Charles's feelings for Harriet fall into place alongside the strength of his sense of obligation to Clementina, without either weakening the other. His behaviour in the library, and his incoherence at the end, also become even more poignant and understandable, and for perhaps the first time in the novel Richardson's hero can command undiluted sympathy. Moreover this is increased, as we learn for the first time what happened as he left the library in high discomposure. He asks Dr Bartlett to advise him, and help him compose himself, and he tells the Doctor three things we have never seen clearly. He has no hope of conquering the opposition of all the Porrettas. He cannot help resenting the way they have treated him. And above all, he has no doubt that even were they to comply with his terms, he would be happier with Harriet because of the differences in nationality and religion. Moreover, though Dr Bartlett admires Clementina and is very sorry for her, he "next to adored" Harriet . . . and he advises Sir Charles accordingly.

This makes the question whether or not to continue to feel bound to Clementina even more agonised than we knew, and brings the first stage of the moral argument to the sharpest possible focus. But Sir Charles meets the challenge admirably. He reminds the Doctor, and himself, not only that Clementina never refused the proposal, but that the terms were acceptable to her and "she even besought her friends to comply with them." If he was determined to await either her recovery or her release before he met Miss Byron, "will Miss Byron herself, if she knows that, forgive me (the circumstances not changed) for the change of a resolution of which Clementina was so worthy?" The repetition of the phrase about circumstances in this new context removes the objection to it. It clearly means only his change of rank and fortune, and it does not mean that he ignores the difference that meeting Miss Byron has made. Only, he sheds on it a new light that is genuinely delicate and tender to Harriet: the question of whether she would be happy to know that her courtship was based on a broken obligation? The way that Clementina has been treated, for his sake (as she wrote in her disordered letter); the fact that she still wants to see him; the possibility that he could restore her to her right mind; surely these things confirm that he should not try to engage Harriet's affections? "Could I be happy in my own mind, were I to try, and to succeed? And if not, must I not be as ungrateful to her, as ungenerous to the other?" *This* is the real core of the problem: that to break the obligation to the Italian girl is to offer a flawed relationship to the English one. Harriet would not be happy in herself if she knew; and Sir Charles's unhappiness would be bound to affect the relationship still further. Moreover, as things stand, he cannot be responsible for Harriet as he is for Clementina.

Harriet and her friends at Selby House have nothing to say to this; and nor, I believe, have we. It seems to me a complete defence of Sir Charles's behaviour, a satisfactory answer to the whole first part of the moral argument, and the only trouble about it is that it has been left so late that it can no longer inject into the whole of the Italian crisis the inner life and imaginative sympathy that there might have been at the time.

But the second half of the moral problem remains: the question of Sir

Charles's conflicting feelings in Italy, and the nature of their resolution. If anything, it is rendered more challenging by our new knowledge that he would have preferred Harriet before he arrived in Bologna, so that our reading of his letter to Jeronymo was right, and Clementina's was mistaken. Most important of all, his defence of himself has now seized on the crucial point that he can only offer a valid relationship to one girl if he has come to a satisfactory resolution of his feelings towards the other. What was delicacy on Harriet's behalf must be delicacy also on Clementina's, even if there is no "obligation" to Harriet.

Alas—the second half of Sir Charles's self-defence evades the issue in the familiar way. It is little more than a summary, half a page as against the four and a half devoted to the conflict before he left for Italy. He says that Clementina on her restoration, "shone upon us all even with a brighter lustre than she did before her disorder," and that "what was before *honour* and *compassion*, now became *admiration*; and I should have been unjust to the merits of so excellent a woman, if I could not say, *Love*." But the question of love is not and cannot be a question of Clementina's merits alone. We can accept that he now cared more deeply for the Italian girl than ever before, but this does nothing to clarify the nature and the resolution (for both their sakes) of the conflict of loves, unless the answer be that he now genuinely found that he loved Clementina so much more, not than he had loved before, but than he had loved Harriet. But that could not be expressed in terms of "justice" to Clementina. He goes on, that now, concluding himself already the husband of Clementina, the welfare and happiness of Harriet were "the next wish of my heart," and that he rejoiced that he had not entangled her. But he then "devoted myself wholly to Clementina—*I own it, Ladies*—And had I thought, Angel as she came out, upon proof, that I could not have given her my heart, I had been equally unjust, and ungrateful." Again circumlocution and fudging blur the question, by seeking to make love an "ought," a question of justice and not of fact. There could only have been three possible resolutions after a fully honest and searching examination of what he actually felt for both women. He could have decided that he loved Harriet too much to make an honourable husband to Clementina. Or he could have decided that he now loved Clementina so much more than Harriet that the question no longer arose. Or he could have decided that he could not love Harriet so much that it became possible for him to break both his obligations and his new feeling; and that, having proved by painful struggle that it was possible to overcome his feelings for the English girl, he could conscientiously hope to make Clementina an honourable and loving husband. But that would not be loving in "justice" to Clementina's merits; it would be loving despite Harriet's, and his own feelings for her, because his heart and conscience could not be easy over broken obligation. Now Sir Charles's formulation will not allow us to clarify which of the last two of these was the case, since the language of "ought" allows him so easily to sidestep the question of what he actually felt for Harriet at the time. And it is surely very important that Harriet, and we, should know? For the essence of the novel has been Richardson's determination to imagine an *ideal* goodness, even excessively ambitious to overcome, not only normal human frailty and conflict, but also normally sufficient ethics. It might be very human and natural to seek to draw a veil over the actual situation for a normal hero, situated as Sir Charles is situated and speaking to Harriet. But if we have been prepared to repress criticisms based on the normative and the natural, in order to give Richardson's idealism a chance to justify itself, he cannot be rescued by appeals to such standards now. Sir Charles for the one and only time is supposed to be speaking with full truth and plainness about the state of his heart. If the second possibility was the case, then Harriet is his second choice, not a true love barred only by circumstances which have now been removed. If the third possibility was the case, then her delicacy surely might like to pose the question of how much of a struggle it was for Sir Charles to come to his decision. And we have only to reverse the position to see that the same would hold true for Clementina; while the question of whether it was right that she should never know a syllable of the matter until after she had made her decision, is never even raised.

There is perhaps one last gloss that we should look at, before deciding the significance of all this. Clementina was allowed to comment on the letter to Jeronymo, albeit deluding herself over its ambiguity; but Harriet is not allowed to comment on Sir Charles's account of himself to her. What we get instead is a full-blooded endorsement in every detail from Charlotte, in what can only be described as a curtain-lecture. "The Lady's merits shine out with transcendent lustre in the eyes of every one . . . Must they not in *his*, to whom *Merit* was ever the *first*, *Beauty* but the *second*, attractive? He had no tie to any other woman on earth: He had only the tenderness of his own heart, with regard to Miss Byron, to contend with. *Ought* he not to have contended with it? He *did*; and so far conquered, as to enable himself to be *just* to the Lady, whose great qualities, and the concurrence of her friends in his favour, had converted Compasion for her into Love . . . But with what tenderness, with what politeness, does he . . . express himself of Miss Byron! He declares, that if *she* were not to be happy, it would be a great abatement of his own felicity. You, however, remember how politely he recalls his apprehensions that you may not on his account, be altogether so happy as he wishes, as the suggestions of his own presumption; and censures himself for barely supposing, that he had been of consequence enough with you to give you pain." One fears that this disposes of the last possibility that Richardson may have been challenging his readers to surpass his hero in delicacy, by finding the right criticism. The thumping italics sound unmistakably like the Master's foot tapping the floor, and suggest that this is to be taken as the official summing up. And if Charlotte's hero-worship of her brother is always irritating, as providing the first violin in that orchestra of praise which has bespoken our response from the start, it is even more irritating than usual when it betrays the author's miscalculation. For even if we were to grant that love should follow merit so obediently (which is questionable enough), one need only riposte that Harriet too had transcendent merit to show that the real question is being fudged. It may well be that he ought to have conquered his feeling for Harriet—the suggestion is that the third possibility was the right one—but the crux for Harriet's delicacy would be the knowledge of how painful and difficult it was to do so, and that would be important for Clementina too. Lastly, the argument of presumption is just too easy an escape from *all* thought of Harriet. To put oneself in Harriet's place would I think be to prefer his anxiety for her to his "politeness," because it is a truer indication of his love. But even if that were not so, it is precisely the strength of his love for her, and not his responsibility for her happiness, that is the real crux. The too-easy escape about presumption allows all eyes, including the hero's and apparently his creator's, to be averted from the area of consciousness where the real conflict, and hence the real justification, could be found and proved. On the evidence we have, the most charitable account of the hero's behaviour might well be that he simply decided his obligation could not be broken, trusted to luck or providence in complete passivity, closed his eyes to everything but the welcome fact that he found himself feeling more for Clementina than he had done before . . . and was lucky. Yet that is hardly an account of ideal goodness and integrity. Ethical mountains have laboured and produced, alas, a moral mouse—to unmerited fanfares of applause.

I do not myself think that Richardson cheated, though one can see that in some ways his task of bringing Sir Charles and Harriet together might have been made more difficult by greater explicitness about Sir Charles's feelings at the crisis. Rather the evidence seems to suggest that he was uneasy about something in his treatment, yet unsure where that something lay. The close of the last of the second batch of letters, when Sir Charles seems certain to marry Clementina, says simply: " 'In the highest of our pleasures, the sighing heart will remind us of imperfection.' It is fit it should be so."

And though Harriet is not permitted to comment on Sir Charles's final statement— a fact that could point either to deliberate evasion, or to obscure unease—she is allowed one remark that seems to indicate the latter. "But still . . . something sticks with me (and ought it not?) in relation to the noble Clementina!" On the surface, both remarks arise from the awareness that a resolution is being achieved at the cost of others; but both seem to have wider reverberations too. The most interesting evidence of all, however, is Harriet's earlier reactions to the last letter Sir Charles writes in the third phase, when he is fairly certain that Clementina will hold to her resolution not to marry him, but is waiting to be quite sure. He has had letters from England, and has something to say about all the people he cares about, with the careful omission of Harriet. And noticing this, she comments also on the absence of any mention of her in all the letters of the third phase—but she praises him for his justice and delicacy: "For, could Sir Charles Grandison excusably (if, on *other* occasions he remembred the poor girl whom he rescued; could he excusably, I say) while his soul was agitated by his own suspense, occasioned by the uncommon greatness of Clementina's behaviour, think of any other woman in the world?" It becomes clearer than ever how consistently Richardson the imaginative artist has been blinded by Richardson the didactic moralist. The central miscalculation comes from a moral dogmatism, that insists his character must only think what he feels morally authorised to think. But the true artist in Richardson then produces a psychological rebellion of a significantly subversive kind. At the end of the letter, Harriet goes on to draw an apparently complimentary contrast between Sir Charles and Adam, which converts itself in the act of voicing it, to a curious kind of involuntary sarcasm. "But is not his conduct such as would make a considerate person, who has any connexions with him, tremble? Since if there be a fault *between* them, it must be *all* that person's; and he will not, if it be possible for him to avoid it, be a sharer in it? Do you think, my dear, that had he been the first man, he would have been so complaisant to his Eve as *Milton makes Adam* . . . To taste the forbidden fruit, because he would not be separated from her, in her punishment, tho' all *posterity* were to suffer by it?—No; it is my opinion, that your brother would have had gallantry enough to his fallen spouse, to have made him extremely regret her lapse; but that he would have done *his own duty*, were it but for the sake of posterity, and left it to the Almighty, if such had been his pleasure, to have annihilated his first Eve, and given him a second—But, my dear, do I not write strangely? I would be chearful, if I could, because you are so kind as to take pains to make me so. But on re-perusing what I have written, I am afraid that you have taught me to think oddly."

It would not be too much to claim, I think, that its "oddness" makes this the most crucial passage in the novel. For it is not only psychologically acute, as only Richardson could be in the eighteenth century, it also implies a radical diagnosis of what has gone wrong, that would have enabled Richardson to rewrite the crisis and turn disaster into triumph, if he had really understood and trusted what he had been imaginatively driven to make Harriet write.

In the first place Harriet reveals that curious trait of the psychology of reading that makes good characters so hard to draw sympathetically in fiction: the instinctive rebellion of flawed humanity against the depiction of a character who is set up to be better than one is oneself; and the instinctive impulse to find fault. Yet Richardson obviously embodied this without understanding it, or his entire work would have been more tactful. For no human being, least of all the "common reader," only thinks what it is right to think. Secondly, in producing a staggering example of absolute recitude of *conduct*, that is at the same time intolerable inhumanity, Harriet unconsciously places her finger on the gap between "ought" and "is" that Richardson has allowed to be reopened at the crisis. For if we really think about the Sir Charles/Adam, the point is *not* that his conduct could be faulted, and that he would be a better man to behave as the Adam of Genesis did. A. J. A. Waldock, writing not about Richardson but about *Paradise Lost*, cites the passage as part of his argument that the story of the Fall is "a bad one for God." But no Christian or Jew could accept that. Theologically, it can only be a bad story if there is no belief in God's love for man, or man's ability to love God. And imaginatively, in fictional terms, it can only be a bad story for God if there is a failure to make love between man and God as real in terms of consciousness as love between man and woman. If we could be imaginatively convinced of the reality of Sir Charles/Adam's love of God, and just as convinced of the reality of his love of Eve; if after experiencing a really painful inner conflict that guaranteed the power and integrity of both feelings, we were then to see him agonisedly deciding that his obligation to God was the greater, and that his love for his woman must be suppressed, the hatefulness of his conduct would totally disappear, and we would be left with a kind of tragic grandeur. What Harriet puts her finger on, without understanding it, is the intolerable complacency that comes from the absence of realised inner conflict and torn consciousness; the insensitivity not only to what humans are, but also to what they should be, of the idea that rightness of conduct is all, and that the good man is he who feels only as he is authorised.

But this is the single spasm of Richardson the imaginative artist at the crisis, and it remains a sad might-have-been in the Pyrrhic victory of Richard-

son the moralist. Yet Harriet's *jeu d'esprit* also enables us to see how close
the disaster at the heart of *Sir Charles Grandison* was to becoming a triumph,
and to make a critical and not merely a moral diagnosis of what went wrong.
For just as the fault does not lie in the rectitude of the conduct of Sir
Charles/Adam, there is no real objection to the conduct of Sir Charles in
Italy. What went wrong is that Richardson failed to hit on an artistic way
of probing his hero's consciousness. Throughout his work, as it is the purpose of this study to show, Richardson's greater achievements came when
his *form* enabled him to free himself from his moralistic straitjacket.
Clarissa, too, deluded herself that to say she should not feel something, was
to say that she did not feel it. And Richardson the didactic moralist never
budged from his heavy insistence that she felt only "conditional liking" for
Lovelace: that is, that her feeling was conditional on his moral reform. But
the art of Clarissa is far deeper and more subtle than its author in his every-
day didactic self, and it is so because his dramatic form allows him to probe
Clarissa's heart, and reveal that she is indeed in love with her tormentor.
The fact that her letters are scrutinised by Anna, who continually questions
what she says, picks up implications, and insists on her examining herself
more closely, means that she is driven (and her creator is driven) deeper and
deeper into her consciousness. Now it is clear from our analysis of the hints
in the first and second phases in Italy, and from the evidence of Sir Charles's
illnesses, that an inner conflict *did* take place, and that he was indeed deeply
disturbed about Harriet, and not like Sir Charles/Adam in his complacency
about Eve. What went wrong, therefore, was that the absence of a formal
equivalent of Anna meant the absence of stimulus to Richardson to probe
that conflict, unsatisfied by arguments about presumption and rectitude, when
the time came for Sir Charles to face the implications of marrying Clementina, and of being refused by her. Doctor Bartlett could have fulfilled such
a function, particularly since he "next to adored" Harriet and could have
been vigilant in upholding his end of the argument he and Sir Charles had
had in the library. But the correspondence would have had to be confiden-
tial. As things are, Sir Charles is clearly aware that his letters will be read
by his sisters and their husbands, and that they are also likely to be sent to
Harriet, as indeed they are. No baring of the heart is possible under such
conditions—but it need not have been so.

If there had been a probing of Sir Charles's heart and mind, as deep as
Anna's probing of Clarissa, I think it is possible that *Grandison* might have
become an impressive novel of a very unusual kind. It would never have been
as powerful as *Clarissa*; but the battle between a double love and a double
conscience might have been explored with the subtlety and psychological
depth that Richardson at his best could undoubtedly command. The recoil

of turbulent emotions when the apparent resolution was overthrown by the surprise of Clementina's refusal could have provided possibly the greatest psychological challenge in the whole of his work to the "master of the heart." In such a case, I believe the drawbacks of the art of "ought" in the story of Sir Charles up to the library scene would have fallen into place as a necessary part of the total strategy. For the freedom to explore his idealism would have established the "excessive" criteria against which Sir Charles would have to measure himself, while the new conflict between equal "goods" would have ensured that he continued to come alive as he had begun to do in the library. Our objections to the unnatural ease of Sir Charles's conduct, when confronted only with the choice of right against wrong, or the great against the merely good, would have disappeared when we experienced the pain of his struggle between opposing "greatnesses." "Ought" could have been reconciled with "is"; and though the novel would always have had the rarefied atmosphere of Richardson's high conceptions of "delicacy," it could have been an achievement to anticipate the subtleties of James or Proust.

As it is, however, the novel fails at the crisis, and because it fails, the allowances that one had been prepared to make in the first half are betrayed. The method Richardson chose, the separation of "ought" and "is" in the two stories, could only justify itself when the two were brought into effective and illuminating mutual challenge. When, after careful preparation, Richardson failed to make and meet this challenge, the obliteration of "is" by "ought" means that the whole novel collapses into the mode of didacticism, and an unacceptable morality at that. The Harriet story of the first half remains a considerable achievement, and the temporary flickering of Sir Charles into psychological life an unfulfilled promise. Yet the book is broken-backed in the middle, and it must be doubtful whether it could hope for much life in the concluding volumes.

ROY ROUSSEL

Reflections on the Letter:
The Reconciliation of Distance
and Presence in Pamela

Who would not choose, when necessary absence . . . deprive her
of the person of her charming friend, to have a delight in retiring to
her closet, and there, by pen and ink, continue, and, as I may say,
perpetuate, the ever agreeable and innocent pleasures that flow from
social love, from hearts united by the same laudable ties?

Who then shall decline the converse of the pen? The pen that makes
distance, presence; and brings back to sweet remembrance all the
delights of presence; which makes even presence but body, while
absence becomes the soul.
> —The Correspondence of Samuel Richardson

For Richardson, familiar letters are the product of a paradoxical double movement in the writer's consciousness. On the one hand, they are the result of an act of retirement in which the writer closets himself from the world. Written "either morning or evening, before needful avocations take place, or after they have been answered," the letter is composed in the solitude of the self alone and speaks for the almost obsessive need for privacy that Richardson shares with many of his characters. "The pen," he writes, "is jealous of company. It expects, as I may say, to engross the writer's whole self; everybody allows the writer to withdraw: it disdains company; and will have the entire attention."

Yet if letters and letter-writing reflect the writer's withdrawal from the

From *ELH* 41, no. 3 (Fall 1974). © 1974 by the Johns Hopkins University Press, Baltimore/London.

"company" of others, it is not a withdrawal which implies the writer's independence from the world around him. Richardson's letters lack the meditative quality of a mind reflecting on itself which his emphasis on withdrawal might suggest. They are, instead, letters in the true sense of the word; that is, they are written to someone. Even the most didactic of them are not monologues. On the contrary they are extremely conversational; filled with comments and questions which invoke the response of a reader who is there not simply as an excuse for writing but as a full and immediate presence.

The withdrawal of the writer, then, is balanced by a seemingly contradictory movement which carries him to an intimate union with another. If he conceals himself from the company of those around him, it is only to reveal himself in a letter which "will shew soul and meaning" and which is "indicative, generally beyond the power of disguise, of the mind of the writer." If he disengages himself from "needful avocations" it is only to fill the resulting void with "the ever agreeable and innocent pleasures that flow from social love, from hearts united."

The letter is the form in which character manifests itself in Richardson's fiction, and the tension between presence and absence, company and retirement, implicit in his conception of the letter defines an equivalent tension in his conception of human nature. For Pamela and B, this tension is at the center of the conflict between love and society which informs their story.

II

> Wise Providence
> Does various parts for various minds dispense:
> The *meanest slaves*, or those who *hedge* and *ditch*,
> Are useful, by their sweat, to feed the *rich*.
> The *rich*, in due return, impart their store;
> Which comfortably feeds the lab'ring *poor*.
> Nor let the *rich* the *lowest slave* disdain:
> He's *equally* a *link* of Nature's *chain*:
> Labours to the *same end*, joins in *one view*;
> And *both alike* the *will divine* pursue.

This passage, which Pamela cites in an attack on Lady Davers's pride, suggests that Richardson saw society as a divinely ordained structure in which each individual, in fulfilling his "part," fulfills as well his duty to his fellow man and to God. What is important, however, is less the presence of this traditional image of society than the particular tonality it takes on in the novel, and as a key to this tonality the poem is somewhat deceptive. The poem suggests that a reciprocity exists between classes which balances their separation so that each "Labours to the *same end*, joins in *one view*." With the possible exception of Pamela's comments on the duties of her role as B's wife, however, there is little of this sense of communion in the novel. There is little feeling that not only roles but the whole structure of social conventions mediates between people in a positive way.

Instead, Richardson concentrates on the way in which a man's "part" in society allows him to separate himself from others. One of the words which appear obsessively in *Pamela* is the word "distance," and one of its important uses is to define the relation between different classes. His jest, Pamela tells B, "is not a jest that becomes the distance between a master and a servant," to which Mrs. Jervis replies "don't be so pert to his honour: you should know your distance," and Pamela answers, "It is very difficult to keep one's distance to the greatest of men, when they won't keep it themselves to their meanest servants." Altogether, the term "distance" or some variation of it is used in this context sixteen times in the first fifty pages, a frequency which suggests how important this separation is for Richardson and how it overshadows any reciprocity which might exist between classes.

In both *Pamela* and *Clarissa*, however, Richardson uses distance in another way. According to Pamela the most important lesson taught to her by Mr. B's mother was to "*keep the men at a distance.*" Lady Davers advises Pamela in a like manner to "keep the fellows at a distance" and Mr. B asks Mrs. Jervis if Pamela "kept the men at a distance." In these instances "distance" functions to define the clear area which modesty or privacy requires, and the duality of this key term suggests that for Richardson the structure of society—not just the order of classes but the whole system of usages and manners—is important precisely because it serves to protect the self from any outside intrusion. This protective function of social forms is particularly apparent in *Clarissa*. Here Lovelace's need to "open my whole soul" to Clarissa makes him an enemy not only of the distance between them—"I cannot bear to be kept at this distance from you," he tells her—but also of the social properties which Clarissa, "a *lover of forms*," uses to create this distance. "Had she not thus kept me at arm's length," he writes, "had she not denied me those innocent liberties which our sex, from step to step, aspire to; could I but have gained access to her in her hours of heedlessness and dishabille [for full dress creates dignity, augments consciousness, and compels distance] we had been familiarized to each other long ago." The relation between Clarissa and Lovelace, however, is only a reflection of that between Pamela and B. It is clear that when B complains to Pamela during their first meeting in the summer-house that "you always fly me when I come near you" and she replies, "It does not become your poor servant to stay in your presence, sir, without your business required it; and I hope I shall always know my place," her implicit assertion of "the distance that fortune made between us" is less the abstract statement of a social ideology than a deeply felt need to enforce a protective separation between them.

Because the forms of society maintain a distance between its members, men are able to exist at ease with one another in Richardson's world. Without these forms, they would be subject continuously to the fearful uneasiness which assails Pamela after her mistress dies and she no longer has a clearly defined role in the world of B's Bedfordshire estate. But these forms are not sufficient; if they were, there would be no novel *Pamela*. The novel begins with the emergence of another force at the center of the ordered image of society we find in its pages. This force is love. It is love which precipitates the action of *Pamela*, for if it is true that the novel begins at the moment when Pamela's position in B's household is made ambivalent, this is so only because the death of his mother allows all of B's latent feeling toward Pamela to crystalize.

Love is the emergence of a need to be present to another and to be confirmed by another in an immediate way. It is born in the isolation of a self distanced from others in the same way the writer's movement toward union with his correspondent is born in the solitude created by his need for privacy, by his withdrawal from company. The movement of love, too, seeks to transcend this separation. For this reason Richardson always associates it with a loss of rational control, with a loss, in other words, of a sense of independent and self-contained existence, and with the lover's desire to negate the distance on which this existence had been founded. The birth of the violent force of love at the center of a self so frail, so neuralgically sensitive, that it could not bear the closeness of another is the great mystery in Richardson's world, and his characters experience its presence as the presence of an unknown force which leaves them "vexed and confused" at their own actions. "But love is not a voluntary thing," Pamela writes, "*Love*, did I say?—But come, I hope not:—At least it is not, I hope, gone so far as to make me *very* uneasy: For I know not *how* it came, nor *when* it began; but crept, crept it has like a thief, upon me; and before I knew what was the matter, it looked like love."

III

It is with the birth of love that Richardson's characters confront the full demands of selfhood. Born from the struggle between privacy and desire, they can achieve completion only insofar as they can resolve this tension. Such a tension is at the center of both Pamela's and B's experience in the novel, but because love comes most violently to B, it is his story which best testifies to its acuteness in Richardson's world.

The fact that we see B through the eyes of Pamela and, consequently, see him primarily as an aggressor, obscures the references which suggest that a certain defensive privacy has played an important part in his life. Until he met Pamela, Mr. B was a man who was "averse to matrimony upon any terms." His initial objections to marrying Pamela have less to do with his class consciousness than they do with his general aversion to marriage and the involvement it implies. He cannot "endure," he tells Pamela, "the thought of marriage, even with a person of equal or superior degree to myself," and it is clear that before his encounter with Pamela, B is a man in whom the need for union with another has lain dormant, one who has lived at a comfortable remove from those around him.

Mr. B's self-sufficient privacy ends during his meeting with Pamela in the summer-house early in the novel: "I do own to you," he is to tell Pamela later, "that I love you with a purer flame than ever I knew in my whole life; a flame to which I was a stranger; and which commenced for you in the garden." The most immediate effect of this new force in B's life is the destruction of that control on which his previous independence had been based. This scene begins with B presenting himself to Pamela in his role as her master whose "business does require" Pamela's presence. B established this role, however, only to discover himself forced by the "purer flame" of love to abandon it. It is important to understand that when he seizes Pamela and violates both literally and figuratively the distance between them, he is not acting with the cynical callousness of a rake. At this moment, Pamela remarks, B looks "I don't know how; wildly, I thought," and B later says to Mrs. Jervis that he was "bewitched by her . . . to be freer than became me." Instead, as these passages make clear, he is caught in the sudden flood of an emotion which, in carrying him toward an intimacy with Pamela, negates the separateness which is the foundation of his old self.

The movement of B in this scene from reserved master to lover, a movement which characterizes so many of the encounters between B and Pamela, defines again the tension between two opposing concepts of the self. More than this, however, B's experience here reveals why it is that the self's commitment to privacy and distance is not simply swept away by the emergence of love. It explains why B struggles so hard in the summer-house to regain control and, in telling Pamela that "I own I have demeaned myself; but it was only to try you," to reassert himself in his protective role as master. The reasons for this is simple. When B is seized by love and forced to violate the distance between himself and Pamela, he is forced as well to reveal himself to her. One of the words which constantly appear in opposition to distance in the novel is the word "expose." "And so I am to be exposed," B remarks when he discovers Pamela has told Mrs. Jervis about their encounter in the summer-house. "You may well be ashamed," he tells Pamela later, ". . . after your noise and nonsense, and exposing me as you have done." Again, he complains, "I have pert saucy answers from you, besides exposing me by your letters."

To be exposed is to be humiliated, it is to demean yourself. But even more, it is to be delivered into the power of another. In Richardson's world, as in the world of Restoration comedy, access to another brings with it the possession of his identity. The uneasiness which Richardson exhibits toward love drives from the fact that love forces you to reveal yourself, and, therefore, deliver yourself, to another. It is this fact that is behind B's sense that he has been "robbed" by Pamela, as well as behind the feeling we have that because he is in Pamela's power, the roles of master and servant have been reversed. "O how poor and mean must those actions be," writes Pamela, "and how little must they make the best of gentlemen look, when they offer such things as are unworthy of themselves, and put it into the power of their inferiors to be greater than they!"

Richardson's sense of the dangers of exposing oneself to others is revealed in a special way in his correspondence with Lady Bradshaigh. Under the assumed name of Belfour, Lady Bradshaigh had written him to plead for a happy ending to *Clarissa*. During the exchange of letters which followed, she was able to maintain this pseudonym for over a year, and, although their relationship was casual, Richardson was unable to live comfortably with the sense that he was known by Lady Bradshaigh in a way that he did not know her. His letters are filled with intense and repetitious complaints that her refusal to acknowledge her true identity is founded in a "wantoness of power," that she is a "lover of power," and that she is making him "one of her diversions." His feelings that her knowledge of him gave her a power which he did not share were intensified when, in what she later confessed was "a desire to see you, without being known," she persuades him to take Sunday afternoon walks in Hyde Park on the promise of meeting him there. It is a promise which, of course, she did not keep, and Richardson writes bitterly that he would never have appeared "could I have imagined that hating a crowd, a gay crowd especially, it was expected that I walk up and down the Mall, exposing myself, as I may say, to the observation of a lady whom I have never had the honour to see."

Not only Richardson's letters to Lady Bradshaigh, but the tenor of much of his correspondence reminds us how much the tension in *Pamela* between exposure and concealment, distance and involvement, was a part of his own life. Richardson's interest in the novel was certainly centered on Pamela, but it is equally true that his heart was in some way with B and that B's situation of being exposed was one he understood fully. More than this, however, these letters give us an insight into the logic of the fear of exposure in Richardson's world. Despite the most obvious implications of Richardson's emphasis on privacy, it is clear from the extremely abstract quality exposure has both in his work and in his letters to Lady Bradshaigh that it would be a mistake to associate his fear of exposure with any idea that the self in Richardson is defined by something hidden and concrete, such as a secret. Lady Bradshaigh does not know any actual secret concerning Richardson, for example, nor does Pamela know anything about B which makes her a real danger to him. Even when Pamela convinces Parson Williams to tell Sir Simon about her kidnapping his only reaction is to say, "He hurts no family by this." The fear of exposure in both Richardson and his characters is not founded on the practical consequences of revelation. Instead, this fear and the shyness with which it is associated seem to result from another cause. In the beginning, his characters are defined by a role which distances them from others. Defined by this distance, they are defined by the nothingness which surrounds them rather than by their substantial relation to something or someone outside themselves. Since they lack such a concrete relation and the positive sense of self it would provide, their experience of their self is an experience of something ephemeral. Faced with the intuition of their own insubstantiality, they seem to be attempting by their shyness to conceal this unsubstantiality from others.

The exposure which accompanies love is not a threat, then, because it delivers to the beloved the kind of preexisting self which could be associated with a secret that the beloved had discovered. Instead, in Richardson love itself constitutes at the center of the lover's ephemerality a new and more substantial self-awareness. It is a self-awareness, however, whose only source is paradoxically the relationship which love has established between the lover and the beloved. Richardson's lovers exist for themselves more intensely after the birth of love, but the new intensity of their awareness is curiously alienated because its source lies outside them. After the awakening of his love for Pamela, B is defined by the new "shapes" into which love has transformed him. But these shapes are only the forms of his love for Pamela. In the same way, when Lovelace asks Clarissa to "take me to yourself, mould me as you please . . . give me your own impression," he is not delivering his self to her so much as he is asking her to constitute this self for him in a new way.

The fear of exposure in Richardson must be read in this context. This fear grows from the recognition that, with the advent of love, the very form of the lover's new self will be determined by another. The term "expose" expresses both the character's initial experience of love as a rupture of the bounds of his privacy, a rupture which allows the beloved to shape him in this way, and his recognition that because the beloved is now the ground of his self he must continue to remain open to her. Exposure is accompanied by fear in Richardson because, in the world of his novels, this is not a reciprocal relationship. In the beginning, B feels himself defined by Pamela, yet he does not serve in an equivalent way as the ground of her self. It is because Pamela maintains her independence while serving as the source of B's self-awareness that he feels possessed by her.

Since love threatens such a possession by another, its appearance is not a blessed relief from solitude but a trauma. Torn between the need for involvement with Pamela and the necessity for some kind of protective separation which this need makes even more acute, B finds himself literally at the center of a war between love and distance. "He then took me in his arms," Pamela writes, "and presently pushed me from him. Mrs. Jervis, said he, take the little witch from me; I can neither bear, nor forbear her—(Strange words these!)—But stay; you shan't go!;—Yet begone!—No, come back again." The story of B and Pamela is the story of his attempts to resolve those opposing claims.

IV

The most obvious course open to B is for him to turn his back on love, to allow Pamela to return home and to live at his former distance from those around him. Such a strategy is suggested by B's periodic attempts to reassert his role as master as well as by the time when he is actually on the point of allowing her to leave. Yet we never feel this is a real alternative for B; we never feel that once their relationship is opened it can be abandoned by either. Although Richardson's characters first experience love as something alien to their former lives, it is the manifestation of a need so fundamental that, once awakened, it cannot be lain to rest.

If B cannot banish love then he must come to terms with it. To do this, he must somehow redress the balance of power which exists between himself and Pamela. Power over another, however, is a function, as we have seen, of one's ability to gain access to the other's consciousness. Pamela's power over B lies in the access to him which his love for her creates. This imbalance can be equalized only if B can somehow achieve an equivalent access to Pamela's consciousness.

It is the desire for such an equality which is behind even the most physical of B's advances toward Pamela. B's actual attacks on her—the scenes in the summer-house and her room, her kidnapping and near rape—are the first and most basic expression of that movement toward another which comes with the birth of love. As such, they are not intended to neutralize Pamela's threat to B by reducing her to the level of an object. Instead, they attempt, in B's own words to Pamela, to "frighten you from your reservedness." These attacks are efforts to unveil Pamela's self through an act of violence equivalent in effect to the action of love on B's own sense of discrete selfhood; efforts which, if successful, would leave Pamela exposed to B in the same way he is exposed to her.

B's attempt to come to know Pamela through the immediate and forceful destruction of the grounds of her separateness is implicit in the heavily metaphorical weight which dress, and therefore disrobement, carry in the novel. Generally in Richardson dress is associated with those social forms which, in compelling "consciousness" and "distance," protect the privacy of the self. Pamela's care in choosing her clothes when she thinks she will return to her parents illustrates how strongly the association of dress with the distance between classes is present here. More specifically, however, Pamela's dress is the constant hiding place of those letters which contain her "heart" and "private thoughts." It is no accident, then, that Pamela's bosom is both the most frequent hiding-place of her papers and the locus of most of B's advances toward her. This association implies both that her modesty functions to protect a psychological rather than a purely physical integrity, and that B's desire for Pamela is a desire to force access to her self rather than the expression of a physical need.

If violence could destroy Pamela's reserve and force her to reveal herself to B, then perhaps the promise of love could be fulfilled. Each would then have an immediate access to the other and there would exist, in the words of Richardson to Lady Bradshaigh, a "communication so equal, and so just." In this relationship, each would know as he is known. Each would find the ground of his self in the other and their relationship would be one of mutual openness.

The instances of B's aggressiveness toward Pamela, however, record not only his attempt to achieve openness in this manner but the failure of this attempt as well. Those moments when B seems on the point of actually forcing the barrier of Pamela's reserve are precisely the moments when her consciousness disappears. Pamela's fainting spells, which are in each case caused by B's disarrangement of her clothing, are neither instances of feminine hypocrisy nor simply dramatic effects. Instead they reflect the extent to which, for Richardson, the self is initially something ephemeral. This interior consciousness is, it seems, so sensitive and so insubstantial that it cannot willingly stand the direct light of another's gaze. When Lady Bradshaigh writes to Richardson that while she is not precisely "afraid to his face . . . it is something that reigns in my freedom of speech," she is reading the mind of her correspondent perfectly, for there is always a sense in his work that a direct confrontation with an other brings a kind of paralysis and fear which prevents "communication" from developing. Since this is true, the attempt to open another's self by a forceful intrusion into his privacy will fail as the inevitable consequence of its success.

B himself recognizes this when, immediately after his attempted rape, he remarks, "I have begun wrong: for I see terror does but add to her frost; but she is a charming girl, and may be thawed by kindness; and I should have melted her by love, instead of freezing her by fear." B's comment is, however, misleading, for he seems to forget that he has, in fact, tried to thaw Pamela by kindness. Even during the rape itself when he tells Pamela, "You see now you are in my power!—You cannot get away from me, nor help yourself: Yet I have not offered any thing amiss to you," he seems more interested in persuading Pamela freely to reveal herself than he is in forcing her revelation. This is particularly true in the scene early in the novel when B confesses to Pamela that he loves her. Here he adopts a milder, more temperate course. When, in this meeting, he forces himself to "stoop" and "beg" Pamela to "behave yourself with kindness to me" and limits himself to holding her hand B seems to be trying not to negate totally the distance between them but simply to lessen it.

B's restraint here suggests another strategy. Like the way of aggression, this strategy is aimed at affecting some kind of direct access to Pamela, but it hopes to accomplish this through a gradual process. If B could contain his own fear of Pamela, if he could control the initial impulse to violate the other which comes from being exposed, then perhaps Pamela's reaction to him would be less extreme and she could be coaxed rather than forced from her reserve.

No such gradual process takes place, however. B attempts at certain crucial times to restrain himself and to quiet her fears with gentleness, but these attempts always end in frustration. The failure of B's various strategies, but, more particularly, of these more tempered advances, marks the real extent of the self's mistrust of others in Richardson's fiction. This distrust is, it appears, so fundamental that any direct approach to another, no matter how circumspect, appears as a threat. It is this fear which prevents Pamela alone in the novel from recognizing the true nature of B's feelings for her.

It prevents her from seeing B as anything but an encroacher on her privacy, and it inhibits Pamela's love for B, a love which has always been there potentially, from actualizing itself.

V

If these were the only alternatives open to B and, consequently, this fear of the other were the determining factor in the novel, then B would be forced to live continuously at the center of the tension between distance and presence, and *Pamela* would be a tragedy. This is not the case, however, for there is one more course open to B, one final way to resolve the conflict in which they find themselves. This way returns us once more to our starting point: the nature of the letter.

As we have seen, the familiar letter incorporates two paradoxical movements in the mind of the writer. It is the result of an act of retirement from the "needful avocations" of the social life. Yet its function is to present the self to another in a particularly naked way. We remember that the language of correspondence is, for Richardson, perfectly transparent. It is "indicative, generally beyond the power of disguise, of the mind of the writer" and shows "soul" as well as meaning. Because of this transparency, the access to the writer's self which the letter allows the correspondent is not the removed and mediated relationship established by social usages, but instead the same kind of direct and intimate openness which love gives to the beloved.

The letter is, in this way, not only a statement of the tension between love and distance in Richardson. It is also the instrument which resolves this tension. Because it shows "soul" it enables the correspondent to achieve that intimacy with the writer which is signified by Richardson's phrase "hearts united." At the same time, because the writer is protected by that "absence" which "becomes the soul," this intimacy is established without any destructive intrusion into the privacy of the writer. For Richardson, letters do make "distance, presence," and it is the ability of correspondence to effect this reconciliation that allows us to understand the role her journal plays in the marriage of B and Pamela.

Composed largely in the "refuge" of her closet, Pamela's journal is associated with the withdrawal of the writer. It records all her "private thoughts" and, like the letter, records them in a transparent style. "I don't remember what I wrote," Pamela remarks after Mrs. Jewkes finds her papers, "yet I know I wrote my heart." Pamela's journal, moreover, not only embodies her heart, but, with the intentionality implicit in the letter form, reveals it as well. Like Richardson's own letters, Pamela's writings are characterized by their essential reference to a correspondent. Even when she is most isolated, immediately after her kidnapping, she begins her account, "O My Dearest Father and Mother!" although she continues, "I have no hope now what I write can be conveyed to your hands." This epistolary quality of her journal is recognized by both her and B. When B confronts her with the papers his first question is "To whom . . . are they written" and she replies, "To my father, sir."

The referential quality of the journal is apparent not only in these characters' reactions to it. More importantly, this quality is inherent too in its content. Like Richardson's own letters, Pamela's journal is not a record of the mind meditating on itself alone. It records no moment in which Pamela, isolated, finds in her interiority the principle of her own existence. As we have seen, even when she is farthest from others she still addresses her writings to them, and this reference is important because it suggests how, for Richardson, the self exists only in its relation to others. Pamela's journal is significantly different in this respect from, for example, Robinson Crusoe's. Both are records of a conversion; that is, they record the birth of a new self. In Crusoe's case this new self can be described in Christian terms as the birth of the new man from the old, or, in secular terms, as the birth of a form of reflexive consciousness. In either case, however, it is primarily a change in the relation of consciousness to itself.

In Pamela's case, however, the conversion is signified primarily by a change in her relation to the other who defines her. Her journal begins by being addressed to her father. Its initial reference is to a relationship which defines her by her place in society. But its content is the growth of her love for B. It contains Pamela's "private thoughts" but these are only "private thoughts of him." The journal records the development of a new self which forms around this love and which will be confirmed only when the journal is delivered to B and read by him.

It is, finally, the ability of the journal to perform this mediation between B and Pamela, to make distance presence, which most fully confirms its epistolary nature. Since Pamela's papers do embody her "heart," in the transparent style of correspondence, they allow B an access to her equivalent to that which B's love gives to her. The access provided by her writings has always been a mitigating factor between them. Even when B's view of Pamela was limited to the glimpse afforded by her early letters to her parents which B received through John, the "worthiness" which he discovers in her "charming manner of writing" momentarily allays his more paranoid fears of her and allows him to "stoop to beg" her compliance. It is, moreover, the full view of Pamela provided by her journal which stills these fears completely. Here he finds nothing which is not "innocent, lovely, and uniformly beautiful," no "secret of your soul" or "hidden regard for Williams" which would give substance to his feelings that she seeks to manipulate him. And it is because her writings expose Pamela in the same way that his love exposes him, because it establishes a "communication, so equal, and so just" that he turns his thoughts toward marriage. "If my mind hold," he tells her, "and I can see those former papers of yours, and that these in my pocket give me no cause to alter my opinion, I will endeavour to defy the world and the world's censures, and make my Pamela amends."

It is important to understand, however, that Pamela's writings allow B this access in a way which preserves the distance between them. It involves neither the face-to-face confrontation which, Lady B reminds us, "hinders conversation" nor the even more destructive intrusion figured in B's attempted rape. Although they do talk about them together, B never reads her papers in Pamela's immediate presence. Even in the scene where B reads her account of her attempted escape while they are together in the garden, Pamela insists on partially withdrawing. "Let me walk about, at a little distance," she tells him, "for I cannot bear the thought."

Pamela herself implicitly acknowledges the double function of her journal in the first stanza of the song she sings for Sir Simon.

> Go, happy paper, gently steal,
> And underneath her pillow lie;
> There, in soft dreams, my love reveal,
> That love which I must still conceal,
> And, wrapt in awful silence die.

Like the happy papers of Pamela's song, her letters do reveal as they conceal, allowing her to withdraw to a safe remove at the moment of their greatest intimacy. It is appropriate, then, that the final reconciliation of B and Pamela should come through B's letter to Pamela. Motivated by the "affection which they (Pamela's papers) have rivetted upon me" B's letter is in every sense a response to her writings. It is composed at that moment when Pamela, returning home, is furthest from him. Yet it is just this distance which frees B to express most clearly his love for Pamela, and to compose that letter which allows her to discover in him "so much openness, so much affection, so much honour, too, (which was all I had before doubted, and kept me on the reserve)."

VI

The removal of this last "reserve" leads Pamela to her first full confession of her love for B. After this point, their relation is never in doubt, and the meaning of this is clear. In Richardson's world, it seems, men and women must first become correspondents before they can become man and wife. The marriage of Pamela and B appears in this context as a natural development of the knowledge of the other which each has gained through their exchange of letters. Secure in this knowledge, each can accept the power over themselves which love has given the other. "Kind, lovely charmer!" B tells Pamela, "now do I see you are to be trusted with power, from the generous use you make of it!" Because he trusts her in this way he consents to be her "prisoner" and put on "the most agreeable fetters that ever man wore." In an equivalent way Pamela now is able to place a "generous confidence" in B and rest calmly in the assurance that she will be "generously used."

Pamela's and B's marriage seems in this way an embodiment of that just and equal communication which Richardson longed for in his early letters to Lady Bradshaigh, a communication which would mark the harmonious resolution of distance and presence. There are elements in the novel, however, which suggest that this resolution is only a superficial one. Pamela's and B's explicit discussions of the form of their marriage in the last half of the novel imply that this marriage involves a modulation of these principles more than a true resolution of them. In these discussions, for example, they formulate a daily schedule in which the duties of each toward the other are defined. Pamela promises never to "intrude" on B when he is angry and he in turn promises to ask "nothing of her, that was not significant, reasonable and just" so that he "should not destroy her own free agency."

These statements imply that each accepts in the other a limited area of privacy which exists beyond the bounds of their intimacy. Like Millimant and Mirabell in *The Way of the World*, they accept marriage as a form which mediates between essentially separate selves, and this acceptance is in strange contrast to what we have understood of the nature of love in Richardson. When Lovelace asks Clarissa to "take me, take me to yourself; mould me as you please . . . give me your own impression" he is invoking a love which transcends the idea of separateness. This same desire lies behind the intensity of B's need to know Pamela, to negate the distance between them. When B tells Pamela that "love, *true* love, is the *only* motive by which *I* am induced" and Pamela remarks to herself that "this heart is Pamela," they accept their relationship to one another as their definition; and the real form of this relationship is, as we have seen, determined by the nature of a correspondence whose ideal is embodied in the phrase "hearts united."

Something of this tension between the form of their marriage and the nature of the intimacy established by their correspondence appears in B's wish that Pamela continue her writing even after they are married, for this implies that he needs some more intimate access to her other than that provided by their formalized relationship. Such a tension existing at the center of an apparent resolution of principles points to an important difference between the distance created by the writer's withdrawal and the distance created by social usages such as dress, manners and class distinctions. Although both forms of distance testify to the self's nervousness in the face of the other, in the case of the correspondent this distance exists so that it may be transcended, so that he can establish a relation "more pure, yet more ardent, and less broken in upon, than personal conversation can ever be." On the other hand, the primary function of social usages in Richardson, as we have seen, is much more to enforce separation—we remember Lovelace's statement that dress "compels distance"—than to effect a positive mediation.

If it is true that society is inevitably such a world of enforced separation, then the withdrawal of the writer takes on an additional tonality. Rather than being simply a protective strategy, it appears as an act which is necessary in order to escape this separation. He must withdraw from the distances of the social world to a solitude in which, paradoxically, relations can be established without regard to this distance. The withdrawal of the writer is reflected in the retreat of B and Pamela to Lincolnshire, to a place where, literally, they become correspondents. In the case of B this retreat defines the "chasms" which his love for Pamela have made in "my affairs, and my own family." In the case of Pamela, her movement is explicitly to a place where she is outside the law and has no socially accepted role. Yet it is only in this area, it seems, that Pamela and B can escape "the distance that fortune made between us" and unite their hearts.

To recognize that a tension exists between the union of their hearts and the mediated relation of their marriage is to place *Pamela* in a more radical light. As several critics have noted, *Pamela* is concerned with the development of identity in a social context. The pattern of the Fortunate Fall, a pattern which traditionally expresses the movement of man toward God, here describes Pamela's movement from her role as servant through her period of captivity to her new role as B's wife. But if the novel on one level assumes the priority of role, it clearly does not do so in an uncritical way. It is necessary, in this context, to see the book not only from Pamela's but also from B's point of view. Unlike Pamela, whose position is made ambiguous by the death of her mistress, B himself exists at the beginning of the novel in a well-defined social position. The intensity of B's desire for Pamela and his inability to abandon her cannot grow out of the insecurity of a similarly ambiguous social position. It would seem, instead, that his love reflects a sense of an insufficiency at the center of the self which is defined by his role.

There may be many ways of explaining this sense of insufficiency. Perhaps it is enough to say again that roles, because they function in Richardson's world to distance the self from others, do not provide the self with a truly positive ground. Why Richardson experiences roles in this way is another and more difficult question. The most obvious answer is that because he is himself a private person, he naturally understands and uses roles in this way. It may be that just as the eighteenth century gradually lost the sense of the immediate presence of the divine in the structure of the natural world, so it lost a sense of its presence in the structure of the social world. The negative experience of distance would express, then, the way in which the social world, like the Newtonian universe, has become something mechanical and lifeless. In any case, it is the need to escape the sense of ephemerality and isolation, to find an immediate union with someone who will grant a more positive sense of self, which is the source of love in Richardson.

If the birth of love is a result of the inadequacy of social usages to confirm the self, then the failure of Pamela and B to incarnate the union of their love in the form of their marriage implies that this inadequacy is not simply a starting-point or a temporary condition. Since their marriage involves an inevitable separation, since society is inevitably a world of distinctions and differences, there will always be some degree of emptiness surrounding the self as it exists in society. In this sense, *Pamela* reveals a profound scepticism toward the ability of society to provide an adequate ground for the self.

This is not to say that Richardson himself accepts the scepticism wholeheartedly. Conservative by temperament, he was committed to the structure of society and obviously attempts to reconcile B's and Pamela's love with his structure. Yet it is just as clear that this reconciliation is not complete. It seems the particular nature of Richardson's genius that he saw more than he would have liked, that he intuited more than he was inclined to exploit. The conflict between love and society in the novel reflects, on this level, a tension between Richardson's intellectual commitment to a structure of society which is the product of "Wise Providence" and his felt experience of society's "parts," as something which distances and isolates the self. Such a tension is apparent in the contrast between "needful avocations," and "hearts united," in his definition of the letter. It is equally apparent in the tenor of his correspondences with Lady Bradshaigh and Sophia Westcomb, correspondences which in their intense sentimentality obviously fill some void in his public life.

VII

The distance defined by the letter-writer's withdrawal, then, is in its most fundamental implication the sign of a revolt. Like the force of love, this withdrawal seems, on this level, a rejection of the isolation of the self in society. But the act of correspondence is not only a rejection of this self. Insofar as it is the form of love, it involves the choice of another as the ground of a new identity. Richardson's characters do not choose to love. Love comes "like a thief." But at crucial times both Pamela and B do choose to affirm the movement of their love toward one another. They choose to be defined by this relationship, and this choice is signaled by their exchange of letters, by Pamela surrendering her papers to B and by B sending the letter which brings her back to Lincolnshire.

For Pamela to say "this heart is Pamela" and to give B her journal is for her to make this choice and to define herself by it. The association of love with such a choice of identity is itself suggestive. It places their relationship in one tradition of Renaissance love poetry in general and in that of the sonnet sequences in particular. In this tradition, the lady is no longer seen as the mediator between the lover and God but becomes herself the final resting-place of desire. She takes upon herself the attributes of the Divine and provides a still center in a turning world. Thus Donne's lovers in "The Good-Morrow" find in one another a ground which seems to allow them to transcend distance and death, and Shakespeare in Sonnet 116 hopes to find in his love an "ever fixed mark" which "is not time's fool."

In an important way, *Pamela* is a domestication of the effort to find in "the marriage of true minds" a relationship which offers such transcendent stability and fulfillment. In this, it reflects certain realities of eighteenth-century English society. Philippe Ariès has shown in his *Centuries of Childhood: A Social History of Family Life* that the eighteenth century was in fact a time when the family began to define itself as a special area of intimacy centered around the wife and children and, in Ariès's words, to "hold society at a distance, to push it back beyond a steadily expanding zone of private life." It is a time when people are turning to a private world defined by the relationship between husband and wife and set in opposition to society.

More specifically, perhaps, *Pamela* looks forward to the investigation of this attempt in the English novel. The marriage of B and Pamela in the isolation of Lincolnshire prefaces the retreat of Booth and Amelia at the end of *Amelia*, the relation of Catherine and Heathcliff in *Wuthering Heights* and the love of Pip and Estella at the end of *Great Expectations*. Each of these novels is centered around a recognition of the inability of society to provide the ground of authentic identity: the image of society as a prison in *Amelia*, the effeteness of Lockwood in *Wuthering Heights*, the hollowness of Pip's great expectations. Each, in turn, investigates the ability of the self to find in its love for another a more substantial sense of self.

From this point of view, *Pamela* is an important document in the history of desire. Such a history, detailing the loss by love of a transcendent object and the effects of its subsequent confinement to the temporal world, would be necessary to any complete understanding not only of *Pamela* but of the development of the English novel. This investigation is, of course, far beyond the scope of an essay, and I am concerned here simply with the idea of the letter as the sign of a choice.

Again, this is a focus which emphasizes radical elements in the novel, elements which Richardson clearly wanted in some sense to avoid. He has gone to great lengths to cleanse Pamela of any trace of ambition, to make her passive in her elevation to the status of B's wife. But with that ambivalence which characterizes his work, the very structure of *Pamela* frustrates his attempt. Like *Pamela*, *Tom Jones* is organized around the motif of the Fortunate Fall. The difference in the way the pattern exists in the two novels is, however, significant. When Tom, having left an orphan, returns to Paradise Hall as its future owner, his new status is not, fundamentally, the result of anything he has done during his wanderings. It is rather the result of a preexisting relationship to Allworthy. His adventures lead him only to discover his true nature, a nature defined by his past, by his parentage. Pamela, on the other hand, has no such preexisting relationship to B. Their marriage is the result of the love which develops between them in the course of the novel. For this reason, *Pamela* is a story of the creation rather than the discovery of the self.

It is because *Pamela* is concerned with such a creation that writing has the status it does in the novel. Pamela's manuscript is not simply the record of her and B's love. The manuscript is also its cause, the central factor in their marriage. Consequently their marriage and the self which it defines for her inevitably appear as the product of her act of writing. Writing in this way becomes associated with the freedom to choose an identity by choosing a new relation to another, and this new identity, because it is the product of writing, comes in turn to be associated with fiction. It becomes something which has been literally written into existence.

The sense that Pamela's story is fictional is not simply implicit in the logic of the book. It is suggested, too, by the reactions of the other characters to Pamela's manuscript. What is significant about these reactions is how often they are reactions appropriate to a literary object. When B reads Pamela's version of the 137th Psalm for Lady Jones and the two Miss Darnfords, they react primarily to her skill as a versifier and her ability to turn a line. When Lady Davers asks to read Pamela's journal, one of her motives is that she "should take great pleasure to read all his stratagems . . . on one hand, and all your pretty counter-plottings . . . for it must be a rare and uncommon story; and will . . . give me great pleasure in reading." And when Lady Davers returns to London, she hopes to use this manuscript to "entertain Lady Betty with, and another lady or two."

The tenor of these reactions characterizes many of B's comments as well. When, after their engagement, he asks Pamela to give him the rest of her journal, his motive is, "the pleasure I take in reading what you write," and he later relates this pleasure to her "easy and happy manner of narration." B's reactions in the important scene when he confesses the full effects of Pamela's journal on him, however, go further. They make explicit the associations between the status of writing and the status of the self which flows from this writing. In this scene B first acknowledges that part of the fascination of the journal derives from its literary effect. "I long to see the particulars of your plot," he tells her, "and your disappointment, where your papers leave off: for you have so beautiful a manner, that it is partly that, and partly my love for you, that has made me desirous of reading all you write." But more than this he sees their marriage not simply as something which results from these qualities. He sees it as something which completes them and shares their nature. "Besides," he continues, "there is such a pretty air of romance, as you relate them, in *your* plots and *my* plots, that I shall be better directed in what manner to wind up the catastrophe of the pretty novel."

B is not only Pamela's lover. He is also her most acute critic, and the explanation for this is clear. *Pamela* is concerned not only with the development of Pamela's self but of B's as well. Its subject is the process of mutual definition which occurs between them. Just as the growth of Pamela's relation to B is associated with a kind of fictionalizing, so is B's relation to her. Lady Davers points to this when, after she discovers that Pamela and B are wed, she asks Pamela to "walk before me . . . that I may see how finely thou can'st act the theatrical part given thee." Her comment is, however, only a gloss on B's own statement above that Pamela's journal is a "romance." The reference here is not to Pamela's reading but to his own comment to Pamela, early in the novel, that "you are well read, I see, and we shall make out between us, before we are done, a pretty story in romance." This reminds us that *Pamela* contains not only Pamela's letters but also B's. Like the identities which it defines, it is a story which they have composed together, which is made up, as B understands, of "*your* plots and *my* plots."

VIII

When Pamela remarks that "my story surely would furnish out a surprising kind of novel" or B calls her papers "the pretty novel" they remind us that these letters are the novel *Pamela* and, in doing so, allow us to see *Pamela* as Richardson's definition of the genre. It is no accident that Richardson thinks of the letter and the novel as fundamentally related forms. Since he conceives of human identity as an intersubjective relationship, he is led naturally to the letter as the most appropriate medium to express it. More than this, the letter describes for him not only the general but also the specific conditions which govern this identity. Generated from the emptiness which initially surrounds his characters from the distances imposed on them by social usages, the letter incarnates the movement of love and defines, in this way, the choices open to his characters.

In *Pamela*, moreover, Richardson attempts to make the letter serve as the resolution of this tension, the agency which reconciles distance and presence, the self defined by society and the self defined by love. As I have tried to show, it is a resolution which is qualified even in *Pamela*. Certainly viewed in the abstract this opposition is too complex and too intense to be bridged by any concept of correspondence, and certainly Richardson realized this by the time he began *Clarissa*. It is not in such a reconciliation, however, that Richardson's concept of the letter is most fundamentally a definition of the novel, but in the fact that the letter does describe a choice and is, therefore, the sign of the freedom which his characters have to write their own selves into being. It is this freedom which, although it appears in different forms, most clearly characterizes the protagonists of novels. Sometimes, as in the cases of Don Quixote or Robinson Crusoe or Lord Jim, they reject the self which is offered to them and choose freedom. Sometimes, as in the cases of Oliver Twist or Pip in *Great Expectations*, they are orphans who, offered no initial identity, find this freedom thrust upon them.

Pamela, with the particular ambivalence Richardson has given his novel, falls into both categories. She is forced to embrace her freedom both by the death of B's mother, which robs her of her defined place in the household, and by the distance which separates her from her parents. But she also chooses it by her reluctance to return to her parents and the place they provide. Like Quixote she sees her life not as something given to her by a higher source but as a story she must tell. It is a story which, because it must be told to others—must be, in fact, woven into the threads of their stories—is in reality a letter.

JINA POLITI

The Miracle of Love

I. REWARD AND "REWARD"

I will now write to your question—whether there was an original ground-work of fact, for the general foundation of Pamela's story. About twenty-five years ago, a gentleman with whom I was intimately acquainted . . . met with such a story as that of Pamela.

("To Aaron Hill," *Selected Letters of Samuel Richardson*)

But, my Friend, the whole narrative is such a Misrepresentation of Facts, such a perversion of Truth.

(*An Apology for the Life of Mrs. Shamela Andrews*)

The Pamela controversy does not originate in a concern over the truth or falsity of the fact as such, but in a culture's prepossessions as to what it is desirable to consider as probable and possible, and what as improbable and impossible. Anti-Pamelist critics were not out to defend an ideal aesthetic canon but a group's notion of verisimilitude which rested on a theory of class-psychology. Fielding and the anti-Pamelists espoused as valid the image with which the ruling class operated in its dealings with the lower class, Richardson and the Pamelists were out to challenge these cultural prepossessions by

From *The Novel and Its Presuppositions: Changes in the Conceptual Structure of Novels in the Eighteenth and Nineteenth Centuries.* © 1976 by Jina Politi. A. M. Hakkert Ltd., 1976.

arguing that human behaviour, whether of the upper or lower classes, was ultimately unanswerable to a higher order of morality that emanated from the inward man.

The controversy proper rests on extra-textural grounds. Fielding and Richardson, like Mr. B. and Pamela, the Deists and the Fundamentalists, used the same terms to mean very different things but there was no ambiguity in their minds as to what each one meant. The disagreement over the right meaning and use of ethical terms which generates conflict in *Pamela*, generates the controversy over *Pamela*. It also explains Richardson's aversion to the morality of *Tom Jones:* "In the character of the weak, the insipid, the Runaway, the Inn-frequenting Sophia as in the character of her illegitimate Tom, there is nothing that very common persons may not attain to."

Fielding's criticism of the novel is based on the prepossession that disinterested morality, if practised at all, can only be practised by the leisured class. When a member of the lower classes appears to practise disinterested morality this can either be seen as "enthusiastic" religious lunacy, or as dissimulation at the service of self-interest. Fielding sees Pamela motivated by both these attitudes and his suggestion for a proper reading of the novel is: before every account which Pamela gives of her actions and reactions insert the words "I pretended." By this simple device Pamela is transformed into Shamela and the novel into a tale of intrigue. Had Pamela not been a servant girl but a young lady of *quality*, no one would have questioned her intentions and there would have been no anti-Pamelist criticism. The Gothic Novel, however, would have had a premature birth.

That the controversy was not over aesthetic but over class prejudice and role allocation is made evident in the sequel to *Pamela*. Richardson, under pressure, conceded to the opponent. Mrs. Pamela B. makes it ever so clear to her maid Polly not to harbour any illusions as to Lord H.'s intentions. In this life, saints are saints, maids are maids, and lords are lords.

Had Richardson not cast his title in the form of an alternation and had left out the "Or Virtue Rewarded," the controversy may have been less heated. But this title seemed like a deliberate challenge. Virtue and its rewards, vice and its punishments, as was briefly discussed in chapter three, were the occasion of great disputes at the time. The anti-Pamelists saw "virtue" functioning as a synonym for Pamela and thus reduced virtue to a specific name. Like the Deists, they argued that virtue should be its own reward. If virtue ceased being disinterested and became goal-directed, it lost its moral quality and acquired something of the character of hypocrisy. Pamela's duplicity lay in the fact that she practised virtue not for its future heavenly rewards (even this expectation was judged by the Deists to be reprehensible) but for immediate, temporal gains at the expense of a foolish young man. Although the doctrine of virtue for virtue's sake seemed a higher system of morality than that of punishments and rewards, actually, it hit at the root of religious eschatology and undermined belief in the Christian plot of fall and redemption.

If "virtue" is seen as a specific name, "reward" is narrowly interpreted to mean, as in the language of trade, Pamela's socioeconomic triumph. However, as in the Bible, the term "reward" occurs frequently in the novel and is used by different characters to mean different things. It is these different and often contradictory uses of ethical terms such as reward, virtue, duty, honour, justice, that generate conflict and stasis in the novel. Once the characters come to share meanings, conflict is resolved and harmony established.

If "virtue" is seen to function generically then "reward" does not attach only to Pamela. It will be noticed that all the characters are in the end rewarded. Pamela's reward is of less significance precisely because it is temporal. But Mr. B.'s conversion from an agent of darkness to an agent of light, in fact a whole society's emergence into a world of light, is virtue's great and proper reward. Pamela may have risen in the social scale, but Mr. B. rose from hell to heaven.

The conceptual structure in *Pamela*, as in *Tom Jones*, is strictly dualistic. It postulates two independent, antagonistic principles, good and evil, whose cosmic strife generates human plots with a teleological structure. Both novels, by analogy, are imitations of the Christian plot which posits a happy outcome at the end of time and the eternal reign of light and love. Both world-models presuppose the active participation in the affairs of mankind of a divine providence. Fielding's imitation of the Christian myth is enlightened and urbane and his primary interest is to draw the analogy with the world of manners. Richardson's imitation is mystical and a-social and his primary interest is to draw the analogy with the inward man. Their difference lies in the fact that Fielding's world model is worldly while Richardson's other-worldly: "An outward *Morality*, a *Decency* and *Beauty* of Life and Conduct with respect to this world, arising only from a *Worldly Spirit* has nothing of salvation in it. He that has his *Virtue* only from this world, is only a *Trader* of this world" (William Law, *An Appeal to all that Doubt, or Disbelieve The Truths of the Gospel*). This was the criticism which the Fundamentalists directed against a morality of decorum and prudence.

Once the obvious point about the dualistic structure of *Pamela* is accepted it becomes by definition impossible to justify an anti-Pamelist reading. For, either one has to suppress the religious and literary tradition upon which the novel is so explicitly modelled, or, like Fielding, one has to subvert the roles and see Mr. B. as angel and Pamela as temptress. But surely this is pure sophistry since it is Mr. B., like Blifil, who disrupts concord and order to satisfy his wicked desires. Like Master Blifil, Mr. B. is unaware of the fact that the plot originates in an otherworldly region and that, paradoxically, he functions as the instrument for advancing the cause of virtue.

Fielding's epilogue to *Tom Jones* gives us a valuable clue for explaining his anti-Pamelism, a clue which can serve as evidence that the reasons were topical and extratextual. In the light of this evidence, modern anti-Pamelist readings may appear as imitative elaborations of Fielding's biased reading and hence groundless. Unless we are to accept that these ideological differences on class and religious belief are so deeply embedded in the culture that after two centuries they can still generate similar responses.

At the conclusion of *Tom Jones*, in the summary given to the reader concerning the future of the characters, we read the following about Blifil: "He is also lately turned *Methodist*, in hopes of marrying a very rich Widow of that Sect." Fielding's prejudice speaks for itself. Pamela's fervent, sometimes hysterical, naively articulated faith smacked of "methodism" to Fielding. The label sufficed to generate the type. Fielding, to save himself from the accusation of a biased reading, very ingeniously made Parson Oliver the anti-Pamelist spokesman in *Shamela* and Parson Tickletext the Pamelist one. Both names have nonconformist connotations since an "Oliverian" meant a Puritan and "Tickletext" could be interpreted as either one who is tickled by the text *Pamela*, or one who teases the text, i.e., a "textualist," "one learned in the text of the Bible; one who adheres strictly to, and bases his doctrine upon, the text of the scriptures." If two nonconformists disagreed about Pamela, then surely the fault lay in her character and not in the reader's mind.

Neither Richardson nor Fielding were interested in composing religious allegories. For both, the primary aim of fiction was probability and it is for this reason that their mind models are made complex and the characters not represented as pure, ideal types. Therefore, to see Pamela's hesitations, fears, decisions and choices, her human failings and natural responses, in other words, to see all those character traits that make her be Pamela and not disembodied Virtue as proofs of her duplicity, is to accuse Richardson for writing a novel and not a morality play. If Fielding is dubious about the sincerity of a servant girl's motives and accuses Richardson on the grounds of improbability, one may accuse Fielding of the same failing by arguing that he invents plot to confound fact.

Richardson's *Pamela, or Virtue Rewarded*, is an expression in fiction of the reaction against the rational and pragmatic tendencies of the Age which were reducing God to a mechanic, the world to a machine, and the language of morality to the language of trade. It is also expressive of a desire to preserve alive for the culture a religious and ethical ideology which had its roots deep in mysticism and hence could not be easily eroded by being modernised. Richardson's opposition to Deism is expressed in his letters, in the third part of *The Apprentice's Vade Mecum*, and in his refusal to print for the Deists. That he printed the works of his nonconformist friend John Leland, one of their severest critics, is not without significance; that he printed works of the mystical divine William Law shows not only where Richardson's inclinations lay, but what was the source from which he drew inspiration for the conceptual structure of his novels.

II. THE VANITY OF TIME

In the small county of Bedfordshire between a master and his servant the cosmic drama of the clash of good and evil is enacted. Like the unfortunate princess in medieval iconography, Virtue chained is at the mercy of the fierce dragon. St. George (Parson Williams) will not be the deliverer. As in Uccello's version, gentle Virtue at last subdues the beast and makes it follow her on the chain. All evil ultimately serves good and works for its triumph:

> All the Evils of Contrariety and Disorder in fallen Nature are only
> as so many Materials, in the Hands of infinite Love and Wisdom,
> all made to work in their different Ways, as far as is possible,
> to one and the same End, *viz.* to turn temporal Evil into eternal
> Good.
>
> (Law, *The Spirit of Love*)

Richardson's world is the world of fallen nature. Nature is not a system of immutable laws whose discovery reveals to man God's infinite, scientific wisdom, but a restless world torn by internal strife and disorder, labouring to transcend its sinful temporality and regain eternity in the bosom of God's "abyssal" love:

> The Elements of this World stand in great *Strife* and Contrariety,
> and yet in great Desire of *mixing* and *uniting* with each other;
> and hence arises both the *Life* and *Death* of all Temporal Things.
> And hereby we plainly know that the Elements of this World were
> once *one undivided* Thing; for union can *nowhere* be desir'd, but
> where there has first been a *separation*.
>
> (Law, *An Appeal*)

Good and evil are not propensities in man's disposition which can be governed by the light of reason, but the very principles of temporal existence which inhere in nature, man, beast and plant:

> The Elementary Nature *in* Man and Beasts, was in the *same*
> Disorder with the *outward* Elements and Stars. . . . For the
> Elements *in* and *without* man were of the same Nature, and
> therefore acted upon one another.
>
> (Law, *The Grounds and Reasons of Christian Regeneration*)

As male and female, Mr. B. and Pamela are the two terms in an opposition.
But the fundamental opposition of wrath and love is to be found separately
in each of them, though the mixture of the hostile elements varies in their
natures. Their strife, inward and outward, conceals the cosmic yearning for
union, the overcoming of separation which can be brought about by the death
of the old, wrathful self, and the birth, through repentence, of the new, loving self. The mediating principle that inspires these regenerations is not reason
but the divine spirit of love: "Amor si dolce mi si fa sentire."

Mystical thought accepts temporal nature in all its gross materiality as
it accepts saintliness in all its angelic spirituality. It does not suppress the
realities and passions of flesh and blood, or the raptures of beatific wonder
for the sake of an enlightened humanism. Its language, unlike the language
of reason, is not abstract and refined, but concrete and sensuous. Richardson's psychological realism has its roots in mysticism which stressed the inward man.

Pamela begins with a series of letters exchanged between a servant girl
and her parents. The letters of Goodman Andrews, though few, are of extreme importance because they do not form part of Pamela's point of view.
It is the beliefs and attitudes expressed in these letters, rather than Pamela's
virtue, that generate the novel's dualistic structure and indicate the manner
of its development:

> I, too, have written a long Letter: but will say one Thing more,
> and that is, That in the midst of our Poverty and Misfortunes,
> we have trusted in God's Goodness, and been honest, and doubt
> not to be happy hereafter, if we continue to be good: tho' our
> Lot is hard here.

The "hereafter" for Goodman Andrews is the fundamental condition of existence and therefore ever-present in man. The "here" is a transitory state
where "the whole Creation is travelling in Pain and Laborious Working, to
be deliver'd from the *Vanity* of Time" (*An Appeal*).

Pamela's beliefs concerning the master of our temporal existence are in
direct opposition to Mr. B.'s:

> Surely your Honour ought to be more afraid of God Almighty,
> in whose Presence we all stand in every Action of our Lives, and

to whom the greatest, as well as the least, must be accountable,
let them think what they list. . . . Well, Well, *Pamela*, said he,
no more of this unfashionable Jargon.

Goodman Andrews's tone is one of humility and resignation to the will of
God, whereas Pamela's betrays an element of pride. Goodman Andrews em-
phasises God's goodness, Pamela his stern, equalitarian justice. To Mr. B.,
all this is "unfashionable jargon" because he situates himself in historical time
and accepts it as the only reality. The "hereafter" is to him a discarded
metaphysical system which had no foundation in empirical fact. Mr. B. expresses himself like an eighteenth-century atheist, a young man of progressive
ideas who considers that beliefs and the language expressing them are subject to the laws of change.

Both Pamela and Mr. B. are very young to have tested their ideas by
experience. Their stubborness and rigidity, as advocates of two opposed
systems of morals, seem more like an exercise in self-persuasion than a debate.
When left to their thoughts, or led to a proof of their beliefs in action, they
waver in youthful confusion—witness Mr. B.'s unsuccessful attempts at rape
and Pamela's at escape. The action of the novel will centre around the testing
of these beliefs. Experience and disputation will lead Pamela to a realisation
that humility is a prerequisite to virtue, and Mr. B. to an inward assent to
all the tenets of "unfashionable jargon."

It is not only the wicked characters that undergo a regeneration in the
novel. Pamela's white angel may be carrying on a fight with Mr. B.'s black
one, but Pamela's black angel is not sitting still. Pamela is not exempt from
inward strife and pride. Self, William Law maintained, was responsible for
all the "Disorder and Corruption, and Malady of our Nature." When the
novel begins, Pamela is far from "the Sacrifice and Destruction of *all
Selfishness*, as well spiritual as natural that must be made before our regeneration hath its perfect Work." If the hysterical, fanatical protection of her virtue seems at times unconvincing, this is not because Pamela is a hypocritical,
calculating little schemer, but because:

> In all this Shew and Glitter of Virtue, there is an *unpurified Bot-
> tom* on which [these virtues] stand, there is a *selfishness*, which
> can no more enter in to the Kingdom of Heaven, than the
> Grossness of Flesh and Blood can enter into it.
>
> (Law, *Christian Regeneration*)

This theme of the overcoming of self which in *Pamela* brings to the
characters the rewards of a happy life in temporal nature, informs the tragedy
of *Clarissa*, whose purification eradicates "the *deepest root* of all selfishness"

and leads her to that saintly state of humility, which is "the *most absolute Resignation* of our whole selves unto God."

Goodman Andrews, therefore, indicates the difficult path to humility which virtue has to tread before she can claim her rewards: "O my Child! Temptations are sore things; but yet without them, we know not ourselves, nor what we are able to do." Goodman Andrews cautions his daughter of the dangers of pride and admonishes her that "it may be too presumptuous to trust too much to [her] own strength." Richardson avoids the tragic tone in the representation of the rape scenes because he wished to stress the physical conflict of two proud, warring wills. Pamela will never reach Clarissa's state of moral excellence. She is not opposing spirit to corrupt matter, but a higher passion to a lower passion.

The stark, matter-of-fact representations have led, quite erroneously, some critics to read in the rape scenes elements of the comic. Pamela's detailed descriptions of the stages in her undressing, her prattling on to Mrs. Jewkes, etc., etc., have given rise to all sorts of comment. Yet Pamela's detailed and eager descriptions could be seen simply as the style of an honest, lower-class girl who has not lost her spontaneity in the twists and turns of wit and who is ready to communicate her experiences without applying the rules of reserve and decorum, trusting that her listeners are as eager to "have it all" as she is eager to transmit it. When Pamela, in the middle of the night, rushes back to the house and arms of her once cruel master, upon waking up the next morning she makes the following entry in her journal: "I am deadly sore all over as if I had been soundly beaten. I did not think I could have liv'd under such fatigue." Only a culture which considers it a virtue to conceal personal emotions and sensations (unless they be expressed in poetry or in the third-person point of view) could feel ambiguously about Pamela.

In *The Rise of the Novel*, Ian Watt observes that Richardson "was very careful to locate all the events of his narrative in an unprecedentedly detailed time-scheme." Watt seems to have misconstrued Richardson's handling of time. A "detailed time-scheme" supports the claim to formal realism by assuming that the author's intention was to represent time historically and to model his conceptual structure on the implications which such a notion of time entails. The actual time of the novel is, roughly, seventeen months. But where is one to place these months? The years are not mentioned, not even the months. Pamela's letters bear no date and when they do it is simply to name the day or the hour. This is not accidental. Years succeed one another in an inexorable, linear fashion, days and months occur and recur in cycles. To view human time and life historically is to accept change and the finite. Richardson wishes to rescue his world model from the contingencies of history. It is not Mr. B.'s notion of time that determines the novel's structure but Goodman Andrews's, for whom time means the repetitive and unrelaxing exercise of duty, the joining of one's forces with "that Goodness of God, which created Time and all Things in it, to have a happy End in Eternity" (Law, *An Appeal*). Thus, a cyclical time-pattern is formally established in support of an ever-recurring, archetypal theme. The characters in Pamela, though situated in a temporal-historical world, are enacting the timeless drama of the miracle of love: "Let it be . . . supposed, that God by a Miracle of Love entered into the *fiery root*, or essence of this fallen Angel, and by a *new Birth* made it again to be a flame of *Love*" (Law, *Christian Regeneration*).

When the novel begins we realise that the first letter is just another letter in a series. A significant past already exists, one to which constant references will be made because it is the shaping, determining force of Pamela's present and future: "I owe every thing next to God's Goodness, to your Piety and good Examples, my dear Parents." Time has been flowing evenly for virtuous Pamela. The year, the month, the day, the hour are measured by the order and fulfilment of obligations and duties. The daily cycle is an imitation in minature of the right pattern which man's life in time should exhibit. When Pamela's good Lady dies, the even flow of time and letters is disrupted. The pious lady is succeeded by her atheistical son, a master who imposes on the house a government reflecting the disorder of his inward condition: "But then, what comes next? Why it pleased God to take my good Lady: and then comes my Master. And what says he? Why in Effect it is, *Be not virtuous, Pamela*."

Lust, like the soul in its fallen state, burns with a "dark firebreath, an anger fire, that must heat and torment itself with its own inward burning strife, and yet be unable to reach, touch, or obtain any spark of light and love, to make its fire-life sweet and amiable of such a flame of fire as angels are said to be" (*Christian Regeneration*). Mr. B.'s transgression divides houses, characters, nature and language into two hostile worlds: the city of God and the city of man. Conflict in *Pamela* is generated by these two world conceptions, one which sees the temporal world as governed by a world above, and another which sees the temporal world and its functional relationships as ends in themselves. The rapidly changing social scene and the theories of Government which had curtailed royal prerogative, and had demythicised the divine right of kings by shifting decision-making more to the people, had shaken faith in the myth of a divine government of the world as well. Richardson in Pamela questions Mr. B.'s absolutistic form of government, but liberalisation comes about only when Mr. B. declares his obedience to a Master above, and acquiesces, like Pamela, to the status of a servant.

Mrs. Jervis is a good servant in this and the other world, standing by her duty to her divine Master when moral and social duty conflict. Mrs. Jewkes serves no Master other than her temporal one. However, to follow blindly the orders of a temporal master means to have lost that independence of spirit which the moral sense grants and which inspires the humble to rise in revolt against the proud.

The distribution of characters follows this opposition and the action is modelled in such a way as to show the injustices and perversion of Mr. B.'s temporal government. The good characters who side with Pamela fall from social grace and are exiled from their social paradise. The bad ones wax in worldly power at the expense of their everlasting happiness: "The *old natural Man*, or the *rational* Man of this world, the the *dark fallen* Nature, enlightened *only* and solely with the Light of this outward World; it is the diabolical Nature" (*Christian Regeneration*). The oppositions generated are multiform. Thus we have:

eternity	temporality
Divine Master	worldly master
pious servant	wicked servant
poor materially	rich materially
rich spiritually	poor spiritually
humility	pride
merciful	wrathful
oppressed	oppressor
love	lust, hate
light	dark
white angel	black angel
virtue	vice
female	male
cottage	mansion
sunflower	bull
inward	outward

The opposition love-hate and the confusion of the contraries appear early in the book: "Is it not strange," reflects Pamela, "that Love borders so much upon Hate? But this wicked Love is not like the true virtuous Love, to be sure: *That* and *Hatred* must be far off, as *Light* and *Darkness*." Hate is associated with lust and pride which keep the individual imprisoned in the self. "Black-hearted Wretch! How I hate him!" exclaims Pamela. "If I hate or despise any one man in the world, I hate something that God cannot hate, and despise that which he loves . . . no love is *holy*, or religious, till it becomes *universal*" (Law, *A Serious Call to a Devout and Holy Life*). Pamela has a long way to travel before she achieves the state of humility and universal love:

A man naturally fancies, that it is his own exceeding love of virtue that makes him not able to bear with those that want it. . . .
If this had been the *Spirit* of the Son of God, if he hated sin *in
this manner*, there had been no redemption of the *World*.

(*A Serious Call*)

When despondency leads Pamela to the pond of destruction, the thought
of ending her life by drowning deprives the element of water of the grace
of baptism and regeneration, and pollutes it with the sin of death. Luckily,
Pamela's sensibility awakes to the fact of her own sinfulness, and to the
knowledge of her true enemy which is her inward pride:

> But, Oh! my dear Parents, rejoice with me, even in this low, Plunge
> of my Distress; for your poor *Pamela* has escaped from an Enemy
> she never thought of before; and was hardly able to stand against;
> I mean the Weakness and Presumption, both in one, of her own
> Mind! which had well nigh, had not divine Grace interposed, sunk
> her into the lowest, last abyss of Misery and Perdition!

It is not accidental that Pamela mixes here the first- and third-person
point of view. This distance enables her to articulate her sudden realisation
of the dual nature of every man and of his inward strife and disorder. In
the pond scene Pamela applies to herself the terms which up to now were
reserved for Mr. B. Her mind is "benighted," God sees "all the lurking vileness
of her heart," she is "presumptuous," "the guilty aggressor." This agony in
the garden matures Pamela in humility and mercifulness:

> Just now we heard that he had like to have been drowned in cross-
> ing the stream, a few days ago, in pursuing his game. What is
> the matter, that, with all his ill usage of me, I cannot hate him?
> . . . He has certainly done enough to make me hate him; but yet,
> when I heard his danger, which was very great, I could not in
> my heart forbear rejoicing for his safety.

Mr. B., while pursuing his game (as he has been pursuing Pamela), runs like
her the risk of death by water. The plunge into the baptismal stream marks
the awakening of repentence in the heart of Mr. B. Pamela may be the narrator in this novel yet behind her limited point of view stands another author
who moulds the plot in divine Omniscience.

III. THE INFOLDING WILL

Upon reading *Pamela* the reader cannot fail but notice that the outdoors
is rarely mentioned. Together with Pamela the reader moves from interior

to interior totally disconnected from the outside world. Distance, separation, disconnection, frustrate communication between the characters, and between Pamela and the world. Selfishness, or the infolding will, is mirrored in the novel's topology. Human space reflects the cosmic heaven-hell division as well as the coexistence of contraries in nature and man. Place acquires the characteristics of the actions that occur within it. Goodman Andrews's cottage is transformed into a paradise lost to which Pamela yearns to return after her fall from social grace. The stately Bedfordshire mansion, once a paradise, is transformed into a hellish place which is identified even grammatically with its libidinous master: "We would have you flee," Goodman Andrews writes to his daughter, "this evil Great house and Man." The Lincolnshire estate also undergoes a metamorphosis, in Pamela's words: "My prison has become my palace."

The projection of moral traits and inner feeling onto place accords with Law's conception of the external world: "For the outward world is but a glass, or representation of the inward; and every thing and variety of things in temporal nature must have its root, or hidden cause, in something that is more inward" (*Christian Regeneration*). The visible world in *Pamela* reflects the inward states of Mr. B. and Pamela. Darkness, secrecy, plotting, fear, imprisonment, separation, tension, wrath, lust, these terms describe it. Richardson creates this atmosphere by studiously avoiding to relate places through descriptive links, or through the movement of characters in space. Like letters, which are infolded, sealed and discontinuous communications, places stand isolated, each holding its secrets within its walls.

While in Bedfordshire, we see Pamela outdoors once. It is when she is peacefully sitting in the garden at work with her needle. When Mr. B. appears, and forgetting his distance offers freedom to his servant, Pamela rushes into the house for safety, and neither she nor the reader see the outside world again until Mr. B. orders her removal by coach to Lincolnshire. It is significant that in her account of this drive Pamela never mentions the surroundings but keeps herself and the reader safely in the coach. The only external impressions which she records are the sight of a church and the setting sun, symbols of the eternal, the temporal, death and regeneration.

The sensuous world is identified with Mr. B. whose restless passions are a manifestation of the wrath and disorder of fallen nature. Nature assumes the aggressive animality of the unloving male, and to Pamela's eyes "Horrid bull," "hideous Mr. Colbrand" and "hideous master" are as one. Pamela rarely uses similes but on the few occasions when she does her analogies come from the world of nature: "But he kissed me with frightful Vehemence; and then his Voice broke upon me like a Clap of Thunder." Thunder in mystical symbolism is a manifestation of the wrath, turbulence and strife of the contraries of nature. The spatial world, then, is under a hideous metamorphosis while Pamela's trials last.

In myths and folktales the agent who (for good or for evil) transforms men, things and places is personified. It is the magician, the fairy, Satan, or an Olympean god. The metamorphoses in these fictional modes always assume external, visible shape. In myth or folktale Mr. B. would figure as giant or beast finally transformed into handsome prince. In *Pamela* the transforming agent has no material shape and the proof for the transformation is no longer empirical. The transforming power is now an inward disposition of the heart and the metamorphosis of the characters occurs within. The change is not one from passion to reason, as the Age of Enlightenment would have it: "For the distinction of our Reason from our Passions is only a distinction in Language, made at pleasure" (Law, *The Case of Reason or Natural Religion*). Richardson, as was mentioned earlier, did not share his Age's admiration for this faculty and together with William Law and other mystics placed the heart above the head. [T. C. Duncan] Eaves and [Ben D.] Kimpel are wrong when they say that Richardson "is never very clear about the 'heart' and it is useless to try to extract from him a consistent belief." The consistency of his mystical world models in Pamela and Clarissa make abundantly clear his beliefs about the 'heart':

> When you place the power of your salvation in your *intellectual* light, or the strength of your *own reason*, you place it in your *weakest* part, in the *poorest*, most *trifling* and *insignificant* thing that belongs to you and upon that which has the least effect in human life. . . . For this light of bare reason or the reasoning faculty of the mind has no contrariety to the vices of the heart; it neither kills nor is killed by it.
>
> (Law, *A Demonstration of the Gross and Fundamental Errors of A late Book*)

The "happy Change" which comes in the lives of Pamela and Mr. B. is not the outcome of reason but of a change of hearts:

> But in that *light* of the *heart*, or *attraction* to God, which . . . is common to all mankind in and through Jesus Christ, all is contrary. As it is a gift and grace of God, so it is a *real life*, a living thing, a *sentiment* of the hearts and so far as it grows and increases in us, so far it destroys all that is bad and corrupt within us. It has the same contrariety to all vices of the heart, that light has

to darkness, and must either suppress or be suppressed by them.

(*A Demonstration*)

Space and place in *Pamela* will reflect the happy change effected in the characters.

The idea of space in *Pamela* is not restricted to physical representation. The concept of distance acquires various meanings in the text. Pamela is in physical distance from her parents and in social distance from her origins; Mr. B. is in great distance from God; Mr. B. and Pamela are separated by great social distance: "I again reflected upon the Distance between us." Mr. B. forgets this and offers liberties to his servant. Pamela is accused by Mrs. Jervis: "Pamela, don't be so pert to his Honour: you should know your distance." Distance separates, and separations in temporal nature are effected by the dark forces counteracting the spirit of love. All oppositions holding in the text, all notions of distance, geographical, social or spiritual, will be resolved once the spirit of love triumphs over the antinomies of self:

> When Love is the Spirit of your Life, it will have the *Freedom* and *Universality* of a *Spirit;* it will always live and work in *Love* not because of *This* or *That, Here* or *There,* but because the Spirit of Love can only love, where-ever it is, or goes, or whatever is done to it. For the Spirit of Love is always the same Course; it knows no Difference of Time, Place, or Persons.
>
> (Law, *The Spirit of Love*)

Before the spirit of love, the world automatically sheds its bull-like mask and sunflower light replaces darkness. Rooms, gardens, houses and world establish communication through open windows and unlocked gates. Pamela, once proud, incorruptible virgin, is taken for breakfast to a dairy. Mr. B., once playboy of the world, sits in his closet meditating on the awful subject of death. Pamela's writings, which were her only means of imposing order to a chaotic existence (even though this order was only a narrative one), once sealed and private communications, now see the light and are transformed into instructive and delightful literature for the benefit of the minds of "the Youth of both Sexes." And we, shameless peeping Toms, are transformed into regular, respectable readers. As in the eighteenth-century theatre, a mere change in lighting has changed the effect of the whole set. "These are the Mysteries of Love and Mercy" (*Christian Regeneration*).

IV. "THE UNLAWFULNESS OF STAGE ENTERTAINMENT"

The reader of *Pamela* finds himself in the embarrassing position of peeping into something private. He cannot identify with the recipients of the letters, nor with Mr. B. who intercepts and reads them. Like Mrs. Jewkes, the reader is forced into becoming a voyeur. Indeed, the story is a very private affair, a secret. Mr. B. urges Pamela to keep things secret, his gifts to her are seen by her parents as hiding "a design," Pamela is "suspicious and fearful," letters are stolen and never reach their destination, Pamela has secrets with Parson Williams, actions take place within walls, within closets, and keys, real and symbolic, keep everything imprisoned.

On the first level, the secret appears to be rape. The secret, however, goes beyond the mere act and becomes a method on how to corrupt. Pamela, having crossed the threshold of society, becomes an obstacle to its ways. The values which she advocates are values proper to the illiterate, lower class and are meaningless in Mr. B's world. Pamela defends them on the grounds that they are eternal and absolute, Mr. B. tries to persuade her that they are relative and that it is in the power of his class to impose, or to change them. Mr. B., once victim of scheming middle-class mothers and daughters, becomes an intriguer himself and uses every art to entangle Pamela in the net of corruption: wooing, threatening, force, temptation. Pamela's incorruptibility creates an unresolvable conflict.

The action assumes the form of repetition without much variation. Every incident, physical or verbal, repeats the same theme: attack-resistance-attack. Since incidents perpetuate the same pattern, causality is negated. The letter form is not suited to reproduce the flow of time and change. When each letter ends, continuity in time and action end with it. The time-gap is shrouded in silence and darkness. What will happen between letters is entirely unpredictable. What is certain is that another letter will follow. Time is arrested within the letters and events do not, of themselves, form causal links. As each letter, however, repeats the same theme, the reader, by force of habit, learns to predict.

There is no playful confusion in *Pamela*, as there is in *Tom Jones*, about the right sequence and causal arrangement of actions in time. The element of suspense in *Pamela* is not the result of plot but of the frustration of plot. Both Pamela and the reader know who intercepts the letters; Mr. B. soon finds out Pamela's plot with the parson; before the gypsy-plot materialises, Mr. B. has changed his mind. Secret designs are frustrated whether for good or for evil. It soon becomes obvious to the reader that the course of events is not in the hands of the characters or of the narrator. The "secret" then was only deceptively such. Causality will not manifest itself in the factual arrangement of incidents in time. It will not be logical but intuitive and will concern the order of values.

The first-person narrative point of view appears to enhance the air of secrecy. A subjective narrative presupposes that the thoughts and feelings of the writer are shared with no one but the reader. Pamela's feelings and thoughts, however, are freely expressed. She does not present a different person in her letters and a different person in her actions. Mr. B. learns nothing from the letters which Pamela has not already directly expressed to him. What Pamela tried to hide are certain of her actions, such as keeping a diary, or planning to escape. These, though, do not make a narrative subjective. The concealment of action is a cliché in novels of plot where the point of view is omniscient.

Thus, though we are made to feel that we are peeping into a world of secrecy, secrets don't have their way. Early in the book the characters, unknowingly, make the right prophecies about the future. Mr. Jervis says: "Yet I believe he loves my good Maiden, tho' his Servant, better than all the Ladies of the Land; and he has try'd to overcome it, because he knows you are so much his Inferior; and 'tis my Opinion he finds he can't." In novels where the plot resolution is made dependent on an external scheme of things, whether providential as in Richardson, or deterministic as in Hardy, the end is foreshadowed early in the book to serve as deductive proof of the inevitable outcome. Mr. B. tells Pamela (and the reader) what the outcome of this adventure will be: "O my good Girl! We shall make out between us, before we have done, a pretty Story in Romance." A literary genre is invoked to give shape to unformulated experience, and as the reader knows, romances, after many tempestuous adventures and reversals of fortune, culminate in a happy end.

Richardson, though not as fervent in his condemnation of it as was William Law, nevertheless mistrusted the pleasures of the stage. Yet, in his novels he relied for many effects on theatrical conventions. Pamela's narrative is, by virtue of the point of view, subjective and yet it manages to achieve dramatic distance. When she reproduces scenes her authorial commentary sounds like artful stage direction: "He gave her five guineas!—She made him a low Curchee, and pray'd God to bless him; and look'd to me, as if she would have spoken to me." "And so I rose up, and was forc'd to lean upon my Master's Elbow Chair, or I should have sunk down." "My master . . . seem'd a little mov'd, and took his Handkerchief out of his Pocket and walked to the Window." "He then took me in his Arms, and presently push'd me from him." "I threw my Apron over my Face, and laid my Head on a Chair, and cry'd as if my Heart would break." Movement and pose are described in a manner which enables the reader to visualise the scene. We are asked to imagine the characters as upon a stage, an eighteenth-century stage where actors spoke their lines facing the audience. Pamela's scenic method enables the reader to gather information which the subjective narrative point of view could not communicate. Since in plays the writer is almost invisible and no one seems to be manipulating the action but the forces inherent in it and the personality of the characters, the scenic method in *Pamela* creates a balance with the subjective point of view and consequently Pamela cannot properly be accused of "telling the story in the way she likes." The reader as voyeur is no more guilty than a theatre-goer.

Motion in *Pamela*, as on the stage, acquires an ideal representation. The reader has no experience of the physicality of motion in space which in novels is usually connected with the process or progress of the action. In *Tom Jones*, where the novel is likened to a journey, space and motion play an integral part in the development of the plot. But in *Pamela* nothing moves. The action is static, conflict culminates in deadlock, Pamela is physically imprisoned, what Mr. B. does when he is offstage no one knows. He appears when the part requires it, disappears when it does not. Pamela in her narrative suppresses the connective links which create the illusion of motion through the illusion of a continuous space. When, for example, she is summoned to appear before Mr. B., she never describes the parts of the house through which she has to pass to arrive in his presence. As in the theatre, we are aware of the lifting of the curtain that reveals a new set. Stasis, which characterises the action, is formally reflected in the narrative method.

The set "Bedfordshire" and the set "Lincolnshire" delimit Pamela's area of motion. She travels from the one to the other and back to the first one again. Though space follows the cyclical and apparently unprogressive pattern of time, something of vast significance does change. Pamela and Mr. B., like the pilgrim, have been in continuous motion through paths that seem to lead nowhere but which suddenly lead to a world of light. Mr. B. had been physically free but morally imprisoned; Pamela physically imprisoned but morally free. Both hero and heroine win complete freedom once they come to accept the insoluble bonds of marriage: "And bless the Goodness of that Providence which has, thro' so many intricate Mazes, made me tread the Paths of Innocence and so amply rewarded me, for what it has itself enabled me to do!" The divine master is as living a presence in the novel as the worldly master. If not a character, he is the maker of the theatre and the play: "God *can* touch his Heart in an Instant" (italics mine).

V. LANGUAGE AS GESTURE

The cosmic strife between good and evil and the temporal one between a gentleman and his servant girl is reflected in the conflict of opposed linguistic conventions. Language, like walls, separates: "All words have a meaning,

a significancy and effect, according to the nature of him whose they are"
(Law, *A Demonstration*). In *Pamela*, one feels that language is struggling
to resolve the tensions but only manages to entangle things more: "The words
of man are as men are, *weak, vain, earthly* and of a *poor* and narrow
Signification" (*A Demonstration*).

Pamela speaks the language of order which admits of no relativity in
the meaning of its terms since they are fixed, absolute and objective. It is
a language characterised by consistency and one which does not depend on
the character's subjective variability. Its terms correspond to, and mirror inward and outward realities. It includes descriptive terms for nonobservable,
universal entities. Mr. B. speaks the language of chaos which is characterised
by confusion, contradiction and perversion in representation. It is imper-
manent and its terms are those of immorality, unbelief and materiality. To
Pamela's ideal terms, Mr. B. proffers terms of bartering. Mr. B.'s confusion
over the right use of terms is expressed early in the book:

> She has written letters . . . in which she makes herself an Angel
> of Light, and me, her kind Master and Benefactor a Devil Incar-
> nate!—(O how people will sometimes, thought I, call themselves
> by their right Names!)

As long as there are two languages which affix contradictory meanings to
terms, communication is impossible and the purpose of language frustrated:
"Well, Mrs. *Jewkes*, said I, I shall not at this Time dispute with you about
the Words *Ruin* and *Honourable;* I thank God, we have quite different Notions of both." The devaluation of language in mystical thought accords with
the idea that things communicated to man by God are of such supernatural
significance, so much beyond the categories of human experience that
language accommodates, that it can serve poorly as an instrument for the
transcription of divine communications: "The common Rules of Speaking
are like other things that are common amongst men, *viz*, poor, empty, and
superficial, hardly touching the *outside* of the mere human things we talk
about" (*A Demonstration*). Pamela's tone, however, betrays an influence of
the empiricist attitude to language and communication which, for other than
mystical reasons, devalued the effectiveness of speech.

The resolution of contraries in the universe of action establishes the
language of order as the true and proper one. As there is no disagreement
now about the meaning of terms, language can be shared and made to sym-
bolise union and concord. When the miracle of love unseals Mr. B.'s heart
and understanding he tells Pamela: "I tho' I doubted not effecting this last
Plot, resolv'd to overcome myself; and . . . part with you, rather than to

betray you under so black a Veil. . . . But, perhaps, it would have come too late, had not your white Angel got the better of my black one." However, besides the two languages which create disorder and confuse characters and reader, there exists another form of communication which is nonverbal and simple.

Gesture is important in drama as it makes for economy by communicating information to the audience in a nonverbal way. In novels, however, the narrator can articulate for the reader all those messages which on stage gesture communicates. It is for this reason that in novels, nonverbal information is minimal before symbolism. Richardson's use of gesture in *Pamela* is of great significance. As in pantomime, it communicates in silence the development of the story and the intentions and feelings of the agents. Gesture supplies the causal structure which the narrative was unable to provide and thus becomes more "eloquent" than speech. The significant gesture in *Pamela* is the touching of hands.

In the first scene between Pamela and Mr. B., we see him taking her hand twice: "And for you, *Pamela*, (and took me by the Hand; yes he took my Hand before them all.)" "And indeed he was not angry for he took me by the Hand." When Mr. B. declares his wicked intentions, the taking of Pamela's hand is not considered by her to be an honour but a threat: "I stood still confounded, and began to tremble, and the more when he took me by the Hand."

The disorder to which lust throws Mr. B. is reflected in the gesture: "Equivocator, again! said he and took my hand. . . . Sir, said I, and fain would have pulled my Hand away." "Stay here, stay here, when I bid you; and snatch'd my Hand, I trembled, and said, I will! I will! for he hurt my Fingers, he graps'd me so hard."

When force proves ineffectual, Mr. B. tries gentle deceit: "He took my Hand in a kind of good-humour'd Mockery . . . it would be Pity, with these fair soft Hands, and that lovely Skin (as he call'd it.)" "He sat down upon a rich Setee; and took hold of my Hand, and said . . . holding both my Hands in his." "The guilty wretch took my left Arm and held it under his Neck, and the vile procuress held my Right . . . there was nobody to help me: and both my Hands were secured."

After the second attempt at rape, when God has touched Mr. B.'s heart, the aggressive gesture takes on a different meaning: "He said, taking my Hand, now will I vow to you. . . . And now *Pamela*, said he, give me your Hand, and say you forgive me. . . . I held out my trembling Hand which he vouchsafed to Kiss." Pamela's hands, up to this moment, have been passive and unresponsive. Mr. B. exercised a right upon them as upon his property.

Pamela has been for him an object of desire and an object which by law he owned.

When sensibility enters his heart and awakes remorse, Mr. B. begins to see Pamela as a human being worthy of respect and love. Pamela's hand begins to respond: "I boldly put my Hand before his mouth, hardly Knowing the Liberty I took." "And with this ambiguous Saying he saluted me . . . and lent me his Hand."

When the wicked master is metamorphosed into a virtuous prospective husband, Pamela's interpretation of the gesture is transformed too: "This, said he, (and honour'd me by kissing my Hand.)" In the first scene, naive Pamela took as an honour a gesture which hid wicked designs. Now that order has been established, right words fit with right gestures. "And so I had the Boldness to kiss his Hand."

The struggle of immature, proud and restless wills had placed an insurmountable distance between the lovers which the touching of their hands eloquently expressed. The distance is effaced by their symbolic joining in the mystery of marriage: "The joining of our Hands . . . the Declaration of our being marry'd." The plot woven by the hands cannot be said to be the product of Pamela's narrative artistry, or of her "methodist" duplicity. It speaks for itself and answers the anti-Pamelist.

Pamela does not end in Christian tragedy as *Clarissa*, but in the happy choice of the second manner of Christian life. The epilogue to the book bears striking similarities to the description given by the Church Father Eusebius, as quoted by Law in *A Serious Call:*

> [The second manner of Christian life] is of a lower form and suiting itself more to the condition of human nature, admits *chaste wedlock*, the care of children and family, of trade and business, and goes through all the employments of life under a sense of piety, and fear of God. Now they who have chosen this manner of life, have their set times for *retirement* and *spiritual exercises*, and particular days are set apart for their hearing and learning the word of God. And this order of people is consider'd as in the *second state* of piety.

Thus, adventures which are providentially directed to further the cause of virtue make Miss Sophia get her Mr. Jones, and Pamela her Mr. B. Fielding and Richardson can go on disputing about the question of improbability in fiction.

JEAN H. HAGSTRUM

Sir Charles Grandison:
The Enlarged Family

Richardson's last novel is considerably better than can be easily imagined by those who have only heard about it. But admittedly it represents a falling off after *Clarissa*, just as *Amelia* is a decline from the heights of *Tom Jones*. The portrait of the ideal husband in *Sir Charles Grandison* (1753) followed two years after Fielding's portrayal of the faithful and loving wife in *Amelia*, whose model of domestic loyalty is perhaps in the end more persuasive than Richardson's paragon. But if the palm for aesthetics must go to Fielding, Richardson comes off with greater intellectual honors, for Amelia does not sparkle with the many intellectual, spiritual, moral, and political facets of Richardson's diamond: Sir Charles is a modern Anglican knight of sensibility, more successful at disarming than destroying opponents, an early Broad Churchman hopeful of reconciling Englishmen and Italians, Anglicans and Catholics, Anglicans and Methodists. Despite broad, even international concerns, here as everywhere Richardson's canvas is chiefly the domestic life. The centrally important relationships of the novel are those of Sir Charles: with the ingénue Emily, who, though only fourteen, loves the hero with passion; with Olivia, the violent and volatile black-haired beauty from Florence whose fierce temper forever obviates a union with the hero; with the lively sister Charlotte, a parallel figure to Anna Howe; with the Lady Clementina, an Italian beauty whom the English gentleman would have married had religious differences between reconciled; and supremely with Harriet Byron— a delicate, beautiful heroine with a fresh country skin and a set of the highest

From *Sex and Sensibility: Ideal and Erotic Love from Milton to Mozart.* © 1980 by the University of Chicago. University of Chicago Press, 1980.

principles, whom Sir Charles, when he is free of all debts of honor, makes his wife in an ideal union.

We are on familiar ground, since many—perhaps most—of the ideas and ideals we have seen developing since the Restoration here attain their climax. The term "hero" is obsessively applied to a new kind of man, the pacifist Sir Charles, who has disciplined his naturally violent passions into a religiously and rationally controlled order. Cliché terms from the heroic plays are also applied to Harriet, who possesses greatness of soul, and to Clementina, who reveals the same quality when she shows herself able to renounce passion for principle, that is, adherence to her Roman Catholic faith and Italian nationality. Richardson's novel thus represents a climax in the domestication of heroism, realizing nobility of action in the spheres of love, marriage, and quotidian duty. It is also a climax of sensibility in love and friendship; and tears are shed copiously and unashamedly not only by the heroine but also by the hero as their hearts unite and as they feel the warm presages of ultimate bodily copulation. Feeling, along with virtue, extends outward from the loving couple to their environment as they work toward uniting the good and redeeming the evil. Sir Charles's Christian heroism is forever active in obstructing the cruel, providing for the needy, encouraging the defeated, enforcing prudence in domestic arrangements, reconciling former enemies. Above all, *Sir Charles Grandison* is the portrait of how a good marriage should be created and sustained. Marriage is an "awful rite," yet for all its majestic solemnity it is not stoical but rests on love and even sexuality at its base. Sir Charles, as Harriet says of him, may make no "ostentatious pretension to religion" though he is unmistakably a Christian; but he does, somewhat ostentatiously, protest his susceptibility to physical love: "A susceptibility of the passion called *Love*, I condemn not as a fault; but the contrary. Your *brother*, Ladies (looking upon all three [the group includes Harriet, his adopted sister, who will become his wife]) is no Stoic." Love must rise—need I say it?—far above the physical to the nobly spiritual; but in the calm of this novel, much more clearly than in the hectic world of *Clarissa*, Richardson makes crystal clear what I have assumed to be true everywhere in his thought and art, that the best love arises from physical attraction, grows with sympathy of mind, and achieves permanence only when two minds fully commit themselves to virtue and benevolence. Were not the excitements of sexuality placed well beneath the surface in this novel, it would be more widely read than it is now or has been in our century. But they exist and bubble underground like hidden springs. They make it clear that Richardson's model for love is the Miltonic, fusing the physical and the spiritual, not the Platonic, rising above and so transcending sexuality.

Two aspects of Richardson's treatment of love appear clearly in *Sir Charles Grandison* for the first time: the portrayal of love madness and the sense that true love is an extension of the familial. Clementina's wits are temporarily disordered by her great love for Sir Charles and its frustration by her family and life in Italy. Richardson's picture of love melancholy was greatly praised in the eighteenth century: Joseph Warton called it "deeply interesting," rating it above the madness of Lear and that of Orestes in Euripedes. But to a modern it seems remote and enormously long in the portrayal, in part an abandonment of what Richardson does so brilliantly in "writing to the moment." It is unredeemed by the psychological depth one finds elsewhere; and even the political-religious contrasts, though of some interest, are not realized graphically. Transalpine, Catholic life was outside Richardson's ken—perhaps outside his sympathies, too (his index to the novel refers to "Men, Women, and Italians"); and though the laments of Lady Clementina have some lyrical beauty, they remain general and effusive, without redeeming particularity.

The presentation of the love of Harriet Byron and Sir Charles as an easy extension of the familial is successful and enormously suggestive to the student of English culture. Richardson continues his familiar polemic against parentally forced marriage and in favor of a child's freedom to choose a partner. He desires reform of the family into a community of love in which personality can freely flower. He is clearly a prophet of that great modern social movement toward Lawrence Stone's "affective individualism," which Richardson not only preaches but embodies in plastic literary forms. The environment of virtuous love which he creates attains its serenity—even its relaxation, I might say—because laughter and tears are both present. Charlotte Grandison possesses real wit and liveliness of mind, and these qualities are not overcome by tragedy as those of Anna Howe are in the greater novel. Even newer habits of love and "bonding" can be treated with relaxed lightness: when Charles kisses Harriet on the lips, Charlotte cries out, "O Lud! O Lud! how could you bear him afterwards in your sight?" Tears are also a sign of personal rapport and goodness in action rather than tension, frustration, or fear. The lachrymose is called, with perhaps a slightly bemused touch, "kindly gush!" and it is regarded as divinely sanctioned: tears are "Dew drops of Heaven!"

A potentially darker side to the familial in this novel must be analyzed perhaps less for its own sake than for what it seems to prophesy about the future direction of love-sensibility. Richardson's love fantasies in *Grandison* have been with some justice called polygamous. His paragon is loved fervently by at least four women, and the question of whom he will choose for a life partner is left decidedly open until very late in the action. And once the decision is made, the former rivals, with some severe obstacles remaining, cease being that and accept their several positions in a relation of tearful love to one another. But in the end "polygamy" is not the appropriate word for the enlarged family over which Sir Charles presides; his own perspective is fraternal: "Men and women are brothers and sisters." Richardson was religious enough to believe in the family of man and to give new meaning to that concept in exploring the love relationship. The hero's rescue of Harriet from the clutches of the rich, vain, hot-tempered, rakish Sir Hargrave Pollexfen brings her into the Grandison family, where she becomes virtually a sister. That role is thrust upon her, but she accepts it gladly. She is obviously in it when she falls in love with her rescuer, and it is from the position of a kind of father-brother that he woos her. His endearments are mixed with instruction, exemplary deeds, practical leadership; lover and head of family are not alternating but fully blended functions as the two move through courtship to marriage. Thus the "company of angels" Harriet falls into is a "family of love," consisting of "true brothers and sisters," and she will surely look upon the husbandly love that eventuates as simply an extension of "all the tenderness of a brother," which her rescuer has been manifesting toward her ever since she joined the family. He also regards the relationship in that fashion: he obsessively calls her his new sister. Since Harriet was orphaned at the age of eight, one thinks back to Otway's famous and influential play in which there is no blood relationship but the orphan has taken a place as a sister before the amorous action begins. Richardson knew Otway's work well; but it must be said that *Sir Charles Grandison* is entirely lacking in the morbidity of *The Orphan*, even though the novel loosely repeats the play's situation, though not its action, and certainly implies that close similarity, if not consanguinity, is a deep attraction. One reason that Clementina, for all her loveliness and piety, will not do as the hero's wife is that she comes from afar—she is dark, Catholic, Italian. Harriet is an English "sister," and the ceremony of marriage is preceded by what can be regarded as an antecedent ceremony—Sir Charles formally taking the orphan into his family. Richardson made of the brother-sister relation in the Grandison family— both the actual blood tie and the symbolic one—something noble, chivalric, and deeply sustaining, endowing it with all the respect and idealism he was prepared to accord to true heterosexual love. The dynamics of Richardsonian love must have been influential; perhaps unconsiously the pre-Romantic, Romantic, and Victorian sensibilities were attracted to the Grandison ménage precisely because it seemed to give so high a sanction to the indigenous and the similar.

And yet it would be wrong to exaggerate this quality in Richardson's concept of love, which would be seriously distorted if morbidities were allowed to intrude. The novelist was in fact an enemy of the narcissistic and the inbred. He was careful to make the lesbianism of Mrs. Jewkes in *Pamela* completely odious, and in this novel his heroine turns away from the irregular embraces and kisses attempted by the violent and mannish Miss Barnevelt, who apparently admires unbaptized ancient heroes and makes us wonder if Richardson was anti-Greek partly because he saw sexual deviance in that culture. Richardson, it can be said rather dogmatically, is not consciously drawn to the abnormal. If anything, it is the forcefully heterosexual that attracts him. In *Sir Charles Grandison* the paragon has a "keeping" rakish father, who is nevertheless respected and obeyed, and a goatish and gouty uncle (a brother of Sir Charles's saintly mother), for whom a wife is provided in the course of the novel in one of the hero's redeeming actions. The hero is himself sexually attractive, with a delicate complexion, curling auburn locks, a manly stature and air, sparkling intelligence, and athletic prowess. This paragon has an eye for feminine beauty, and one of his greatest satisfactions arises from his having wooed and won "one of the most perfect beauties he had ever seen." If one wishes to see clearly Richardson's ideal of love, an ideal that perhaps did not change much in its essential features during his writing career, *Sir Charles Grandison* is an admirable source: as a novel of normality and daily life it is a corrective to the greater *Clarissa*, with the latter's hectic evil passions and almost equally hectic transcendence of even good passions. The later novel enables us to see clearly that "transcendence," not "denial," is the proper word to describe the sanctification of Clarissa. In the love between Charles and Harriet we have passionate-virtuous love realized in the social sphere, much to its edification. Indeed, that love becomes an example of what could in fact transform mankind into a family and so obviate the drive toward death and the afterlife that so powerfully motivates Clarissa when her earthly love falls in ruin.

All of Richardson's novels together enable us to see his achievement as one of the eighteenth-century climaxes in realizing the Miltonic ideal of friendship, love, and marriage and also the post-Edenic frustrations of that ideal. His range is as impressive as his penetration, and his entire treatment of love through all the novels is so encyclopedic that it is as much in need of an index as his last novel, which, like Pope's *Iliad*, was provided with one as a convenient guide to its sentiments. What an exploration of the recesses of the heart is stimulated by a full and careful contemplation of the following relations: Pamela and Mr. B; Pamela and the coarse, bisexual Mrs. Jewkes; Clarissa and Lovelace; Clarissa and the squat, toadlike Solmes; Clarissa and her sensible-fervent friend Anna; Anna and her meek lover, Hickman; Clarissa and the reformed rake, Belford; Lovelace and Anna; Harriet and Charlotte; Sir Charles and each of his women; Sir Charles and Lady Clementina's brother Jeronymo; Harriet and her other "sisters." Even to give a partial list is to suggest the richness, the essential health, and the ambiguities: a richness that fulfills the adumbrations of Lee, Otway, Dryden, Pope in *Eloisa*, Rowe, Steele, Lillo; a health that impressed Samuel Johnson, Jane Austen, and the Victorians; and the ambiguities that have titillated Gothicists, Romantics, and Freudians. Richardson, as decades of adverse criticism and neglect have shown, is not hard to dismiss or ignore. But, as our age has come to realize, to dismiss him for his surface conventionality is to dismiss one of the most richly nuanced psychological artists English literature has produced. It is a pity that the length of his works and the frequent piety of his tone make him unavailable to many. In a study of eighteenth-century love he will have to be regarded as a watershed.

RITA GOLDBERG

Clarissa Lives:
Sex and the Epistolary Novel

Clarissa, then, has delivered herself into the hands of her complex and dangerous suitor, Lovelace. Once she leaves Harlowe Place, the interplay of plots, the confusion between authentic and manufactured identities, the counterpoint of voices, create such a dense fabric that any analysis leaves as much behind as it accounts for. If we were to make comparisons between *Clarissa* and other art forms, indeed, we could choose the opera, a genre which was of great interest to Diderot and Rousseau. What is lacking, however, is that staple of operatic menus, the lovers' duet. There are quarrels in abundance between Clarissa and Lovelace, but only one occasion (the day before the rakes come to supper) when tenderness prevails on both sides. Even then, Clarissa only admits some affection for Lovelace, and that grudgingly, in a letter to Anna Howe. There are no direct confessions of true feeling between these troubled lovers. The area of actual contact between them is always a battlefield. Only after the skirmishes are over do they retreat and reflect on the reality and depth of their love (or hatred).

The few letters which *are* exchanged between the two protagonists are invariably misinterpreted. "Never was there such a pair of scribbling lovers as we," remarks Lovelace in a letter to his confidant, John Belford, "yet perhaps whom it so much concerns to keep from each other what each other writes." The most famous example of such a failure of communication is Lovelace's misunderstanding of a letter which Clarissa sends him near the end of the novel. "Sir," she writes,

From *Sex and Enlightenment: Women in Richardson and Diderot.* © 1984 by Cambridge University Press.

> I have good news to tell you. I am setting out with all diligence
> for my father's house. I am bid to hope that he will receive his
> poor penitent with a goodness peculiar to himself; for I am over-
> joyed with the assurance of a thorough reconciliation, through
> the interposition of a dear, blessed friend whom I always loved
> and honoured.

Lovelace believes that the Harlowes have taken her back. Overjoyed, he ex-
ults in a letter to Belford about the happiness he will now enjoy with Clarissa.
Belford, engaged in other matters, cannot enlighten him about the true state
of things until very much later. Clarissa, of course, is referring to her immi-
nent death: by "my father" she means God. She is thinking allegorically, as
if she were only half present in the literal world.

We can compare this spiritual *double entendre* to the many examples
of sexual *double entendre* which are so common in French novels of the same
period. It is curious, after all, that a work which is so deeply concerned with
sexuality has so little to do with romantic love. It has been commonly said
that the gap between love and sex, and indeed between marriage and love,
was far greater in the social life of upper-class Paris than it ever was in London, and there seems little reason to doubt the assertion. But if we turn to
the novels of Diderot and, later, Laclos for confirmation of these social facts,
we must also remember that they reveal as much about their literary origins
as about their social environment. Diderot and Laclos had perhaps the deepest
insights of any of their contemporaries except Rousseau into the Richardsonian world view. While Rousseau chose to amend the original vision by giving love an ascendancy over sex, Diderot and Laclos recognized that Richardson was exploring the assault on individuality through sex, and they took
this notion to extremes that would probably have shocked the English
novelist.

Clarissa, then, would most likely make a bad opera because there are
no love-scenes, no opportunities for harmonious reconciliation, in this mer-
ciless world of letters. This seems quite surprising when we think about letter-
writing. Correspondence has been a favoured means of expressing and even
enlarging romantic love; but it does not function in such a way in *Clarissa*.
The epistolary technique, however, is enormously subtle, because it reflects
the tensions in and the development of character under stress. One can take
the changing attitude of John Belford as an example: he grows from a rather
passive defender of Clarissa into her executor, and becomes the main source
for an account of her death. It allows us to learn of subplots which parallel
and illuminate the main action: the lively Anna Howe's courtship by the dull
but virtuous Hickman, for instance. Through it, we may be treated to several

versions of the same events, so that we can know the true depth of Lovelace's duplicity and of Clarissa's innocence. Much has been made of the intimacy of the epistolary structure. We see the characters at their most "relaxed," as it were, because they are writing to their closest friends, who are sometimes critical but never dismissive. But in another way, the epistolary structure also distances us. We learn of events at second hand; they are always being retold.

Clarissa's raving after the rape, for example, is recounted entirely by Lovelace. Here the epistolary style is used most advantageously. We can observe the counterpoint between Lovelace's account of her behaviour and his own commentary upon it. The breakdown is a time of self-revelation for Clarissa. All the while we are aware of the irony in learning of these truths from the man who has brought Clarissa to them through his duplicity. The effect of the lengthy ellipsis is stunning: we are slowly led to realize the enormity of the rape through its repercussions. It is the great unmentionable, like a religious epiphany, and we are told what happened only after Clarissa has had the presence of mind to escape from the brothel for good. This long first "absence" prefigures Clarissa's death: it is followed by a great deal of writing from her. When she grows too weak to continue, detailed accounts from Belford to Lovelace take over. After her death there is a flood of posthumous letters from her, while the novel ends with Lovelace's death. In this way, her consciousness dominates the book.

But throughout the novel it has been a strangely disembodied consciousness, just as Lovelace's has been. When we consider Richardson's emphasis on the integrity of the person, it is odd that the active expression of the self through deeds carries relatively little weight. We are given direct access to thoughts and emotions, but not to events: it is as if plot were an outer shell, an encumbrance like Clarissa's richly dressed suits, to be got rid of as soon as possible. This attention to the inner life seems extremely modern today, and helps, again, to explain the novel's ineligibility for opera. There is very little spectacle, very little dialogue between the main figures. As Johnson said in a celebrated remark: "Why, Sir, if you were to read Richardson for the story, your impatience would be so much fretted that you would hang yourself. But you must read him for the sentiment, and consider the story as only giving occasion for the sentiment."

On the other hand, the contortions of the plot certainly make for liveliness when they occur, but they depend largely on a misreading of one character by another. Lovelace can trick Clarissa into thinking that Tomlinson is a deliverer, and that the prostitutes are ladies, by playing on her ignorance of the world. But *we* are not allowed to be ignorant. We are co-conspirators, and the moving principle is dramatic irony. The plot doesn't function the way a thriller's would, for example, and there are few surprises.

Even Lovelace's stratagems are literary or dramatic: we have impersonation, forged letters, tampering with correspondence, and *coups de théâtre* such as the escape from Harlowe Place or Lovelace's appearance at Hampstead dressed as an old man, after Clarissa's flight from Mother Sinclair's and before the subsequent rape. They are not developed for or from the novel as such, the way they might be in Balzac, Dickens or Tolstoy. The social context and events in themselves have little meaning and no independent momentum. Even when the prostitutes have Clarissa arrested, the situation and language suggest that we are confronting something which is not so much a narrative event as a linguistic and moral one. In this case, it centres around one of the preoccupations in the novel: the proper sphere and content of Law.

From Clarissa's point of view, criminality has little to do with conventional ideas about law. This ambiguity of definition is one of the great ironic currents in the novel. "The Law shall be all my resource: The Law, . . . The Law only shall be my refuge!" she cries, on the verge of suicide after the rape. It is quite clear that she is not referring to the law of the land, nor even to conventional religious notions of legality, since she is about to plunge a penknife into her heart. After all, she has refused to litigate with her father for the control of her estate (which would have granted her freedom from her family and from both her suitors); and she never consents to bringing charges against Lovelace. Shortly after her escape from him, she is arrested on false charges. The description of the scene of the arrest, as related by Belford to Lovelace, who has had nothing to do with this particular trick, is illuminating.

> As she came out of the church, at the door fronting Bedford Street, the officers, stepping to her, whispered that they had an action against her.
>
> She was terrified, trembled, and turned pale.
>
> *Action*! said she. What is that? I have committed *no bad action*! Lord bless me! men, what mean you?
>
> That you are our prisoner, madam.
>
> *Prisoner*, sirs!—What—How—Why—What have I done?
>
> You must go with us. Be pleased, madam, to step into this chair.
>
> With *you*! With *men*! I am not used to go with *strange men*! Indeed you must excuse me!
>
> We can't excuse you: we are sheriff's officers. We have a writ against you. You *must* go with us, and you shall know at whose suit.

This little scene, like so many others in the book, is full of precise detail. The officers meet Clarissa on the Bedford Street side of the church; she trembles and goes pale; every turn of dialogue is recorded. But it is also fraught with the quality of nightmare. For Clarissa, the encounter is an effect without a cause. She is being arrested without having committed a crime, without even a clue as to what she might be accused of. As in a dream, she misunderstands what the men are saying. Her *malentendu*, however, reveals another awareness: it serves to reinforce the strong sense of her own identity, made deeper by suffering. She is terrified, because she *does* have a secret, the rape, and she has no idea how much the sheriff's men know about her. We may look at part of the passage again: "the officers, stepping to her, whispered that they had an action against her . . . *Action*! said she. What is that? I have committed *no bad action*!"

Indeed she has not. Clarissa's story is of a passion, in the Christian sense, which must be strongly distinguished from mere passivity. Like all moral passions of this kind, her suffering is purposeful, and offers a direct challenge to society. While we think of the Christian martyr as one who rejects the flesh in favour of the spirit, we have in Clarissa a heroine for whom the flesh is essential. It is true that she transcends earthly rewards in her death, but it is important to remember that the source of her spiritual triumph has all along been her insistence on the integrity of the person, body and spirit. It is this consciousness that gives her the courage to refuse Solmes, and that destroys any hopes for worldly happiness after the rape. In the passage under discussion, the men "have an action against her." It is not difficult to see that by now Clarissa identifies men with action and action with evil. Hence her disbelieving reply: "Action? . . . I have committed *no bad action*!"

Here, the legal word "action" functions in several ways. It brings home to Clarissa the constant necessity of defining her own limits, of being clear in her mind that *she* is not guilty of the rape. But the men, by bringing an "action" against her, force her into the polar thinking which we have desscribed. Men are active, but do not feel; women are feeling, but cannot act; therefore she cannot have committed a *bad action*. Action has become a sexual distinction, because all Clarissa's experience of men shows that they cannot both feel and do. The brilliantly changeable Lovelace, champion of freethinking, is but the most extreme example.

If we continue further in our analysis we notice, of course, that the passage identifies "action," which is both male and negative, with the law, which comes apparently out of nowhere to punish Clarissa. The charge has actually been brought by the prostitutes, who are women in complicity with men. This blurring of sexual roles has some importance in other contexts, particularly in connection with Diderot. But the significant point in this bit of dialogue is that the undertones tell us about Clarissa's consciousness and the impressions that events (which are always secondary in importance to their human impact) make on it. Even her misinterpretations of the world are characteristic.

One can contrast this view of action (which takes its sexual form in the rape) with Ian Watt's. "In the realm of action," writes Watt, "the rape itself, when Clarissa is unconscious from opiates, may be regarded as the ultimate development of the idea of the feminine sexual role as one of passive suffering: it suggests that the animality of the male can only achieve its purpose when the woman's spirit is absent." This view, while a common one, is mistaken. Many critics and novelists have seen Clarissa in this way, and the trivializations that followed her *have* portrayed "the lass with the delicate air" (to borrow loosely a chapter heading from *Pamela's Daughters*, that amusing book by Robert Utter and Gwendolyn Needham), for whom sex itself is the ultimate evil. But it is nonetheless curious that even so perceptive a critic as Watt has not seen that this novel centres on a rape, not on conventional expressions of sexuality. Faced with this particular violation, many readers seem to lose their literary alertness. Instead of seeing the rape as a kind of murder of the identity for which the sexual aspect is only a metaphor, they are reduced to conventional phrases about female masochism and sexual passivity, as Watt is later in the same passage.

But Watt has touched on the deep mythological structure in *Clarissa* (indeed, it is difficult not to do so, since it informs the text at every point). The male world in *Clarissa* is seen as potentially criminal, though individual men are not necessarily evil. We can reflect, however, that even the wise and decent cousin Morden becomes a duellist and a murderer, though he deliberately breaks his promise to the dying Clarissa to do so. At the least, one may conclude from a reading of *Clarissa* that the institutions which men have created are powerful, and therefore not to be trusted by their victims, who are usually women. Indeed, the very scantiness of energetic action and its consequences.

We can again consider Clarissa's reluctance to litigate with her father for her estate, which would give her independence, or to bring Lovelace to court for rape. Lovelace plays upon this ambivalence in Clarissa and knows that she will never bring suit against him. Indeed, even before Clarissa's rape (which has already been planned and is included in his exalted reverie) he fantasizes about raping Anna Howe, whose letters he has been intercepting, and even Anna's mother. He includes his band of four rakish friends in the enterprise, describes in detail what the rapes would be like, and goes on to consider the consequences:

> Well, but shall we not be in danger of being hanged for three such enormous rapes . . .?

Yes, to be sure, when caught. But is there any likelihood of that? Besides, have we not been in danger before now for worse facts? and what is there in being in *danger*? If we actually were to appear in open day in England before matters are made up, there will be greater likelihood that these women will *not* prosecute than that they *will*.—For my own part, I should wish they *may*. Would not a brave fellow choose to appear in court to such an arraignment, confronting women who would do credit to his attempt? The country is more merciful in *these* cases than in *any others*: I should therefore like to put myself upon my country.

If caught, he continues, he would turn the trial into a triumphant occasion. He compares himself to a public figure, a general mayor, or ambassador, and ends the elaborate description complacently:

Then we shall be praised—even the judges, and the whole crowded bench, will acquit us in their hearts; and every single man wish he had been me!—the women, all the time, disclaiming prosecution, were the case to be their own. To be sure, Belford, the sufferers cannot put half so good a face upon the matter as we. . . .

Well, but suppose, after all, we are convicted; what have we to do, but in time make over our estates, that the sheriffs may not revel in our spoils? There is no fear of being hanged for such a crime as this, while we have *money* or *friends*. And suppose even the worst, that two or three were to die, have we not a chance, each of us, to escape? The devil's in 'em, if they'll hang five for ravishing three!

I know I shall get off for one—were it but for family sake: and being a handsome fellow, I shall have a dozen or two of young maidens, all dressed in white, go to court to beg my life. And what a pretty show they will make, with their white hoods, white gowns, white petticoats, white scarves, white gloves, kneeling for me, with their white handkerchiefs at their eyes, in two pretty rows, as his majesty walks through them and nods my pardon for their sakes!—And, if once pardoned, all is over: for, Jack, in a crime of this nature there lies no appeal, as in a murder.

Lovelace is, of course, justified in his confidence that the law—the law of the land, that is—would be on his side if Clarissa or Anna were ever to bring suit. In the eighteenth century as in the twentieth, it is the victim who is on trial when an accusation of rape is brought before a court of law. As we shall see, Richardson amplifies this insight in a variety of ways throughout the novel. But this passage is also typically Richardsonian in its use of a real social situation as a reflection, or perhaps even refraction, of a character's imagination. The description expands from a hard-hearted perception of Lovelace's legal position into an inflation of the external world in which the rake becomes a public figure, almost a god, accompanied by his vestal virgins, over whom only a king has authority.

Political comparisons abound in Lovelace's letters. Tyrants, kings and generals from ancient history are often invoked. The real helplessness, in legal and social terms, of the women Lovelace encounters contributes greatly to his sense of his own power. But his power is exercised almost entirely in fantasy. The impulse to remake the world in the image of that fantasy breaks into actual deeds only now and then: the discarded plans, the almost hallucinatory exaltations, are evidence enough that an internal life only slightly enlarged by contact with real women is quite enough for Lovelace. He is no Robespierre: he is on the side of authority, and knows it to be his friend. It is quite striking that he has no political or military aspirations at all, unlike real-life eighteenth-century rakes such as John Wilkes. His dominion is internal. He is really a sportsman, like his aristocratic ancestors, but he stalks ideas and identities rather than the game-birds with which he so often compares his female prey. The imperial parallels which he frequently draws remind us of the society and tradition which support and affirm him.

Clarissa may therefore be looked upon, with reason, as the perpetual victim, the unjustly accused political prisoner in a male world where rapists and the rapacious alike go free. Clarissa's crime, if it could be called such, is her unwillingness to go against an inner principle of wholeness. Anna Howe points this out early in the novel (and Clarissa's awareness of her own integrity remains a constant topic in the correspondence). The famous passage in which Anna points out that virtue itself marks Clarissa off from her persecutors is a constant point of reference throughout the novel. Clarissa's insistence upon chastity as a vehicle of integrity has perhaps led to her lack of popularity in our own century. Readers have tended to see her as a representative of the most unpleasant side of the Puritan ethic, that which treats women as property, and unwed deflowered girls as damaged goods (even though Clarissa herself makes numerous comments on the interaction of love and property relations). It is confusing that Clarissa was seen, even in her own time, as an apotheosis of womanhood: for us this blurs the clarity of her moral struggle. But in the novel she is singleminded, a person absolutely unable to compromise, whose will cannot be broken or even bent by anyone. Such behaviour hardly conforms to an ideal of female passivity.

ROSEMARY BECHLER

Reading the Fire-Scene
in Clarissa

Musing upon the "concept of irreconcilable opposites" which informs the tragedy of *Clarissa*, Margaret Doody comments that it is "an extremely odd novel, noticeably different from the dominant fictions of Richardson's own day." Richardson himself, beseiged with demands for a happy ending, often complained that the work had been misunderstood. If, in his postscript to the final volume, he is not more explicit about the "great end" he had "in view," it is because, in a period hovering perilously between a notion of nature as a moral resource and as no moral resource at all, *Clarissa* constituted a most daring project. For Samuel Richardson, nature manifests the fatal divide between the light and the fire, the love and the wrath of God, in a tragic conflict which is at the same time the essence of life as well as the necessary condition for sustaining the possibility of progression back to the original unity. In this battle between good and evil, "The No is an opponent of the Yes, or of truth, in order that the truth may become apparent" (Jacob Boehme, *Theosophische Fragen* [trans. M. H. Abrams]). Instead of a system of immutable laws revealing to man God's infinite, scientific wisdom, this "odd novel" posits a world of restless "Strife and Contrariety" which serves the purpose in human time of expressing its meaning. Structured around its "double yet separate correspondence" (author's preface), *Clarissa* seeks to express in fiction a profound fundamentalist reaction against the rational and pragmatic tendencies of the age.

Further research needs to be done into the extraordinary circle with whom Richardson was intimate during the years in which he planned and

---

© 1987 by Rosemary Bechler. Published for the first time in this volume.

penned *Clarissa*—a circle which notably included his friend and physician, George Cheyne, until his death in 1743; the "English mystic" William Law and his disciple John Byrom; Dr. John Heylin and the well-known surgeon, also Richardson's doctor and close neighbour, John Freke, who published his *Treatise on the Nature of Fire* in 1752. But it is clear that throughout the 1740s and early 1750s, Law, Byrom, Freke and Richardson at least, collaborated closely on the printing and publication of a series of texts. It was this circle, he told Aaron Hill, who saw *Clarissa* in its early stages—all persons "whom I could not deny." Freke's treatise on fire, written during this period and applauded by William Law, takes an obscure line from Horace as its epigraph, later quoted by Lovelace. In 1750, we find Richardson and Freke correcting the proof sheets of Byrom's poem "Enthusiasm" based on Law's *Appeal* of 1742—an occasion Byrom celebrated with some sprightly verses attacking Aaron Hill's popular manual on the *Art of Acting*, but complimenting the author of *Clarissa*: "Nevertheless,—with freedom may I speak? / Yes, to be sure, to R——n, or F——ke!—." In 1749, Richardson had printed another poem by Byrom, "An Epistle to a Gentleman of the Temple," which upheld Law's position as expressed in the *Spirit of Prayer:—OR The Soul rising out of the Vanity of Time into the Riches of Eternity* against the Bishop of London in a controversy concerning the fate of man. In 1752, he printed Law's *Way to Divine Knowledge*, having handled all Cheyne's works from 1733 onwards.

We know that "the Brethren" not only have the Tory and Non-Juring or Jacobite sympathies of their Collierite predecessors in common, but that like Richardson they had "always shown a Relish for spiritual and internal Religion." This particular commitment to an enthusiast pietism is inspired by writings in the hermetic tradition which go back to the early seventeenth-century works of the German mystic Jacob Boehme, and to his subtle and influential innovation upon the Christian form of the Neoplatonic circle of emanation and return. To some Pietists in Germany and a number of Inner Light Puritans in England, he bequeathed the compelling vision of a fallen universe which is constituted throughout by an opposition of quasi-sexual contraries. These contraries are at once mutually attractive and repulsive, their momentary conciliations giving way to renewed attempts at mastery by the opponent powers. What then clearly distinguishes the works of this circle is the resulting dialectical emphasis on God's inclusivity. God's wrath is only His love effected by the principle of separation or division from the source. If, throughout Richardson's novel, Clarissa's "Sunclad power of Chastity" which blazes upon Lovelace, "as it were, in a flood of light" is starkly contrasted with his fiery lust which threatens at every moment "to scorch her into a cinder" like another Semele, nevertheless fire only becomes destructive if it is "unable to reach, touch or obtain any spark of Light and love, to make its fire-life sweet and amiable" (William Law, *The Grounds and Reasons of Christian Regeneration*). For Richardson, as for Law and Freke, there is a fire which illuminates and purifies and there is one which destroys because it "cannot help itself to that which it wants, but is always working against itself." But in the end they are the same. Moreover, as male and female, Richardson's protagonists are the two terms in an opposition, but the same opposition can be found separately in each. Both characters have to develop through conflictual time to a greater or lesser extent. In the opening letter of *Clarissa*, Anna Howe refers to the heroine's "deserved motto," "rather useful than glaring," and adds, "tho' now, to your regret, pushed into blaze, as I may say; and yet blamed at home for the faults of others."

It is furthermore typical of this group that they follow the strict demarcation which the seventeenth-century Inner Light Puritans draw between enthusiasm as the public display of controversial innovation, and enthusiasm as very private, not to say secretive, piety. Cherishing that mysterious communication which is the growth of God within, they all directed some of their fiercest polemicizing against what they regarded as the scandal of the age, public desecrations of God's power. William Law first came to prominence with the *Absolute Unlawfulness of the stage-entertainment fully demonstrated* in 1726; Freke's treatise is an attack on those popular public experiments which turned natural philosophy into a vulgar "raree-show"; Richardson's earliest publications include a pamphlet attacking the contemporary stage and the *Apprentice's Vade Mecum* (1733), which is full of Collierite argument. He repeatedly refers to that "taste even to wantonness for out-door pleasure and luxury" as *the* justification for his own writing. Divided from controversialists such as the Methodists by this distaste for exposure, Richardson's circle was marked by public conformity to the rituals of the church, whilst quietly destroying all evidence of their correspondence. This of course has important implications for the novelist's chosen epistolary form, supporting and enriching Roy Roussel's insights into that "paradoxical double movement" in the writer's consciousness whereby his "withdrawal . . . is balanced by a seemingly contradictory movement which carries him to an intimate union with another." It further ensures that the tension between the privacy of the novel form and theatre as public performance is a main arena of the battle between Clarissa and Lovelace.

Richardson's initial concern was not that his readers would succumb to Lovelace's charms. It was enough to show conclusively in the deadlock of wills that he was loveless. But as the first readers misread Clarissa's "delicacy" over his offers of marriage as prudery, and in the gathering out-cry against the tragic ending, Richardson was forced to spell out what Lovelace was. To the second edition he adds the notes which emphasize his premeditated baseness, but in the third edition he "replaces a page of report by thirteen of dramatic argument" in the form of another false proposal scene which is then the first in a series of four.

William Beatty Warner comments astutely that by adding this, "Richard-son tries to make all that subsequently happens seem preordained." Warner's own reading of this sequence of scenes as "melodramatic struggles to con-trol Clarissa's body" which "often resemble nothing so much as two flames contending" is the most suggestive of modern accounts, not least because it is so thoroughly "Lovelacean." Thus, the "parallelism" he detects in their approaches and withdrawals "invites the reader to . . . join two lovers ap-parently only separated by the unlucky timing of their moments of obstinacy." Clinging to evidence that Lovelace's proposals are sometimes "genuine," such a reader scours those scenes for the moments of promise "where the story of Clarissa and Lovelace suddenly opens out to comedy and love." Lovelace similarly projects the possibility of a comic resolution to a drama he is in-clined to entitle, "The Quarrelsome Lovers" and whose scripting and direc-tion he believes are within his power.

What reader within living memory of a Congreve ending would not enter-tain the glorious possibility:

> MILLAMENT: Why does not the man take me? Would you have me give myself to you over again?
> MIRABELL: Aye, and over and over again, for (kisses her hand) I would have you as often as possibly I can.

Yet one might as well argue that Romeo and Juliet are "only separated" by the non-arrival of a letter from Verona to Mantua, or Cathy and Heathcliff, by the latter's "unlucky timing" in vacating the kitchen settle. As in those other manuals of Romantic Love, the possibility of comic resolution haunts the central impasse as a measure of its tragedy. In itself, it is no solution. Warner complains, "By dying without any explicit 'cause' for doing so, Clarissa allows blame for her death to spread and infect everyone who has touched her life." But this is precisely Richardson's argument, "to rescue her from a Rake, and give a Triumph to her not only over him, but over all her Oppressors, and the World besides." The cause lies in the scale and intran-sigence of that impasse. In his new fourth proposal scene, it is this totality and deadlock which as ever, Richardson is concerned to prove.

The most obvious effect of the addition, and it is an important one as we shall see, since it is the basis on which we would be asked to reject the Millament-Mirabell concept of consummation, is to increase the sheer repetitiousness of the succeeding proposal scenes. But within the scene itself, Richardson mainly resorts to strengthening his hints about Lovelace's relationship to fire.

Clarissa opens with the announcement, "We have had warmer dialogues than ever yet we had . . . he is such a wild, such an ungovernable creature (*He* reformed!), that I am half-afraid of him." When he snatches her hand, pressing it to his lips "in a strange wild way" crying "But to give you up upon *cold* conditions, D——n me . . . if I either will or can!" Clarissa comments "his behaviour was so strangely wild and fervent that I was perfectly frighted. I thought he would have devoured my hand. I wished myself a thousand miles distant from him." Lovelace's own account confirms that he is "a rapid, a boisterous Lover," that he was "ready to devour" her hand, and adds, "There was, I believe, a kind of phrensy in my manner, which threw her into a panic, like that of Semele perhaps, when the Thunderer, in all his majesty, surrounded with ten thousand celestial burning-glasses, was about to scorch her into a cinder." He explains that although he had recently undertaken to act a "*gentle*" and "*polite* part," he had failed to command the necessary restraint, concluding with the characteristic pun on *l'honnête homme*, "It is exceedingly difficult, thou seest, for an honest man to act in disguise: As the Poet says, 'Thrust Nature back with a pitchfork, it will return.' " This account comes shortly after Lovelace's complaint that Clarissa is "almost *eternally* shutting up myself from him"; his assertion that the light of the Bible "is too glaring to be borne"; and the express wish to get at Clarissa's correspondence, although a "detected invasion in an article so sacred, would ruin me beyond retrieve." It is immediately followed by the denial that he is the cause of the Harlowe family's anger: "I only point the Lightning, and teach it where to dart without the Thunder. In other words, I only guide the Effects: The Cause is in their malignant hearts" and by a new resolve to make Clarissa "acknowledge a *lambent* flame, a preference of me to all other men, at least: And then my happy hour is not far off." Lovelace is not the only one with a warm temper. The Harlowes are "flaming and malevolent spirits," and even Anna Howe will shortly burn a letter before her mother's face rather than let her read it, and have to be begged "not to be inflamed," and to terminate her correspondence with Clarissa, "lest I should be thought an *inflamer*."

Against a general background of real and potential conflagration which will reach one kind of culmination in the fire-scene, we are asked to consider, as in so many Restoration comedies, the true character of the rake. The quotation from Horace, "Thrust Nature back with a pitch-fork, it will return" is the best clue of all, since as the epigraph to John Freke's 1746 *Essay to shew the Cause of Electricity*, it plunges us straight into the battle which had raged over the last five years between Freke and the leading natural philosopher of his day, Benjamin Martin, concerning the real nature of fire. At the time, it was not at all clear that the natural philosopher had the upper hand. His desperate campaign to differentiate his "noble science" from its "vile prostitution" by "quacks and illiterate pretenders" ended in bankruptcy and a failed suicide attempt, while Richardson's friend was a Fellow of the Royal Society and one of the great men of Tory London. He was defending the "learned Professions . . . *Physics* and *Divinity*" against the encroachment of experimental philosophy in a key controversy over the spirituality of matter.

At the centre of the contention were the enormously popular electricity lectures which gave the miraculous phenomenon of electricity a privileged place in the culture of the 1740s. Natural philosophy set itself the task of producing dramatic and wonderful active powers by the manipulation of inert matter, thus proving the immanence of divine power in the material world. A rapidly improved apparatus allowed a repertoire of such spectacles as "the electrical Venus," "the beatification" in which a crown would emit a halo of sparks round the head of the wearer, the Lightning, the Ignis Fatuus, the Shooting Stars and Aurora Borealis. In evoking wonder, such spectacles reached the consciences of the audience, making them aware of the rational powers of the human mind to discover God's laws governing the most inanimate matter.

The moral validation of natural philosophy thus lay in the performance itself, in its ability "to represent the principal Appearances of Nature to the *view* of the Audience." Martin's notes were available only at his lectures. There are important links here with the theatre of moral sensibility as in Steele's preface to the trend-setting *Conscious Lovers* (1722) where again performance is preferred to reading: "for the greatest Effect of a Play in reading is to excite the Reader to go see it; and when he does so, it is then a Play has the Effect of Example and Precept." Martin spelt out the theatrical appeal of his method of instruction in his most popular lecture commentary, the *Philosophia Britannica* (1747):

> That vast variety of things which here present themselves may
> have the pleasure that attends variety heighten'd and increased
> by emerging fresh to the view as he passes along, and regaling
> him with something still novel and unexpected. Annotations seem
> to answer the end of scenes in a play: they present the whole most
> agreeably in parts, which thus more immediately affects us and
> gives us the greatest pleasure and entertainment.

Freke like Richardson is quick to point out the danger of such a theatre of susceptibility to credulous minds. These are so many "Tricks like Ledgerdemain . . . performed by him whose Time is little worth," "Bizarreries . . . to raise the Astonishment it is wont to do in uninformed Minds."

But he has much more fundamental objections to Martin's scheme. Taking his inspiration from Law's most eloquent analysis of the Behmenist doctrine of fire, the *Appeal to all that Doubt or Disbelieve The Truths of the Gospel* (1740), Freke argues that electric powers are not active principles placed in matter by God and released by the machines of the experimental philosophers, but an emanation of the divine fire which is the source of life and the spiritual property of all material things, the desire of all things "to return to their first state of glory":

> Quench this Desire, and suppose there is nothing in the Matter
> of this World that desires to be restored to its first Glory, and
> then all the breaking forth of Fire, Light, Brightness and Glance,
> in the Things of this World, is utterly quenched with it.

Originally dispersed harmoniously throughout the universe, this principle, which Freke claims should be called "Vivacity" rather than electricity, is conserved and circulated through nature by the agency of the Sun, "a machine or engine." But when its distribution is upset through death, disharmony or "the Contrivance of Man," the divine fire becomes visible as the wrath of God. When "more of this Fire" was "crowded together, than was intended by the Author of all Uniformity," it would be "no Wonder, in this confined state, if that . . . which would be gentle and beneficent, should, with all the Power that belongs to it, break out at the first Door which is opened for its Passage from this tortur'd state" (*An Essay to shew the Cause of Electricity*). It will blaze out, devour, invade and comminute into separate parts. Or when the surplus "*Capsula*" of "lambent flame" meets the resistance of a dead body such as an insulator, it will display all the qualities of electrical phenomena, alternate attraction and repulsion, sparks and electric glow. There is no virtue in such a display. It is the wrath of God as the self-torment of nature. A true understanding of the divine can come only through illumination, not demonstration.

The inner light is the only path to salvation. Thus Freke scornfully concludes, "is it not a great Disgrace to the Learned to employ this great secret of Nature . . . and with such mean Tricks to go on in contenting themselves rather with the Shew of it than seek into the Cause of its amazing greatness?" (*Treatise on the Nature and Property of Fire*). Those "whose Time is little worth" with their "Kill-Time" amusements commit a grave offence indeed, since "as every intelligent Creature is its own *Self-mover*, so every intelligent

Creature has Power of *kindling* and *inflaming* its Will, Imagination, and
Desire as it pleases, with Shadows, Fictions, or Realities; with Things carnal
or spiritual, temporal or eternal" (Law, *An Appeal*). What the illumined may
understand from the workings of fire is that in nature, as in human nature,
desire "perpetually generates either life or death in us."

Lovelace the contriver does not understand. Resisting the light of God,
as of Clarissa, his own fire, "bound, compacted, shut up and imprisoned,"
he attributes his anger to her resistance, and directs his yearning to be restored
to glory, against her. His "frenzy" is a desire kindled with "things carnal,"
an essential confusion of flesh for spirit. Thus in wanting to make Clarissa
"acknowledge" a lambent flame, he both mistakes the nature of her love and
forces her into an increasingly clandestine correspondence. Again, adopting
the position of the natural philosopher, he claims only to "point the Lightning . . . without the Thunder" of the Harlowe anger. But he consistently
refuses to understand the dual nature of fire, its potential either for "life or
death in us." Where he claims to "only guide the effect," he forces the wrath
of God within the family into visibility and thus malignancy. For the wrath
of God is not in its "causes" malignant as he maintains: "The Fire of a Can-
dle is of the same Kind as that which burns a House" (Freke, *Treatise*). In
not understanding this, Lovelace must tragically misapply Freke's epigraph.
Freke gives the Horace quotation a dual application corresponding to the
dual aspect of divine fire. In revealing the cause of that electrical fire which
is tortured into visibility by the experimentalists' apparatus, he also reveals
its divinity. But for Lovelace, to act gently is to "disguise" the true aggression of his fervour. The "honest man" is a devourer. In a later moment of
victory, Clarissa, we are told, "taking one of the lights . . . turned from us;
and away she went unmolested!" Clarissa's turning away and her secret correspondence is indeed "sacred." It is a preservation of hidden "Vivacity." But
Lovelace misinterprets hidden fire as disguised fire which then must blaze
out to destroy what it loves. His confusion can only increase that self-torment
which is the separation and death of things.

It is here Richardson engages in an earlier sister controversy over whether
or not "a reformed rake makes the best husband," prompted by the play which
announced the arrival of sentimental comedy. In Colley Cibber's *Love's Last
Shift* (1696), Loveless (frequently misspelt Lovelace by Collier and others)
is reclaimed from his libertine vagrancy by his virtuous wife, Amanda, who
poses as a courtesan and having "charm'd him even to a Madness of impure
Desire" and satisfied it, reveals her identity, thus happily reconciling virtue
and pleasure. If the official moral of the play holds that "there are Charms
in Virtue, nay, stronger and more pleasing far than hateful Vice can boast

of," Loveless's case is at least as central to the dramatic argument: "Most of your Sex confound the very Name of Virtue; for they would seem to live without Desires; which cou'd they do, that were not Virtue . . . for who can boast a Victory when they have no foe to conquer?" Cibber was nothing if not calculating: "Such out-of-fashion Stuff! / But then again, / He's lewd for above four acts, gentlemen! / For faith, he knew, when once he'd changed his fortune / And reformed his vice, 'twas time to drop the curtain";—while Thomas Davies recorded that at this redemption of the rake, the audience shed honest tears. But his "reformed" comedy also provoked one of the great plays of the 1690s in gentlemanly reply.

Scornful of the ambiguities of Cibber's feminine ideal as of his rake's reclaim, John Vanbrugh's *The Relapse* (1696) is about real temptation, and as Aubrey Williams has shown, distinguishes carefully between Probationis, in which God tempts and tries His children, and Seductionis which is an attempt to seduce, overcome, undo, including the gratuitous seeking out of "occasions of sin." Loveless's relapse is the result of his confusion of the two. Resolving to test his new-found virtue in the "uneasy Theater" of London, he claims, "This Winter shall be the *fiery Trial* of my Virtue, / Which, when it once has proved, / You'll be convinced 'twas of no false Alloy / There all your cares will end." The attractions of the "uneasy Theater" are not so lightly disclaimed, and Loveless falls. Rescripting Worthy as a sophisticated libertine, Vanbrugh provides his Amanda with a real temptation which she victoriously withstands. Jeremy Collier objected violently—particularly to Worthy's sudden conversion:

> what can be more improbable than that so Profane and finished a Debauchee, so weak in principle, and so violent in Passion, should run from one extreme to another? Should break through Custom, and Metamorphose Desire at so short a warning? To solicit to Rudeness, and talk Sentences and Morality, to be Pious and Profane in the same Breath must be very extraordinary.

Here was a much more insidious confusion of virtue and pleasure. It was an argument the beleaguered Richardson would be forced to revive.

But when Elkanah Settle entered the debate with *A Farther Defence of Dramatick Poetry: Being the Second Part of the Review of Mr. Collier's View of the Immorality and Profaneness of the Stage* (1698), it was clear that the "fiery trial" under discussion was that embodied in the theatre itself:

> Virtue cannot very well be wrought up to any *Dramatick* Perfection, nor sparkle with any considerable Brightness and Beauties,

unless it stands a Temptation, and surmounts it. We have a Proverbial Saying, that will hardly allow that Woman to be truly chaste, that has never been try'd . . . Thus the Relapser's Amanda crowns her Character even with a double Laurel; not only by Illustrating and (I may, not improperly, say) Aggrandizing her own Invincible Virtue in the Assault she has repuls'd; but likewise, in the Conversion of her Assailing Libertine. 'Tis not supposed therefore that the *Dramatick* Poet must be oblig'd to borrow his Characters of Virtue from Lazy Cells, and Melancholy Cloysters, a Copy from a *Hermit*, or an *Anchoret.* No; His Characters of Virtue must come forth into the gay World, with Levity, Vanity, nay Temptation itself, all round them. They must go to the Court, the Ball, the Masque, the Musick-Houses, the Dancing-Schools, nay, to the very Prophane Play-Houses themselves, (to speak in Mr. Collier's Dialect) and yet come off unconquer'd. These are the Virtues that, to be Instructive to an Audience, are what should tread the Stage.

This is a masterpiece of provocation; nor, to the opposition, could it have been more improper. The especial piquancy of the challenge resides in the way Settle hovers, as he avers, "not improperly," between what we may call a mimetic and a materialistic defence of theatrical pleasure. On the whole, the men of wit, in not so dignified retreat, had been forced to regroup with increasing discomfort behind a vocabulary of representation, illustration and exemplary imitation.

The attack on them was well under way by the time Collier joined it, and the point of contention, once again, was the spirituality of matter. This core of Collier's argument Richardson fully grasps in the *Apprentice's Vade Mecum*, where the theatre must be shunned not only because of the notorious "great Resort of lewd Women to those Places," but because these *are* "Places where the Temptation is made the stronger, by the Impressions which the Musick and the Entertainment are liable to make." For Collier, "*Love* has generally a *Party Within*; and when the Wax is prepared, the Impression is easily made. Thus the Disease of the *Stage* grows Catching: It throws its own *Amours* among the Company, and forms these Passions when it does not find them." He endorsed Bossuet's memorable statement that men "become Vicious by committing Vice in Effigie." His own vocabulary, as in his favourite metaphor of contagion, is a constant denial of the protection afforded by the proscenium arch: "A Moral Sentence at the Close of a Lewd Play, is much like a Pious Expression in the Mouth of a Dying Man, who has been wicked all his Life time," "the acting of a religious Play upon the modern Theatre, would be next to a Libertine's preaching in a House of Prostitution." Its provocative juxtapositions of flesh and spirit not only anticipate the elegant similes of Law's campaign against Enlightenment reason—"You might as well write the Word, *Flame*, upon the outside of a *Flint*, and then expect that its imprisoned Fire should be *kindled* by it"—but provide Richardson with the metaphors of his art.

Settle's defence moves vauntingly in the opposite direction. The "Perfection" of virtue is that which the theatre can make "sparkle" with "Brightness and Beauties." Amanda, let it be said, not only illustrates virtue, she aggrandizes it, and this because her temptation is the splendid one of the theatre itself. Nay, Virtue can be no mere "Copy," no borrowed character, but she who must "come forth" into the public places. If she is to be "Instructive," it is because, in flesh and blood, she treads the stage. Recalling its heyday and the great pun of Nell Gwynne's epilogue to *Tyrannick Love*, this is a triumphant evocation of that hybrid being, the Restoration actor-character. Settle's argument is outrageous. Whether or not "a reformed rake makes the best husband," who else could know what a really good woman is?

This is, of course, Lovelace's point of view. "As gold is tried by fire," he chants, "and virtue by temptation, so is sterling wit by opposition." Two days later, he is hoping "in a while to get her with me to the public Entertainments . . . These diversions will amuse. And the deuce is in it, if a little Susceptibility will not put forth." A Worthy who has received Settle's blessing, he can to himself justify submitting Clarissa to a "complete trial." He can, moreover, "in a strange wild way" and in words uncomfortably close to Collier's, imagine his sudden conversion: "Mould me as you please: I am wax in your hands: Give me your own impression, and seal me for ever yours." But has not Worthy, like Lovelace, confused the two temptations? Are they not both seducers?

Richardson counters Cibber and Vanbrugh here, for in both plays the libertine takes the execution of temptation upon himself in his own interests. Not only this, but he assumes the credit and issues the reward. Lovelace also not only creates and worships a false goddess in Clarissa, but sets himself up as a false god to judge her. But who is he to judge, and what is the trial for? Again the point at issue is the status of material causes, or in Richardson's terms the question, what is the status of fire? to whom does fire belong? Lovelace believes that it is his fire which tests Clarissa, as he believes that it is this which destroys her. Like Worthy, he sees the highest possible outcome of his temptation as the emergence of a woman who can say no to him reluctantly. But Lovelace's contradictory endeavour has an even more paradoxical effect. For in destroying Clarissa, as he does, he also helps to create a saint. Lovelace is "a machine at last, and no free agent." The fire which indeed fragments her, which opens bodies, is also the alchemist's agent of transmutation. Lovelace's seduction is the work of the devil, but God turns defeat into victory. What the rake, whose credo depends upon the cynical separation of flesh and spirit, can never understand, is the spiritual destiny of all desire:

> that every Time you see a Piece of Matter dissolved by Fire, you have a *full Proof*, that all the Materiality of this World is appointed to a Dissolution by Fire, and that then, (O glorious Day!) Sun and Stars, and all the Elements, will be delivered from Vanity, will be again that *one eternal, harmonious glorious* Thing which they were, before they were compacted into *material* Distinctions and Separations.
>
> (Law, *An Appeal*)

That this joint provocation of natural philosophy and the theatre is Richardson's starting point, is borne out by the preface to *Clarissa*. The famous defence of "writing to the moment" is, point for point, Martin's prospectus:

> The following history is given in a series of letters . . . All the Letters are written while the heart of the writers must be supposed to be wholly engaged in their subjects . . . So that they abound not only with critical situations, but with . . . *instantaneous* Descriptions and Reflections . . . affecting Conversations; many of them written in the dialogue or dramatic way . . . *Much more* lively and affecting . . . in the height of a *present* distress.
>
> (Preface)

If there is any difference it lies in a degree of inwardness, since here it is the heart of the writer, rather than the audience and before the reader, which is immediately affected and "wholly engaged."

But when, ironically enough, Richardson was forced to defend the fire-scene against the charge of indecency, his argument was very close to Vanbrugh's own. Lovelace is an object of "Aversion." How then was Richardson's experiment different from Vanbrugh's or Martin's? The "Passion I found strongest in me, whenever I supposed myself a Reader only, and the Story real, was *Anger*, or *Indignation*." It is this emphasis on reading which makes the difference. For this is not one of those "fictions" which "kindle and enflame" the carnal will. It is the truth, and we consume it not in the flesh but in the spirit, with a righteous indignation—with that inward apprehension which Richardson's epistolary novels demand. We can begin to see what lies behind Byrom's apparently casual compliment to Richardson in 1750, that unlike the men of theatre his novelist's art can "distribute thus / All that is worth the notice in a play," for it is Richardson's strategy to claim for his novel all those attractions which the opposition offered, but to place them in the context of this very different spiritual drama.

Take Martin's emphasis on the "fresh," the "still novel," the "unexpected." Tony Tanner, commenting [in *Adultery in the Novel*] that without Lovelace there would be no novel and that "newelty, that was the man's word, was everything with him," asks, "what is a novel without 'newelty' and plot?" But within *Clarissa*, Richardson proceeds to place this quest for novelty as irredeemably loveless. It is Lovelace waiting for the fire who gloats, "I love to write to the *moment*"; Lovelace's "vehement aspiration after a novelty" which he thinks, "set me upon a desire to become a goddess-maker"; Lovelace who justifies the "life of honour" on the grounds that it "keeps Love in a continual fervour . . . . The happy pair, instead of sitting dozing . . . over a wintry Love, always new to each other and always having something to say"; and Lovelace who thinks that "my frequent egresses will make me look new to her, and create little busy scenes between us." The quest for novelty is idolatry, lust and artifice and is revealed as such in the course of Richardson's novel.

One method of exposure is gradually to reveal the sheer repetitiousness of events, so that Lovelace speaks more truly than he knows when he admits, "like Solomon, I can say, There is nothing new under the Sun." It is a method which finds concise formulation in the curious writings of James Harris, best known as the author of *Hermes: Or a Philosophical Inquiry Concerning Universal Grammar* (1751), which was printed by Richardson and received at least his formal approbation. Taking the same central text from Ecclesiastes as his source, Harris outlines a doctrine of reminiscence fused with one of historical recurrence in which ignorance "of what is similar in Events which return (for in every returning Event such Similarity exists) is the forgetfulness of a Mind uninstructed and weak; a Mind ignorant of that great, that PROVIDENTIAL CIRCULATION, which never ceases for a moment thro' every part of the universe." To such a mind, what is near us in time erroneously appears more important, more striking, because it appears novel. Lovelace's encounters with Clarissa gradually become repetitious, a Kill-Time amusement repeated "over and over again," until they seem like two of Freke's electrified bodies: "And so it will be repeatedly attracted to it, and be repell'd *toties quoties*." While Lovelace sees each encounter as a new opportunity, Clarissa, who will enter the officer's house with the words "Was she not a prisoner?— . . . Let her have the prisoner's room," begins to discover "what is similar in Events which return." Despite all his plots and contrivances, when in the fire-scene the question is again raised, "*Am I then a villain, madam?*" she flees to Hampstead.

The new proposal scene confronts the reader with this choice. Either we can see it as the first of a series of demonstrations of "the sudden gust of passion, which had like to have blown me into her arms." Or we may recognize, in the anticipation of the fire-scene, that this is an illuminating history, in which things gradually become what they essentially are, and use our time accordingly. Each encounter is the return of nature, but we may understand that nature if we so wish, for every scene contains "this great secret"of fire. "The No is an opponent of the Yes, or of truth, in order that the truth may become apparent."

The fire-scene is, amongst other things, a compact critique of the theatre of sublime effects. If Benjamin Martin is worried by the "vile prostitution" of his "noble science," Lovelace's account commences with the same false scruples: "Altho' the subject is too hallowed for profane contemplation, yet shalt thou have the *whole* before thee as it passed"; and Richardson shows that Martin's art rightly belongs in a brothel. If Martin is embarrassed by "illiterate pretenders" and christens his opponents "*hominiform* Animals, or Creatures in the *Shape of Man*," then Sinclair and her crew, bearing names such as Sally Martin or Dorcas Martindale, will find themselves characterized accordingly: "Creatures who, brought up too high for their fortunes, and to a taste for pleasure, and the public diversions, had fallen an easy prey to his seducing Arts," "nymphs . . . dressed out, to captivate, or to ape Quality," led by "the old dragon." Sally Martin is particularly keen to see the divine Clarissa prostituted, mimicked and sold for their profit, a keenness Freke purportedly had detected in Martin.

But this critique is itself designed to reveal the nature of Lovelace, for this is his plot, and what does it make him? When he starts a fire, insisting that it is "real" as Clarissa will be "convinced in the morning by ocular demonstration," claiming as his provocation Clarissa's unparalleled resistance, he is the natural philosopher. This is a misuse of elemental fire which can only cause confusion, an attempted imposition on the credulity of his audience, a trick and a lie. But it is more than this. As it is a fiction, so it is carnal, a strategy to gain access to Clarissa's body. The true relationship between these two aspects of Lovelace's art is a crucial one. As we have seen, Lovelace thinks he wears a disguise because he is a villain. Rather, in playing a villain, "committing Vice in Effigie," this is what he becomes. It is he who in hardening his heart against Clarissa's light, converts his love for her to lust. He has a choice, but it is not the one he recognizes. For Lovelace thinks he plots his own plots and chooses his own disguises. Convinced that his trick fire is real, "*And so it was, Jack!*" he thinks that he controls it for his own ends, as he creates his own identity through the power of his own will.

Here we touch upon the central Behmenist mystery of the Fall in which evil is a turning away from God to nature in the attempt to be its "own Self-full Maker and Creator," a turning away which does not know that it is a return to God. In denying that he may choose his own nature, but insisting that he can forge his own destiny, Lovelace exactly reverses the significance of the paradox of Boehme's Fall. Hence the profound irony of his complaint that the plot has been ruined by his "capacity of being moved by prayers and tears. Where, where, on this occasion, was the *Callus*, where the flint, by which my heart was said to be surrounded?" for in denying that his heart is a flint, Lovelace is denying what is Law's favourite image for the spiritual potential of all fallen things. The flint is "dead, or in a State of Death," yet "every Particle of the *flint* consists of . . . *compacted fire*." When on this occasion Lovelace is moved and Clarissa saved, it is by no mere fashionable sensibility, but this "capacity" alone. This is the "real" fire of the fire-scene.

Lovelace is then the Collierite actor as perceived by "the Brethren," who, "when the Vehemence of any Passion is to be represented, there is a necessity of forming and blowing up those Passions in their own Minds, which must be expressed and conveyed to the Audience by outward Gestures." As William J. Palmer has shown, this dramatic art in all its aspects is one in which Lovelace is particularly skilled. Yet in the fire-scene, he is fatally upstaged by the clear integrity of Clarissa's role: "This was Mine, my Plot!—And this was all I made of it! . . . But why? Because I never before encountered a resistance so much in earnest."

Lovelace's ipecacuanha plot has already revealed his familiarity not only with Congreve's *Love for Love*, but with those popular manuals of histrionics to which Aaron Hill's *Art of Acting* (1746) belongs. Hill's recommendations seem to confirm the Collierite analysis: "1st. The imagination must conceive a *strong idea* of the passion. 2dly. BUT that idea cannot *strongly* be conceived without impressing its own form upon the muscles of the *face*" and so on "in their natural and not-to-be-avoided consequences" through body, voice and gesture. Byrom's poetic response, dedicated to Richardson and Freke, wryly concedes the similarity: "This is the System, if I take it true, — / The Art which, as he says, is Nature too. / Grant it,—But what kind of nature? In terms subtly and humorously couched for the cognoscenti, Byrom makes two points about acting.

Firstly, he hints at a much more serious argument in the poem they had just completed proofreading, that when "We think our Wishes and Desires a Play, / And sport important Faculties away / Edg'd are the Tools with which we Trifle thus, / And carve out deep Realities for us." And so he warns, "Yet all this while, this Art of Looks and Limbs / Is ill-bestowed upon

Theatric Whims." This is a lesson Lovelace will learn too late, for he also thinks that he may doff his disguises at will and reverse their effects when-soever he chooses. To "trifle" is not to take "Theatric Whims" for the "realities" they are. Secondly, where Hill's analysis of the actor's inspiration traces the effects of "th'inspiring WILL," Byrom's parody is an account of "The Soul": "The Soul, it seems, what passes by observes / From some snug Place behind the Optic Nerves." Through this simple substitution, Byrom interrogates the materialist reduction implicit in Hill's "idea" of a passion. What can be the connection between the soul's observation and the optic nerve? When Hill directs that grief is expressed, "by neither muscles nor eye intense,—but both languid," when Lovelace coaches, "That won't do. That dropt jaw and mouth distended into the long oval, is more upon the Horri-ble, than the Grievous," what they ignore is no more nor less than, in Byrom's words, "the Meaning of the Soul."

Yet it is this which defeats Lovelace the actor-dramatist, who like Dryden's "Poet," endeavours "an absolute dominion over the minds of the Spectators." Clarissa quickly detects Lovelace's "treachery," while his account of her extreme reaction testifies despite itself to her earnestness: "Her eyes running over, yet seeming to threaten future vengeance: And at last her lips uttering what every indignant look and glowing feature portended." Such a "natural . . . consequence" may seem to endorse Hill's system, yet no "system" could ever capture this beauty. As the description proceeds, Byrom's false seeming, the simile which is theatre, is turned into a portent of the truth: "her charming tresses fell down in naturally shining ringlets, as if officious to conceal the dazzling beauties of her neck and shoulders; her lovely bosom too heaving with sighs and broken sobs, as if to aid her quivering lips, in pleading for her." It is not only the harmony of thought and appearance which makes this so different from an art of exposure and enticement. There is an artistry here but it is a divine artistry which stops Lovelace in his tracks, penetrating even *his* heart. As the scene thus reveals the source of Clarissa's beauty and integrity, it also exposes that terrible division between inner and outer of the actor; the gap between words and actions; the extraordinary mixture of violence and suave premeditation which is his repressed excite-ment: "I mentioned the morrow as the happiest day of my life." We may view it as an "ocular demonstration," as Lovelace sees the "assemblage of beauties offered . . . to my ravished sight," in which case we shall be served by "That Muse, which histrionic Wits applaud," whom "The Wise will think no bet-ter than a Bawd"; or we may seek those higher causes which are mere ap-pearances to him, "seeming to threaten," "as if officious," "as if to aid."

Henry Fielding, as the definition of exemplarity offered in the dedication of *Tom Jones* might suggest, "for an Example is a Kind of Picture, in which Virtue becomes as it were an Object of Sight, and strikes us with an Idea of that Loviliness, which *Plato* asserts there is in her naked charms"— with an immaculate command of the hilarious, coolly chose the former option. If, as has been argued, the most insistent anti-Jacobite politics of *Tom Jones*, including its setting in England at the moment of the 1745 rebellion, are the product of a late, hasty revision on Fielding's part in 1748, this might well account for the "sudden outburst of bitterness against Fielding" and "many signs of enmity on Richardson's part at least" which Eaves and Kimpel document as occurring immediately after its publication in 1749. Nor would it be surprising if Richardson regarded himself, together with the novel which was the current toast of the town at the time of its revision, as the central and highly vulnerable target of a masterfully insinuating joint attack on Jacobite treachery and Behmenist belief. Certainly, the satire against John Freke in book 2, chapter 4, and book 4, chapter 9, of *Tom Jones*, charging him with a disastrous combination of snobbery, prudery and vulgarity, is equally a satire against the author of *Clarissa*. As such its target is precisely the "higher cause" of the fire-scene. Indeed, this is one of the jokes at Richardson's expense, since he becomes, in himself, one of those invisible higher causes which receive such short shrift; a shadowy presence lurking behind Fielding's explicit quarry, and one cruelly cut off from any riposte since his best hope must be that few outside Fielding and "the Brethren" would detect his presence or fully understand why he was there.

Fielding first employs a plethora of secondary causes to wreak havoc in the Behmenist doctrine of the dual potential of fire. The pretext of the first sally is a discussion of the mysterious reconciliation between Mr. Partridge and his wife who, "as she could be extremely angry, so could she be altogether as fond" and "yet, on extraordinary Occasions, when the Passion of Anger had raged very high, the Remission was usually longer, and so was the Case at present." The reconciliation begins when Partridge treacherously negotiates with his wife an original cause for Jenny's dismissal, saying, "She was grown of little Use as a Servant, spending all her time in reading, and was become, moreover, very pert and obstinate." Fielding promptly gives us the real cause of this capitulation: "For indeed she and her Master had lately had frequent Disputes in Literature; in which, as hath been said, she was become greatly his Superior." As if this were not crushingly anti-Richardsonian enough, neatly dispensing with *Pamela*, its effects and aftermath, chapter 4 adds another reason in the shape of "some other matrimonial Concessions, well known to most Husbands; and which, like the Secrets of Free Masonry, should be divulged to none who are not Members of that honourable Fraternity." He then urges "*Mr. John Fr——*, or some other such Philosopher" to "bestir himself a little, in order to find out the real Cause of this sudden Transition . . . for it is our Province to relate Facts, and we shall leave Causes to Persons of much higher Genius."

Fielding's "facts" are extremely materialist ones, and the second trouncing similarly takes the form of a joyous reduction of the subtle conflicts of Richardson's dialectic to a marital squabble. Here the butt is Freke's medicine and electricity together, which Fielding compares with the beating Black George administers to his family to reduce them to "a State of perfect Quiet," concluding, "To say the Truth, as they both operate by Friction, it may be doubted whether there is not something analogous between them, of which, Mr. *Freke* would do well to enquire before he publishes the next Edition of his Book." This is an opportunity for much fun at the expense of the Richardson circle, including a lewd attack on their fear of lewdness and vulgarity, and a blistering paraphrase of Freke's objections to electricity lectures as "only proper for the Vulgar, unless in one single instance, *viz.* where Superiority of Birth breaks out; in which Case, we should not think it very improperly applied by any Husband whatever, if the Application was not, in itself so base." As in this astute substitution of "superiority of birth" for fire, Fielding consistently replaces the Behmenists' "higher cause" with his own hints at their pompous and sordid motives. Thus friction becomes sexual tension; the return to the original unity, a family bullied into submission; the "something analogous" in the Behmenist divine analogy between matter and spirit, an opportunity for publication; and the cast of *Clarissa*, a bunch of rather angry (and rather lowly) people. The two short paragraphs which describe the offensive of Black George, "a peacable kind of fellow, and nothing *choleric*, *nor rash*, yet did he bear about him something of what the Antients called the *Irascible*," is a summary of the process Fielding perceives at work in Lovelace's entire career, centering around his "application" of "a small Switch, a Remedy of wonderful Force, as he had often assayed, and which the Word Villain served as a Hint for his applying."

This is a rewriting of the confrontation between Clarissa and Lovelace in the fire-scene, in which she indeed calls Lovelace villain, provoking both anger and lust: "*Am* I then a villain, Madam? Am I then a villain, say you?— and clasped both my arms about her, offering to raise her to my bounding heart." In it, such self-approving humour as exists in the writings of Byrom or Richardson, consisting of a kind of extended religious pun, is hopelessly debunked by the rapier-like agility of Fielding's wit. Its very concision is part of a masterful comedy of exposure, since even as we unravel his own jibe at the pursuit of hermetic knowledge, "a Remedy of wonderful

Force . . . which the Word Villain served as a Hint for his applying," we know that the search for "higher causes" is redundant in the face of a man and his wife coming to blows. Together, these lampoons comprise the outline of a materialist critique, while their very obliqueness and marginality put "the Brethren" and their dialectic in their place. Here we find no Behmenist economy of fire, but a rather simpler comedy of sometimes sadomasochistic sexual impulse, of which it is all too easy to divine that the greater the anger, the greater the fondness, followed by "perfect Ease and Tranquility." Such are complete reconciliations between ordinary mortals, even Tom and Sophia. These are the "facts" behind the "secrets of . . . that honourable Fraternity."

As the first, notable, "Lovelacean" reading of *Clarissa*, this is not without evidence from the text. It had not taken Lovelace long to transfer his affection for the struggling Clarissa to her struggles: "Her struggles!—O what additional charms, as I now reflect, did her struggles give to every feature, every hint, of a person so sweetly elegant and lovely!" But for Richardson, such confusion of flesh with spirit, opposition for desire, is never the final cause of love even in a Lovelace. Before it becomes a material cause, it is a spiritual perversion, and never loses its sense of loss.

It is difficult for us now to understand Richardsonian sexuality. Modern critics, not surprisingly, tend to detect it everywhere. When Beatty Warner does hint at a "real," it is surely one of his leading candidates for that dubious post: "Right in the midst of struggle is the possibility of union which is the 'other' of struggle—invisible to the combatants—but makes all the oppositions activated by their struggle appear real." Fielding's wisdom makes for a more forthright intervention. Having reached "that happy Hour which had surrendered the charming *Sophia* to the eager arms of her enraptured *Jones*," he concludes his history, "For what Happiness this World affords equal to the Possession of such a Woman as *Sophia*, I sincerely own I have never yet discovered." Yet the question remains of exactly what sexuality is. For Richardson, and there is little else, it is a yearning for a return to the original unity: "The Evil seek Wrong, and the Good seek Right; but they both are Seekers, and for the same Reasons, because this present State has not That which it wants to have" (Law, *The Spirit of Love*). It is the desire for an end to all separation and division in the world, and a return to the Father's house. Clarissa's victory over "a rake . . . all her oppressors and the world besides," is the perfection of her earlier cry, "the World is but one great family. Originally it was so. What then is this narrow selfishness that reigns in us, but relationship rememb'red against relationship forgot?";—by which standard the Harlowes' "darling view . . . of *raising a family*" is one more specious eidolon.

Fielding laughed at a "whole Family" being reduced to "a State of perfect Quiet," and of "something analogous" to "electricity" which "is often communicated through one person to many others who are not touched by the instrument." But *Clarissa*, whose heroine has good cause to remark that "one pace awry . . . has led me hundreds and hundreds of miles out of my path," offers us the vision of a dialectical totality in which there can be no local and autonomous resolution, no personally fulfilling containment of elemental fire: "Now, Madam, if that passion is not little and selfish that makes two vehement souls prefer the gratification of each other, often to a sense of duty, and always to the whole world without them, be pleased to tell me what is." This might have been a direct reply to Fielding's happy ending, such another selfish and limited attempt as Lovelace's to make Clarissa "acknowledge . . . a preference of me to all other men, at least," or to "create beauty, and place it where nobody else could find it." It is this concept of love as a high critique, a standard for happiness as for virtue unwittingly shared by Lovelace and Clarissa, that Richardson bequeathed to European literature. Nevertheless, in an important sense, Richardson's position in history was that of the loser. In the eighteenth century, materialism, natural philosophy, psychology, environmental determinism, did not give way to the divine analogy between spirit and matter—with the arguable exception of Shaftesbury's uneasy combination of Platonism and Lockean sensationism, significantly most important as a theory of art. Properly to trace Richardson's great influence would be to give an account of something gradually forgotten, or never understood, but despite this, a surviving vision.

Chronology

1689	Samuel Richardson born in Mackworth, Derbyshire, to Samuel and Elizabeth Richardson, of London tradesman families.
1699	Family moves back to London.
1701–4	Perhaps attends Merchant Taylors' School; at most he gets "only Common School-Learning."
1706	Apprenticed to a printer, John Wilde.
1713	Becomes overseer and corrector in a printing house.
1715	Made a freeman of the Stationers' Company.
1719	Sets up his own printing business.
1721	Marries Martha Wilde, the daughter of his former master. They have six children, none of whom lives beyond three years.
1722	Takes over the prosperous Leake printing business.
1731	Wife dies.
1733	Marries Elizabeth Leake, of the printing family; they have six children, of whom four daughters survive. Publishes *The Apprentice's Vade Mecum*. Gets contracts to print for the government, eventually including even the journals of the House of Commons. During the 1730s his press becomes known as one of the three best in London.
1739	Publishes a reworked version of L'Estrange's *Aesop*. Begins writing *Pamela*.
1740	Publishes *Pamela, or Virtue Rewarded* anonymously.

1741 Publishes *Familiar Letters on Important Occasions* (model letters for the nominally literate; its full title is *Letters Written to and for particular friends, on the Most Important Occasions: Directing Not Only the Requisite Style and Forms To Be Observed in writing 'Familiar Letters,' but How to Think and Act Justly and Prudently, in the Common Concerns of Human Life*).

1742 Publishes *Pamela in her Exalted Condition*, a sequel meant to replace a spurious continuation of the popular Pamela story.

1744 Probably completes a draft of *Clarissa*.

1747 Publishes the first two volumes of *Clarissa: or The History of a Young Lady*.

1748 Publishes the remaining five volumes of *Clarissa*.

1749 Publishes revised edition of *Clarissa*.

1753 Becomes Master of the Stationers' Company. Publishes the first six volumes of *The History of Sir Charles Grandison*.

1754 Publishes the final *Grandison* volume.

1761 Dies at Parson's Green, near London.

Contributors

HAROLD BLOOM, Sterling Professor of the Humanities at Yale University, is the author of *The Anxiety of Influence*, *Poetry and Repression*, and many other volumes of literary criticism. His forthcoming study, *Freud: Transference and Authority*, attempts a full-scale reading of all of Freud's major writings. A MacArthur Prize Fellow, he is general editor of five series of literary criticism published by Chelsea House. During 1987–88, he was appointed Charles Eliot Norton Professor of Poetry at Harvard University.

IAN WATT is Professor of English at Stanford University. His books include *The Rise of the Novel*, *Conrad in the Nineteenth Century*, and the forthcoming *Gothic and Comic: Two Variations on the Realistic Tradition*.

MARTIN PRICE is Sterling Professor of English at Yale University. His books include *Swift's Rhetorical Art*, *To the Palace of Wisdom*, and *Forms of Life*.

ANTHONY WINNER is Professor of English Language and Literature at the University of Virginia and the author of *Characters in the Twilight: Hardy, Zola, and Chekhov*.

MARK KINKEAD-WEEKES is Professor of English at the University of Kent at Canterbury and the author of *Samuel Richardson: Dramatic Novelist*.

ROY ROUSSEL is Professor of English at the State University of New York at Buffalo and the author of *The Metaphysics of Darkness: A Study in the Unity and Development of Conrad's Fiction*.

JINA POLITI is the author of *The Novel and Its Presuppositions*.

JEAN H. HAGSTRUM is John C. Shaffer Professor of English and the Humanities at Northwestern University. His books include *The Sister Arts*, *Sex and Sensibility: Ideal and Erotic Love from Milton to Mozart*, and *Samuel Johnson's Literary Criticism*.

163

RITA GOLDBERG is the author of *Sex and Enlightenment: Women in Richardson and Diderot.*

ROSEMARY BECHLER is affiliated with Girton College, Cambridge University, and is the author of several articles on Richardson and eighteenth-century fiction.

Bibliography

Ball, Donald. *Samuel Richardson's Theory of Fiction*. The Hague: Mouton, 1971.

Barker, Gerard. *Grandison's Heirs*. Cranbury, N.J.: Associated University Presses, 1985.

Bechler, Rosemary. " 'Triall by what is contrary': Samuel Richardson and Christian Dialectic." In *Samuel Richardson: Passion and Prudence*, edited by Valerie Grosvenor Myer, 93–113. London: Vision, 1986.

Braudy, Leo. "Penetration and Impenetrability in *Clarissa*." In *New Approaches to Eighteenth-Century Literature*, edited by John Phillip Harth, 177–206. New York: Columbia University Press, 1974.

Brissenden, R. F. *Virtue in Distress: Studies in the Novel of Sentiment from Richardson to Sade*. London: Macmillan, 1974.

Brophy, Elizabeth Bergen. *Samuel Richardson: The Triumph of Craft*. Knoxville: University of Tennessee Press, 1974.

Brownstein, Rachel Mayer. " 'An Exemplar to Her Sex': Richardson's *Clarissa*." *Yale Review* 67 (1977): 30–47.

Castle, Terry. *Clarissa's Ciphers: Meaning and Disruption in Richardson's* Clarissa. Ithaca: Cornell University Press, 1982.

Coates, Paul. *The Realist Fantasy: Fiction and Reality since* Clarissa. London: Macmillan, 1983.

———. "Saying 'No,' Saying 'Yes': The Novels of Samuel Richardson." In *The First English Novelists: Essays in Understanding*, edited by J. M. Armistead. Knoxville: University of Tennessee Press, 1985.

Doody, Margaret Anne. *A Natural Passion: A Study of the Novels of Samuel Richardson*. Oxford: Oxford University Press, 1974.

Eagleton, Terry. *The Rape of Clarissa*. Oxford: Basil Blackwell, 1982.

Eaves, T. C. Duncan, and Ben D. Kimpel. *Samuel Richardson: A Biography*. Oxford: Oxford University Press, 1971.

Edwards, Lee. *Psyche as Hero: Female Heroism and Fictional Form*. Middletown, Conn.: Wesleyan University Press, 1984.

Fiedler, Leslie. *Love and Death in the American Novel*. London: Paladin Press, 1970.

Flynn, Carol Houlihan. *Samuel Richardson: A Man of Letters*. Princeton: Princeton University Press, 1982.

Gillis, Christina Marsden. *The Paradox of Privacy: Epistolary Form in* Clarissa. Gainesville: University of Florida Presses, 1984.

Gopnik, Irwin. *A Theory of Style and Richardson's* Clarissa. The Hague: Mouton, 1970.

Hagstrum, Jean H. *Sex and Sensibility: Ideal and Erotic Love from Milton to Mozart.* Chicago: Chicago University Press, 1980.

Harris, Jocelyn. " 'As if they had been living friends': *Sir Charles Grandison* into *Mansfield Park.*" *Bulletin of Research in the Humanities* 83 (1980): 360–405.

———. "Learning and Genius in *Sir Charles Grandison.*" In *Studies in the Eighteenth Century IV*, edited by R. F. Brissenden and J. C. Eade, 167–91. Toronto: University of Toronto Press, 1979.

Hill, Christopher. "Clarissa Harlowe and Her Times." *Essays in Criticism* 5 (1955): 315–40.

Karl, Frederick R. *The Adversary Literature.* New York: Farrar, Straus & Giroux, 1974.

Kermode, Frank. "Richardson and Fielding." *Cambridge Journal* 4 (1950): 106–14.

Kinkead-Weekes, Mark. "*Clarissa* Restored?" *RES* n.s. 10 (1959): 156–71.

Konigsberg, Ira. *Samuel Richardson and the Dramatic Novel.* Lexington: University Press of Kentucky, 1968.

Loesburg, Jonathan. "Allegory and Narrative in *Clarissa.*" *Novel* 15 (1981): 39–59.

McKee, Patricia. *Heroic Commitment in Richardson, Eliot, and James.* Princeton: Princeton University Press, 1986.

McKillop, Alan D. *Samuel Richardson: Printer and Novelist.* Hamden, Conn.: Shoe String, 1960.

Miller, Nancy. *The Heroine's Text: Readings in the French and English Novel, 1722–1782.* New York: Columbia University Press, 1980.

Palmer, William J. "Two Dramatists: Lovelace and Richardson in *Clarissa.*" *Studies in the Novel* 5 (1973): 7–21.

Perry, Ruth. *Women, Letters, and the Novel.* New York: AMS, 1980.

Preston, John. *The Created Self.* London: Heinemann, 1970.

Showalter, Elaine. "Critical Cross-Dressing: Male Feminists and The Woman of the Year." *Raritan* 3, no. 1 (Fall 1983): 130–49.

Warner, William Beatty. *Reading* Clarissa: *The Struggles of Interpretation.* New Haven: Yale University Press, 1979.

Watt, Ian. *The Rise of the Novel.* Berkeley and Los Angeles: University of California Press, 1957.

Acknowledgments

"Richardson as Novelist: *Clarissa*" by Ian Watt from *The Rise of the Novel* by Ian Watt, © 1957 by Ian Watt. Reprinted by permission of the University of California Press.

"The Divided Heart: Clarissa and Lovelace" (originally entitled "The Divided Heart") by Martin Price from *To the Palace of Wisdom: Studies in Order and Energy from Dryden to Blake* by Martin Price, © 1964 by Martin Price. Reprinted by permission.

"Richardson's Lovelace: Character and Prediction" by Anthony Winner from *Texas Studies in Literature and Language* 14, no. 1 (Spring 1972), © 1972 by the University of Texas Press. Reprinted by permission of the author and University of Texas Press.

"The Inquisition (The Final Instalment)" by Mark Kinkead-Weekes from *Samuel Richardson: Dramatic Novelist* by Mark Kinkead-Weekes, © 1973 by Mark Kinkead-Weekes. Reprinted by permission of Methuen & Co. Ltd.

"Crisis, Resolution, and the Family of the Heart" by Mark Kinkead-Weekes from *Samuel Richardson: Dramatic Novelist,* © 1973 by Mark Kinkead-Weekes. Reprinted by permission of Methuen & Co. Ltd.

"Reflections on the Letter: The Reconciliation of Distance and Presence in *Pamela*" by Roy Roussel from *ELH* 41, no. 3 (Fall 1974), © 1974 by the Johns Hopkins University Press, Baltimore/London. Reprinted by permission of the Johns Hopkins University Press.

"The Miracle of Love" by Jina Politi from *The Novel and Its Presuppositions: Changes in the Conceptual Structure of Novels in the Eighteenth and Nineteenth Centuries* by Jina Politi, © 1976 by Jina Politi. Reprinted by permission.

"*Sir Charles Grandison*: The Enlarged Family" (originally entitled "Richardson") by Jean H. Hagstrum from *Sex and Sensibility: Ideal and Erotic Love from Milton to Mozart* by Jean H. Hagstrum, © 1980 by the University of Chicago. Reprinted by permission of the University of Chicago Press.

"Clarissa Lives: Sex and the Epistolary Novel" (originally entitled "Clarissa Lives: 'Let This Expiate'") by Rita Goldberg from *Sex and Enlightenment: Women in Richardson and Diderot* by Rita Goldberg, © 1984 by Cambridge University Press. Reprinted by permission of Cambridge University Press.

"Reading the Fire-Scene in *Clarissa*" by Rosemary Bechler, © 1987 by Rosemary Bechler. Published for the first time in this volume. Printed by permission.

Index

169